Mr. Justice Sutherland

A MAN AGAINST THE STATE

Mr. Justice Sutherland

A MAN

AGAINST THE STATE

BY

JOEL FRANCIS PASCHAL

GREENWOOD PRESS, PUBLISHERS
NEW YORK

TO KATHERINE
AND
LUTHER EISENHART

PREFATORY NOTE

FOR some years now, American readers have displayed a noteworthy interest in judicial biography. This interest springs, I believe, from a growing appreciation of the role of judges in the governing of the American people. Everyone now recognizes that the Supreme Court is something more than a court of law. It is an agency of government operating in a political context. This context may differ from that of the other branches of the Government, but it is still political. I am not surprised, therefore, to find that I have written something which is not so much a biography as an essay in government.

The reader will observe my dependence on the papers left by Justice Sutherland. For making these accessible to me, I should like to thank the Justice's daughter, Mrs. Walter Bloedorn and his grandson, George Sutherland Elmore, both of Washington, D.C. For their unfailing kindness I shall always be grateful. I should say a word or two here about the papers themselves. Included in them are several scrap books consisting mostly of newspaper clippings collected from all over the United States. I have made free use of these clippings and I have no wish, of course, to leave the impression that I was led to them by an examination of the files of the newspapers involved.

Mr. Thomas E. Waggaman, the Marshal of the Supreme Court of United States, generously afforded me access to pertinent materials which he had gathered over the years. I am also in his debt for numerous other courtesies. It is a pleasure to recall personal interviews with Justice Owen J. Roberts and Judge Harold Stevens. Justice Roberts favored me with a colleague's glimpse of Sutherland at work on the Court and Judge Stevens talked provocatively of Sutherland's Utah background. My good friends, Dale F. Stansbury of Duke University, Beverly Lake of Wake Forest College, Brainerd Currie of the University of California at Los Angeles, Harold Shepherd of Stanford University and John G. Dawson of the North Carolina Bar all read the manuscript at various stages and offered many valuable suggestions. Lodwick Hartley, head of the department of English of North Carolina State College, gave me some stimulating criticisms of a general nature and, with characteristic kindness, read the proof.

The staff of the Princeton University Library assisted me greatly with their usual expert skill. For this I am thankful. I am likewise highly appreciative of the care and attention my book has received from the Director and Staff of the Princeton University Press. No author could ask for more considerate treatment. I should like also to thank the *Journal of Legal Education* for permission to use material which previously appeared in its pages.

Professor Alpheus T. Mason has aided me in more ways than I can recount. From his first suggestion that I undertake a book on Sutherland, he has always been ready with whatever was asked. I have experienced in full measure his rare talent for making another's problem his own. Like all others who write on constitutional law, I am under a heavy obligation to Professor Edward S. Corwin; but I am happy to say that my debt is also a personal one.

The encouragement and assistance given me by my father, Dr. George W. Paschal, while I would not minimize either, are but the latest example of a collaboration which extends back to my earliest remembrance. He read both manuscript and proof. He remains, as he has always been, an incitement to scholarly endeavor. Finally, I have had through all the later stages the creative companionship of my wife, Primrose McPherson Paschal.

J. F. P.

Raleigh, N.C., April 17, 1951.

CONTENTS

INTRODUCTION

FOURTEEN years have now passed since that historic April day in 1937 when the Supreme Court of the United States found lodgment in the Constitution for Franklin Roosevelt's New Deal. More and more it is coming to be suggested that the Court's capitulation signified that the American people were thenceforward to live under a political structure different from that they had known for a century and a half. One writer has summarized the change by saying that whereas formerly we had a Constitution of *rights*, we now have a Constitution of *powers*.[1] Another's expression is that a *political* democracy has been substituted for a *constitutional* democracy.[2] Whether or not one accepts these descriptions of the new dispensation, it is hardly open to argument that it is here—and that it is, in some degree, new.

Understandably, the prophets of such a fundamental revolution have been much celebrated. This is as it should be, but it is not enough. Despite the developments of recent years, it is still true that for the greater part of American history, and for a preponderant number of individual Americans, a Constitution of *limitations* has been a cherished American doctrine. And today, even with the experience of total war freshly in mind, one would scarcely dare to say that such an idea is no longer a force in the United States. It is no mere sentimentalism, then, that suggests a study of the life of George Sutherland, one of the last and one of the most effective champions of this peculiarly American notion to sit on the Supreme Court of the United States.

Sutherland was an Associate Justice from 1922 to 1938. Even before 1922, James Bryce had described him as "the

[1] Edward S. Corwin, *Total War and the Constitution*, New York, Alfred A. Knopf, 1947, pp. 171-172. This thesis was questioned by Judge Jerome Frank in the *New York Times Book Review*, May 4, 1947. Professor Corwin replied, *ibid.*, June 1, 1947.

[2] C. Perry Patterson, *Presidential Government in the United States*, Chapel Hill, The University of North Carolina Press, 1947, p. v.

living voice of the Constitution."[3] Sutherland was indeed the voice of *one* Constitution. While he was on the Court, no other justice spoke for the majority in so many great cases.[4] He sketched the limits of executive and judicial power, as well as that of the legislature. His influence extended to every sphere of government. If the Constitution is what the judges say it is, Sutherland was its chief author during his incumbency. Accordingly, he can be regarded as a representative figure in a sense applicable to but few of the justices who have served on the Court. As such, he stands as one of the major landmarks in American constitutional law, the landmark from which the new departure was taken in 1937.

[3] *New York Times*, September 10, 1922.

[4] The following cases, to which others could be added, seem sufficient to prove the point: *Massachusetts* v. *Mellon*, 262 U.S. 447 (1923); *Adkins* v. *Children's Hospital*, 261 U.S. 525 (1923); *Euclid* v. *Ambler Realty Co.*, 272 U.S. 365 (1926); *Tyson and Bro. United Theater Ticket Office* v. *Banton*, 273 U.S. 418 (1927); *Ribnik* v. *McBride*, 277 U.S. 350 (1928); *Williams* v. *Standard Oil Co.*, 278 U.S. 235 (1929); *Liggett Co.* v. *Baldridge*, 278 U.S. 105 (1928); *Frost* v. *Corporation Commission of Oklahoma*, 278 U.S. 515 (1929); *Macallen Co.* v. *Massachusetts*, 279 U.S. 620 (1929); *Bedford Cut Stone Co.* v. *Journeymen Stone Cutters' Ass'n*, 274 U.S. 37 (1927); *Patton* v. *United States*, 281 U.S. 276 (1930); *Powell* v. *Alabama*, 287 U.S. 45 (1932); *New State Ice Co.* v. *Liebmann*, 285 U.S. 262 (1932); *Stephenson* v. *Binford*, 287 U.S. 251 (1932); *Colgate* v. *Harvey*, 296 U.S. 404 (1935); *Rathbun* v. *United States*, 295 U.S. 602 (1935); *Jones* v. *Securities & Exchange Commission*, 298 U.S. 1 (1936); *Carter* v. *Carter Coal Co.*, 298 U.S. 238 (1936); *United States* v. *Macintosh*, 283 U.S. 605 (1931); *United States* v. *Curtiss-Wright Export Corp.*, 299 U.S. 304 (1936); and *United States* v. *Belmont*, 301 U.S. 324 (1937).

Mr. Justice Sutherland

A MAN AGAINST THE STATE

1

THE DEVELOPMENT
OF AN IDEA, 1862-1900

GEORGE SUTHERLAND was born of British parents at Stoney Stratford in Buckinghamshire, England, on March 25, 1862. The circumstance that he was a native of Great Britain was rendered noteworthy sixty years later when he was appointed to the Supreme Court of the United States. Only three justices before him, and none for over a hundred years, had been of foreign birth.[1] His father, Alexander George Sutherland,[2] was of Scottish descent, of a family which had earlier lived in Edinburgh, and earlier still in the extreme north of Scotland. His mother, Frances Slater, was English. Sometime in 1862 Alexander Sutherland espoused the faith of the Church of Jesus Christ of Latter-day Saints, and formed a resolve to emigrate with his new family to the Promised Land that Brigham Young had found for the Saints in the Great American Desert. Accordingly, in the summer of 1863, the Sutherlands, aided perhaps by a grant from the Church, abandoned England and traveled some five thousand miles to settle in the little village of Springville, in what is now the State of Utah.

After a short time the elder Sutherland renounced his faith in Joseph Smith's revelations and pushed on to Montana as a mining prospector. By 1869, however, he

[1] *New York Times*, September 10, 1922, in a feature story on Sutherland's appointment to the Court. The other justices of foreign birth were James Wilson, who was born in Scotland; James Iredell, who was born in England, and William Paterson, who was born at sea while his English parents were on their way to America. To these, the name of David J. Brewer could be added. He was born in Asia Minor but was the child of American parents. Mr. Justice Frankfurter of the present Court was born in Austria.

[2] Sutherland's name was originally the same as his father's but, to avoid confusion, he dropped the "Alexander" on coming of age.

was back in Utah, settling for a time in Silver City and later in Provo. His restlessness and the great variety of occupations he pursued suggest that this Sutherland never achieved more than a moderate economic success. Besides being a prospector for minerals, he was, at various times, mining recorder, justice of the peace, postmaster, and practicing attorney. Both parents lived to see their son rise to high place, the father dying in 1911, and the mother in 1920.[3]

The Utah of Sutherland's youth, although it had been the home of the Mormons for two decades, was still a frontier community. Years later, Sutherland confessed that he was tempted to think of himself as a pioneer and added that if this was not exactly the case, he still could be called a "pio-nearly."[4] His boyhood was, in his words,

a period when life was very simple, but, as I can bear testimony, very hard as measured by present day standards. . . . Nobody worried about child labor. The average boy of ten [undoubtedly referring to himself] worked—and often worked very hard. . . . He milked, cut and carried in the night's wood, carried swill to the pigs, curried the horses, hoed the corn, guided the plow or, if not, followed it in the task of picking up potatoes which had been upturned, until his young vertebrae approached dislocation and he was ready to consider a bid to surrender his hopes of salvation in exchange for the comfort of a hinge in the small of his back.[5]

In a passage which is surely a further self portrait, he described the attire of the typical Utah lad as consisting of

[3] The data on Sutherland's parents can be found in the *Salt Lake Herald Republican*, January 12, 1905, and in the unpublished memoir on Sutherland by Alan E. Gray, formerly Sutherland's law clerk and now of the San Francisco Bar. A copy may be found in the office of the Marshal of the Supreme Court. Mr. Thomas E. Waggaman, the present incumbent, informs me that this memoir was read by Sutherland and approved by him as an accurate statement.

[4] "The Spirit of Brigham Young University," an address prepared by Sutherland to be read at the commencement exercises of the University on June 4, 1941. It was reprinted in the University publication, *The Messenger*, vol. 18, no. 10. The reference is to p. 3.

[5] *ibid.*, pp. 3-4.

a hat of ancient vintage, sometimes with a well developed hole through the crown of which a lock of hair might be made to wave like the plume of an Indian on the warpath; a hickory shirt the worse for wear; a pair of pants handed down . . . held in place by one suspender, or allowed to defy the forces of gravity with the sole and precarious support afforded by the contours of an immature body.[6]

Sutherland was not long in acquiring the rudimentary public education available to him. McGuffey's Readers and Webster's blue-back spelling book were the staples of this discipline.[7] The necessity of earning his own living forced Sutherland from school when he was just twelve years old. At that age he became a clerk in a clothing store in Salt Lake City. Later he served as an agent of the Wells-Fargo Company and held a position in the mining recorder's office. Finally, in 1879, entirely as a result of his own industry and frugality, Sutherland was able to turn once again to the classroom—this time at the recently established Brigham Young Academy in Provo.[8]

2.

This institution, which later became Brigham Young University, was, of course, an enterprise of the Mormon Church. It was presided over by a man of compelling force, Karl G. Maeser. To him Sutherland was always quick to attribute a decisive influence on his life.[9] Maeser was of German birth and had been converted by Mormon missionaries to Saxony.[10] Except for Brigham Young, he

[6] *ibid.*, p. 4.

[7] *ibid.*, p. 6. For an account of the influence of the McGuffey Readers on American life, see Richard D. Mosier, *Making the American Mind: Social and Moral Ideas in the McGuffey Readers*, New York, King's Crown Press, 1947. Mosier pictures the readers as exercising a conservative and a nationalist influence.

[8] Gray, *op. cit.*, p. 1.

[9] Sutherland to James E. Talmage, January 13, 1927; Sutherland to Reinhard Maeser, February 26, 1923.

[10] Maeser's conversion is apparently one of the great epics of the Mormon Church. An absorbingly interesting account of it is given by Jesse R. S. Budge in his *The Life of William Budge*, Salt Lake City,

seems to have been the most powerful of the Mormon leaders. After sixty years had intervened, Sutherland described him thus:

Dr. Maeser's knowledge seemed to reach into every field. Of course there were limits; but they were not revealed to me during my course at the Academy. That he was an accomplished scholar I knew from the first. But the extent of his learning so grew before my vision as time went on that my constant emotion was one of amazement. I think there were days when I would have taken my oath that if the Rosetta Stone had never been found, nevertheless he could have easily revealed the meaning of the Egyptian hieroglyphics. He spoke with a decided accent; but his mastery of the English language, of English literature, and of the English way of thought, was superb.[11]

Maeser's influence was not merely that of an instructor. "He was," says Sutherland, "a man of such transparent and natural goodness that his students gained not only knowledge, but character which is better than knowledge."[12] The Academy's atmosphere and the tone of its instruction were definitely religious. Indeed, Brigham Young's single command to Maeser at the time of its establishment had been: "I do not want you to attempt even the alphabet or the multiplication table without the spirit of the Lord. That is all."[13] To such an ideal Maeser undoubtedly gave unswerving allegiance, but always in a free and generous spirit. The nonconforming Sutherland was never made to feel that his dissent made the slightest difference in the attention he received or the esteem in which he was held. He carried with him for the remainder of his days a vivid

---

The Deseret News, 1915, pp. 63-74. It seems that missionaries were not regarded with favor in Saxony. Accordingly, William Budge expounded the Mormon faith to Maeser in a beer hall where the two could talk without being suspected. I am indebted to Mr. Harold Shepherd, of the Stanford University Law School and himself a grandson of William Budge, for placing this volume in my hands. For other material on Maeser see *The Millennial Star*, December 9, 1926, and Reinhard Maeser, *Karl G. Maeser*, Provo, 1928.

11 "The Spirit of Brigham Young University," *supra* note 4.
12 *ibid.*, p. 9.
13 J. Marinus Jensen, *History of Provo, Utah*, Provo, 1924, p. 348.

and grateful memory of Maeser, acknowledging always that the immigrant Saint had exerted an influence on his "whole life which can not be exaggerated."[14] Maeser, for his part, admired and respected his pupil. He was often heard to remark that Sutherland's essays were invariably models of excellence, and in later years his friends speculated that no one would have been less surprised or more pleased at his pupil's subsequent success.[15]

A full outline of Sutherland's course of study at Brigham Young is not available. It is certain, however, that among other things Maeser discussed with his students the Constitution of the United States. Years later, Sutherland approvingly recalled his teaching that a divine hand had guided the framers.[16] This was in strict conformity with the official doctrine of the Church. Indeed, Maeser had available—and doubtless used—the Mormon scriptures to prove his point. Section 101 of the *Doctrine and Covenants* quotes the Deity thus:

79. Therefore, it is not right that any man should be in bondage one to another.

80. And for this purpose have I established the Constitution of this land, by the hands of wise men whom I raised up unto this very purpose and redeemed the land by the shedding of blood.

There were many other texts which Maeser might have quoted to stimulate in his scholars a reverential feeling for the Constitution. Section 98 of the *Doctrine and Covenants*, for example, contains the following passage:

5. And that law of the land which is constitutional, supporting that principle of freedom in maintaining rights and privileges, belongs to all mankind and is justifiable before me.

6. Therefore, I, the Lord, justify you and your brethren of my church, in befriending that law which is the constitutional law of the land;

7. And as pertaining to law of man, whatsoever is more or less than this cometh of evil.

14 Sutherland to Reinhard Maeser, February 26, 1923.
15 *Deseret News*, September 6, 1922.
16 Sutherland to Mrs. Jeanette A. Hyde, May 28, 1936.

8. I, the Lord God, make you free, therefore you are free indeed; and the law also maketh you free.

These verses, as Maeser believed, were transmitted to the Mormon people by means of revelations received by Joseph Smith in the year 1833. Maeser probably also recalled to his students the belief of the Mormons, voiced by Brigham Young, that some day, when the Constitution should be hanging "upon a single thread," the Faithful would rush forth to save it.[17]

It is not mere supposition that the idea of a divinely inspired law which had for its purpose the freedom of man seared itself into the consciousness of George Sutherland, although he himself was not of the Faith. So, too, with the notion of a last-ditch, heroic defense of this law. More than a half-century later, when it seemed to him that the Constitution was under attack as never before, he wrote a Mormon friend that one of his greatest joys had been derived from the Church's adherence to that document. He went on to add: "I can recall, as far back as 1879 and 1880, the words of Professor Maeser, who declared that [the Constitution] was a divinely inspired instrument—as I truly think it is."[18]

Maeser, however much he relied on sacred writings, led his pupils to an acquaintance with other literature as well. A book published by him in 1898, entitled *School and Fireside*, indicates a preoccupation with philosophical ideas. It reveals him as a thoroughgoing believer in the individualistic doctrines of the nineteenth century. His acceptance of those doctrines in the realm of educational theory was wholehearted and specific. "The fundamental principle of occidental education," he wrote, "is the development of individuality." To this principle he attributed all progress in "politics, commerce, industry, art, and learning."[19] While placing high value on the works of John Stuart Mill,

[17] *The Discourses of Brigham Young*, Salt Lake City, The Deseret Book Company, 1925, p. 553.
[18] Sutherland to Mrs. Jeanette A. Hyde, May 28, 1936.
[19] Karl G. Maeser, *School and Fireside*, 1898, p. 32.

he accorded the first place among philosophers to Herbert Spencer. In a lavish tribute, he termed "this great thinker . . . the peer of Plato, Aristotle, Bacon, Newton, Leibnitz and Kant."[20]

Spencerian notions were so much a part of the intellectual atmosphere of Sutherland's early years that he could not have escaped their influence altogether,[21] and their sponsorship by a revered and seemingly omniscient teacher rendered them irresistible. Moreover, something like a cosmic conspiracy seemed to militate against any later apostasy, for when Sutherland began the study of law at the University of Michigan a few years later, his great teacher, Thomas M. Cooley, was a Spencerian disciple of the highest standing. The oracles of the bench and Sutherland's companions at the bar were also Spencerians. But this was not all. The America of Sutherland's youth was subjected to a constant barrage of Spencerian propaganda by the publicists of the day. Such writers as Christopher G. Tiedman, John Forrest Dillon, and John Randolph Tucker penned, with missionary enthusiasm, elaborate justifications of the Faith. In short, wherever he turned, Sutherland encountered the gospel of laissez faire according to Spencer.

Spencer, then, was not only the initial intellectual influence in Sutherland's life but a persisting one. He provided a basic philosophy which served as a celestial guide for Sutherland in his odyssey as lawyer, legislator, and judge. This philosophy embodied two major conceptions,

[20] *ibid.*, p. 29.

[21] Spencer's enormous influence in late nineteenth century America is attested by both Parrington and the Beards. See *Main Currents of American Thought*, New York: Harcourt, Brace and Company, 1939, III, 197-211; and *The Rise of American Civilization*, New York: Macmillan, 1943, II, 406ff. It was also noted by Justice Holmes. "H. Spencer you English never quite do justice to," he wrote Lady Pollock in 1895, "or at least those whom I have talked with do not. He is dull. He writes an ugly uncharming style, his ideals are those of a lower middle class British Philistine. And yet after all abatements I doubt if any writer of English except Darwin has done so much to affect our whole way of thinking about the universe." *Holmes-Pollock Letters*, Cambridge: Harvard University Press, 1941, I, 57-58.

each universal in scope and application: evolution and liberty.[22] Spencer believed that man, society, and the state were all results of an immeasurably lengthy growth, and that this process was to be continued to the end of time. The dynamic force was supplied by the principle of adaptation. Spencer held that every organism contains within itself an undeniable impulse urging the establishment of harmony with its environment. He insisted that "whatever possesses vitality, from the elementary cell up to man himself, obeys this law. . . . [Man] alters in colour according to temperature . . . gets larger digestive organs if he habitually eats innutritious food—acquires the power of long fasting if his mode of life is irregular, and loses it when the supply of food is certain—becomes fleet and agile in the wilderness and inert in the city—attains acute vision, hearing, and scent, when his habits of life call for them, and gets these senses blunted when they are less needful."[23] So important to Spencer was this adaptive process that he made it the sole criterion of good and evil. That which encouraged adaptation was good; that which prevented it, evil. If some outside agency should prevent the necessary adjustments, the result must surely be death and oblivion.

The second idea, that of liberty, proclaimed the freedom of the individual to effect the adaptation which nature demands. Individual happiness, in Spencer's view, was not to be found in externals; rather it was the result of the satisfaction of certain inner cravings, of self-realization. Accordingly, the essential condition of happiness was the liberty to satisfy these cravings by the exercise of the faculties of adaptation. Given free play, and unimpeded by outside interference, these faculties were certain to

[22] The discussion of Spencer which follows is drawn from his *Social Statics* and *The Man Versus the State*. I have also used Hugh Elliot, *Herbert Spencer*, New York, Henry Holt, 1917; T. J. C. Hearnshaw, *Social and Political Thinkers of the Victorian Era*, London, G. G. Harrap, 1933; and Ernest Barker, *Political Thought in England from Herbert Spencer to the Present Day*, New York, Henry Holt, 1915.

[23] Herbert Spencer, *Social Statics*, New York, D. Appleton, 1883, pp. 74-75.

produce, of their own force, a state of perfect equipoise and bliss. Spencer asserted that

progress, therefore, is not an accident, but a necessity. Instead of civilization being artificial, it is a part of nature; all of a piece with the development of the embryo or the unfolding of a flower. The modifications mankind have undergone, and are still under-going, result from a law underlying the whole organic creation; . . . As surely as the tree becomes bulky when it stands alone, and slender if one of a group; as surely as the same creature assumes the different forms of cart-horse and race-horse, according as its habits demand strength or speed; as surely as a blacksmith's arm grows large and the skin of a labourer's hand thick; as surely as the eye tends to become long-sighted in the sailor, and short-sighted in the student; . . . as surely as the musician learns to detect an error of a semitone amidst what seems to others a very babel of sounds; as surely as a passion grows by indulgence and diminishes when restrained; . . . as surely as there is any effi-cacy in educational culture, or any meaning in such terms as habit, custom, practice; so surely must the human faculties be moulded into complete fitness for the social state; so surely must the things we call evil and immorality disappear; so surely must man become perfect.[24]

The evolutionary progress toward a society capable of highest happiness was cruel, unrelenting, inevitable:

Pervading all nature we may see at work a stern discipline, which is a little cruel that it may be very kind. . . . The poverty of the incapable, the distresses that come upon the imprudent, the star-vation of the idle, and those shoulderings aside of the weak by the strong, which leave so many "in shallows and in miseries," are the decrees of a large, far-seeing benevolence. . . .

Power of application must be developed; such modification of the intellect as shall qualify it for its new tasks must take place; and, above all, there must be gained the ability to sacrifice a small immediate gratification for a future great one. The state of transition will of course be an unhappy state. Misery inevitably results from incongruity between constitution and conditions. All these evils, which afflict us, and seem to the uninitiated the obvious consequences of this or that removable cause, are unavoidable attendants on the adaptation now in progress. Humanity is being

[24] *ibid.,* p. 80.

pressed against the inexorable necessities of its new position—is being moulded into harmony with them, and has to bear the resulting unhappiness as best it can. The process must be undergone, and the sufferings must be endured. No power on earth, no cunningly-devised laws of statesmen, no world-rectifying schemes of the humane, no communist panaceas, no reforms that men ever did broach or ever will broach, can diminish them one jot. . . .[25]

For Spencer, the state was the result of the great increase in population, which had produced a condition in which individuals, in following their adaptive urges, had begun to run afoul of each other. The state emphatically was not the result of a social quality in man. On the contrary, Spencer supposed that man was by nature solitary. Instead of desiring companionship, man wished nothing so much as to be left alone. That man still contained within himself vestiges of this aboriginal predilection for solitude, and had not perfectly adapted himself to the relatively new requirements of the social state, rendered inevitable by the growth of numbers—this was the all-sufficient explanation for the existence of evil, sorrow, and pain.

Since Spencer believed that the state was unnatural, and represented a deviation from the law of liberty, he was adamant in declaring that its activities should be limited to the adjustment of the difficulties which had made it seem desirable. The overcrowding of the earth had presented a new situation. Men were confronted with the alternatives of society or perpetual war. The role of the state, therefore, was to make society possible "by retaining men in the circumstances to which they are to be adapted." When its true function of securing the adaptive process had been discharged, and man's nature had become reconciled to society, the state was destined to wither away and to appear ultimately as the crude expedient of a primitive age.

In such a philosophy, the role of the state was plainly confined to the settlement of disputes and the preservation

[25] *ibid.*, pp. 352-356.

of order. Justice was to be discovered by harking back to the original rights of man as they existed before the state had become necessary. Its administration was to be motivated by a desire to maintain, in so far as possible, all the privileges man had enjoyed in his original solitary condition. This was in accordance with the theory that man, by becoming a member of society, had surrendered no right save that of acting in a manner incompatible with the equal liberty of others.

Spencer, therefore, was certain that when the state passed beyond these confines and attempted meliorative functions it was straying from its true purposes. Moreover, any such attempt was bound to fail; since the evils which the state might seek to rectify resulted entirely from non-adaptation, the only remedy was adaptation, which interference by the state tended to prevent. For example, Spencer believed that any contribution by the state to the relief of the poor was not only an unjustifiable spoliation of the wealthier classes, on whom the burden would fall, but an essay in futility as well. "It defeats its own end," he declared.

Instead of diminishing suffering, it eventually increases it. It favors the multiplication of those worst fitted for existence, and, by consequence, hinders the multiplication of those best fitted for existence—leaving, as it does, less room for them. It tends to fill the world with those to whom life will bring most pain, and tends to keep out of it those to whom life will bring pleasure. It inflicts positive misery, and prevents positive happiness.[26]

Although the state was thus faced with certain failure when it encroached on forbidden territory, this failure was not the only price exacted for the disregard of eternal truths. The assignment of one function to one organ was an essential condition of the highest efficiency. Accordingly, when the state embarked on tasks outside its role of preserving order, there was necessarily a diminution of its ability to perform its legitimate mission. Moreover, such adventures only whetted the appetites of legislators. Once

[26] *ibid.*, p. 416.

the first forbidden step was taken, there was sure to be pressure to follow it with others: "The State's misdoings become . . . reasons for praying it to do more!"[27]

Enough has been said to show that Spencer believed that the state should be a wholly negative force of police, limiting its activities to enforcing contracts, suppressing insurrection, and repelling foreign invasion. It had no warrant for controlling education, for promoting commerce and industry, nor even for enforcing sanitation. Furthermore, once a mistake had been made it was vain to think that it could be rectified by more legislation. "Nature will not be cheated," he declared.

Every jot of the evil must in one way or other be borne—consciously or unconsciously; either in a shape that is recognized, or else under some disguise. No philosopher's stone of a constitution can produce golden conduct from leaden instincts. No apparatus of senator, judges, and police can compensate for the want of an internal governing sentiment. No legislative manipulation can eke out an insufficient morality into a sufficient one.[28]

Forms of government were therefore not considered to be of much importance. Whatever the form and wherever the sovereign power lay, government was perforce the inevitable enemy of liberty. "The divine right of majorities" was attacked as a superstition no less pernicious than that of the divine right of kings.[29] Certainly a majority should have absolute dominion in those matters which called forth the state, but beyond this it had not the slightest authority. In all other matters the right of resistance remained to each citizen, even though he should stand alone against the world. Liberty, not majority rule, was held to be the true index of democracy. The man of genuine democratic feelings was said to love freedom "as a miser loves gold, for its own sake and quite irrespective of its advantages. . . . Flimsy excuses about 'exigencies of the

---

27 *The Man Versus the State*, Caldwell, Idaho, Caxton, 1944, p. 97.
28 *Social Statics*, pp. 295-296.
29 *The Man Versus the State*, pp. 174ff.

state,' and the like, can not trap him into [acts] of self-stultification."[30]

The evidence that Spencer exerted a decisive influence on Sutherland is not confined to the fact that Maeser was such an unquestioning disciple nor to Sutherland's repeated acknowledgment of his debt to Maeser. The remarkable correspondence between Spencer's views and those expressed by Sutherland throughout his public career leaves no room for doubt. This correspondence will be made clear in later chapters. It is enough to say here that Sutherland, throughout his public career, walked in the shadow of Herbert Spencer. He appropriated to his own use the philosopher's ideas of liberty, evolution, and progress. Moreover, he also appropriated the Spencerian method. For all the data with which Spencer buttressed his arguments, he was not concerned primarily with facts, nor did they furnish him his point of departure. Instead, he began with a theory to which the facts must necessarily conform. When they did not conform, it was because the essential ones had not been discovered. This deductive method characterized all of Sutherland's efforts. Always there was a recurrence to first principles. That these principles were those of Herbert Spencer accounts for a major chapter in the history of the interpretation of the American Constitution.

3.

Sutherland left Brigham Young Academy in the summer of 1881 when he became the forwarding agent for the contractors building the Rio Grande Western Railroad.[31] Fifteen months later he made the long trip to Ann Arbor to enter the University of Michigan Law School. When Sutherland matriculated, the Michigan Law School was riding the crest of a nationwide fame. Its students came from all parts of the country in response to a catholic invitation which excluded only those under eighteen years of age and those unable to furnish "certificates giving

---

[30] *Social Statics,* pp. 268-269.   [31] Gray, *op. cit.,* p. 2.

satisfactory evidence of good moral character." The dean of the School was the celebrated judge and scholar previously mentioned, Thomas McIntyre Cooley. Of almost equal eminence was James Valentine Campbell, Chief Justice of the Michigan Supreme Court, a member of the faculty for many years.

The system of instruction was simple, consisting only of lectures and moot-court work.[32] There were ten lectures a week of an hour each. No subject required more than thirty-one lectures for its exposition and several were disposed of with only one or two. Although a state institution, the Law School put no particular emphasis on Michigan law and procedure, but strove, by the inculcation of general principles, to equip its graduates to practice in any common-law jurisdiction.

In Sutherland's day the curriculum included two courses relating to constitutional law and theory. The first was given by Judge Campbell under the general heading, "The Jurisprudence of the United States." Later Cooley lectured on the general principles of constitutional law. After each lecture the two judges entered in their record book the subject covered. From these titles and other materials, it is possible to get a fairly precise idea of the nature of the instruction and its content. Campbell gave thirty-one lectures, all of which dealt with the Constitution and the laws of the United States.[33] Campbell's lec-

[32] The material in this and the following paragraphs is taken from the record book kept by the faculty and the notebooks of De Forrest Paine, Alexander Hamilton, Jr., and Marshall Davis Ewell, students in the Law School in this period. The record book and the notebooks are in the University of Michigan Libraries. I should like to acknowledge here the assistance given me in the use of these materials by Dean E. Blythe Stason.

[33] The lecture topics as recorded by Campbell for the term Sutherland was in his class were: Lectures Introductory to United States Jurisprudence; Historical Antecedents; Legal Position of the Continental Congress; Defects of the Articles of Confederation; General Purposes of United States Constitution; Some Special Considerations; Some Restrictions on State Action; Bills of Credit-Retrospective Laws; Protection of Contracts; Judgments and other Public Acts; Rights of Citizens; Sources of United States Law; United States Law-Places Sub-

tures were especially notable in one particular. In them, he clearly articulated the theory of the foreign relations power which prevails today as a result of two of Sutherland's most celebrated opinions.[34] Otherwise, he made few excursions into the realm of theory. This latter province was, appropriately, reserved to Cooley.[35]

In 1882, when Sutherland was his student, Cooley was conceded to be the "greatest American writer on Constitutional Law" and "the most frequently quoted authority."[36] In 1868 he had published his great *Treatise on the*

---

ject to U.S. Jurisdiction; Law of Nations; Law of Nations; Same Subject; Law of Nations Concluded; Congressional Power; Regulation of Commerce; Naturalization; Bankruptcy; Post Office; Coinage; Maritime Offenses; Copyright; Copyright; Patents; Patents; Patents; Patents; Judicial System of the United States; Judicial Power; United States Courts; Judicial System of United States Concluded.

[34] *United States* v. *Curtiss-Wright Export Corp.*, 299 U.S. 304 (1936); *United States* v. *Belmont*, 301 U.S. 324 (1937). For Campbell's views on the foreign relations power, see Chapter 6.

[35] The Cooley lecture topics were: Introductory Address; Introduction to Constitutional Law; General Principles and Definitions; The Same Subject; The Charters of English Constitutional Liberty; The Same Subject; General Principle of Constitutional Right; The Same Subject; General Principles—The Right of Revolution; Territorial Government— Steps in the Formation of States; The Purpose in Forming a Constitution and Apportionment of Powers; The Checks and Balances of Government—Judicial Powers and Their Finality; The Apportionment of Power by State Constitutions; The Same Subject; Power of the Legislative Department—Vested Rights and Its Control in Respect to Them; The Same Subject—Control of Remedies; Vested Rights—Retrospective Laws; Legislative Control of Estates; Domestic Relations; Due Process of Law; Protection to Civil Liberty by State Constitutions; The Same Subject; Religious Liberty; Protection in Liberty and Property against Unwarranted Judicial Action; Political Rights—the Right to Assemble and Discuss Public Affairs: To Petition, To Bear Arms; The Liberty of Speech and of the Press; Appropriation of Private Property to Public Use—Under the War Power; Under the Treaty Making Power; The Power of Taxation and the Restriction Upon It; Constitutional Protection of Private Property—Appropriation of Private Property to Public Use; The Same Subject. In the discussion of Cooley which follows, for purposes of clarity and convenience I rely on his *Constitutional Limitations* rather than the student notebooks. The same material generally was presented in the lectures as in the book.

[36] Benjamin R. Twiss, *Lawyers and The Constitution*, Princeton, Princeton University Press, 1942, pp. 34-35.

Constitutional Limitations Which Rest upon the Legislative Power of the States of the American Union.[37] Cooley's design is suggested by the title of his book. It is concerned with *Limitations,* and in his preface he specifically avows his "sympathy with the restraints which the caution of the fathers had imposed upon the exercise of the powers of government."[38] In defining the state, he made it quite clear that it was a voluntary association of individuals for their own advantage.[39] He was careful to point out that individual rights were antecedent to both states and constitutions and that the latter did not "measure the rights of the governed."[40] He quoted with approval the following excerpt from a Missouri case:

What is a constitution and what are its objects? It is easier to tell what it is not than what it is. It is not the beginning of a community, nor the origin of private rights; it is not the fountain of law, nor the incipient state of government; it is not the cause, but consequence of personal and political freedom; it grants no rights to the people, but is the creature of their power, the instrument of their convenience. Designed for their protection in the enjoyment of the rights which they possessed before the constitution was made, it is but the framework of the political government, and based upon the pre-existing condition of law, rights, habits, and modes of thought. There is nothing primitive in it: It is all derived from a known source. It presupposes an organized society, law and order, property, personal freedom, a love of political liberty, and enough of cultivated intelligence to know how to guard it against the encroachments of tyranny. *A written constitution is in every instance a limitation upon the powers of government in the hands of agents; for there never was a written republican constitution which delegated to functionaries all the latent powers which lie dormant in every nation and are boundless in extent and incapable of definition.*[41]

[37] Edward S. Corwin has said that Cooley's book is "the most influential treatise ever published on American constitutional law." See his *Liberty Against Government*, Baton Rouge, Louisiana State University Press, 1948, p. 116.

[38] Thomas M. Cooley, Constitutional Limitations (1st ed. 1868), p. 12.
[39] *ibid.* (7th ed. 1903), p. 1.   [40] *ibid.*, p. 68.
[41] *Hamilton* v. *St. Louis County Court*, 15 Mo. 1, 13 (1851). Italics are mine.

From such a conception of the Constitution, it was easy for Cooley to infer that large areas were protected by the "law of the land" from the depredations of legislatures. The plain design of this law was to exclude "arbitrary power from every branch of the government."[42] "The principles upon which process is based" and not "any considerations of mere form" were to determine whether "due process" had been observed.[43] Vested rights were not to be thought of in "any narrow or technical sense," but rather as implying an interest "which it is right and equitable that the government should recognize and protect and of which the individual could not be deprived arbitrarily without injustice. . . ."[44]

In sketching the bounds of permissible legislative action, Cooley regarded as fundamental the axiom that "equality of rights, privileges, and capacities unquestionably should be the aim of the law."[45] If some people were to be deprived of their capacity to contract, it could "scarcely be doubted that the act would transcend the due bounds of legislative power, even though no express constitutional provision could be pointed out with which it would come in conflict."[46] Cooley then advanced the thought—one his zealous pupil committed to memory for use years later—that those who sought to justify such deprivations "ought to be able to show a specific authority therefor, instead of calling upon others to show how and where the authority is negatived."[47] The police power was said to extend only to the enactment of "those rules of good manners and good neighborhood which are calculated to prevent a conflict of rights, and to insure to each the uninterrupted enjoyment of his own, so far as is reasonable, with a like enjoyment of rights by others."[48] It did not include a general power to regulate

[42] Cooley, Constitutional Limitations (7th ed. 1903), p. 504.
[43] ibid., p. 505.   [44] ibid., p. 508.   [45] ibid., p. 562.   [46] ibid., p. 561.
[47] "Freedom of contract is . . . the general rule and restraint the exception." Sutherland for the Court in Adkins v. Children's Hospital, 261 U.S. 525, 546 (1923).
[48] Cooley, op. cit., p. 829.

prices, as such an exertion by the state was held to be "inconsistent with constitutional liberty."[49]

On this point the professor had to contend with the recently decided case of *Munn* v. *Illinois*,[50] in which the Supreme Court sustained price control for storage charges in grain elevators. His point of attack was that eventually used by the Court and Sutherland himself—an emphasis on Chief Justice Waite's rather superfluous quotation from Lord Hale, that businesses "affected with a public interest" could be regulated. "The mere fact," Cooley commented, "that the public have an interest in the existence of the business, and are accommodated by it, can not be sufficient, for that would subject the stock of the merchant, and his charges, to public regulation."[51] Businesses were affected with a public interest, in the constitutional sense, only when they derived some unusual advantage from the state.

Such was Sutherland's introduction to the formal study of the Constitution. As he had learned from Spencer that laissez faire had a cosmic sanction and application, just so he derived from Cooley the conviction that the Constitution affirmed this truth. Indeed, this harmony appeared to be so perfect that Sutherland continued to believe, as Professor Maeser did, that it was the result of divine intervention.

4.

Sutherland did not take a degree at the University. It seems likely that he stayed there only one term, for in March 1883, he was licensed to practice law in Michigan.[52] This suggests that Sutherland may possibly have had some intention of remaining there. If so, his mind was changed for him by a young lady he had met at the Brigham Young Academy, Rosamond Lee. They were married in the summer of 1883. Their union was a happy one, lasting for nearly sixty years. Within the next few years they became

[49] *ibid.*, p. 870.
[51] Cooley, *op. cit.*, pp. 872-873.
[50] 94 U.S. 113 (1877).
[52] Gray, *op. cit.*, p. 4.

the parents of two girls, Edith and Emma, and a boy, Philip.

Immediately after his marriage, Sutherland joined his father in a partnership known as "Sutherland and Son" for the practice of law in Provo. From the first he seems to have done well. If fees were not large they were numerous. An account book kept by the eager young lawyer reveals that he had some twenty or twenty-five clients a month, who paid an average of $15 each. Some charges were only a dollar or two, but there were occasionally fees ranging up to $100.

In the small town of Provo specialization was out of the question, and we have Sutherland's word for it that public opinion would not allow him to pick and choose his clients. Accordingly, he had his share of the rough customers known to every frontier community. Among the first was a group of fifteen Irishmen charged with murder. One of their fellows had been killed and the assassin had been lynched, allegedly by Sutherland's fifteen clients. "Such a multitude," Sutherland recalled later, "all big-fisted and fierce-hearted men, charged with the most serious crime, almost overwhelmed me. Suppose, I thought, all of them are hanged! The possibility troubled my conscience and tore great holes in my nerves. When I slept I could see them dangling from the gibbet right before my self-accusing eyes." His fears were not realized, however. Only seven of the Irishmen were convicted and none was sent to the gallows.[53]

In 1886, the partnership between father and son was dissolved. The younger Sutherland thereupon joined forces with Samuel R. Thurman, later Chief Justice of the Utah Supreme Court. Soon afterward, William H. King, who also was to rise to prominence, joined the firm. As a young lawyer, Sutherland devoted himself to the extra-legal activities usually followed by those similarly situated. He made patriotic addresses and he took part in local politics. Even though the issues were local, and relatively unim-

[53] *Cincinnati Enquirer*, August 13, 1916.

portant, Sutherland discussed them in terms of the great problems of political theory. His first effort along these lines is an interesting one even today. It reveals the essential identity of the mind of the twenty-four year old attorney of 1886 and the Supreme Court Justice of 1937.

The city council of Provo had, in the face of a clearly preponderant opposing sentiment, issued licenses for the sale of liquor. For this disregard of the popular will, the councilmen were soundly berated by the city newspaper. Sutherland sprang to their defense with a reply reminiscent of Burke. The city fathers, he explained, were under no obligation to heed the voice of the people. Indeed, they should not. They had only to satisfy "their own consciences and their own reason of the rightfulness, policy, justice, consistency and legality of any contemplated legislation." When they had done this, he concluded, they could, "with a good deal of propriety, invoke Mr. Vanderbilt's somewhat profane and summary disposition of a stiff-necked and unappreciative public."[54]

In this same year, Sutherland had one of his most important cases at the bar. It concerned polygamy, which in those years was a vital issue in Utah. The reason was that the United States had, after a long period of toleration, commenced an intensive enforcement of the Edmunds Act [55]

---

[54] *Territorial Inquirer* (Provo), December 10, 1886. *Cf.* the following from Sutherland's dissenting opinion in *West Coast Hotel Co.* v. *Parrish*, 300 U.S. 379, 401-402, 57 Sup. Ct. 578, 81 L. Ed. 703 (1937): "It has been pointed out many times . . . that this judicial duty (that of passing on the constitutionality of a statute) is one of gravity and delicacy; and that rational doubts must be resolved in favor of the constitutionality of the statutes. But whose doubts, and by whom resolved? Undoubtedly it is the duty of a member of the court . . . to give due weight to the opposing views of his associates; but in the end, the question which he must answer is not whether such views seem sound to those who entertain them, but whether they convince him that the statute is constitutional or engender in his mind a rational doubt upon that issue. The oath which he takes as a judge is not a composite oath, but an individual one. And in passing upon the validity of a statute, he discharges a duty imposed upon him. . . . If upon a question so important he thus surrender his deliberate judgment, he stands forsworn. He cannot subordinate his convictions to that extent and keep faith with his oath or retain his judicial and moral independence."

[55] 22 Stat. 30.

prohibiting the practice. One of those indicted in the new drive was a man named Grosbeck, who retained Sutherland as his lawyer. The indictment charged him with unlawful cohabitation on two counts. Sutherland objected on the grounds that the offense was a continuing one and that therefore Grosbeck was amenable to but one conviction and one sentence. In a companion case,[56] the Supreme Court of the United States later accepted this view. While he did not appear as counsel before the high court, Sutherland was credited with originating the argument that brought some relief to the harassed Saints. His brief, replete with citations from English cases, was published by the daily press[57] and Sutherland became something of a hero to the Faithful.

5.

This was but one incident of Sutherland's lifelong relationship with the Mormons. The settling of Utah was, of course, directly attributable to them, and they have since retained a dominant position in the state. In this they have been aided by an organization described by one observer as "the most nearly perfect piece of social mechanism with which I have ever, in any way, come in contact, excepting only the German army."[58] The Church is hierarchial in structure and its authority has not been confined to religious matters. Especially was this true in the earlier days. Joseph Smith and later Brigham Young exercised secular powers on a considerable scale. Indeed, under the presidency of Brigham Young, there had been a formal union of church and state, accomplished by his appointment as Governor of the Territory.[59] So long as only Mormons lived in Utah, little opposition was voiced to such an ar-

[56] *Snow* v. *United States*, 120 U.S. 274.

[57] *Territorial Inquirer* (Provo), June 15, 1886; *Territory* v. *Grosbeck*, 4 Utah 487 (1886).

[58] Richard T. Ely, "Economic Aspects of Mormonism," *Harper's Magazine*, cvi (April, 1903), 667-678.

[59] These and other facts of Mormon history are contained in a speech made by Sutherland to the Senate in 1907. See 41 *Cong. Rec.* 1492.

rangement. But the immigration of Gentiles in considerable numbers subjected Mormon social policy to constant criticism and in turn stimulated counter measures on the part of the Church. One of these, of particular importance, was the establishment, in 1868, under the aegis of the Church, of a number of cooperative business enterprises. An intensive effort was made to insure that every Saint should be a stockholder. Those without money were allowed to contribute either labor or goods. The object was confessedly to render the Mormons independent of the oncoming Gentiles. An important corollary was the injunction laid on church members not to trade outside the Church.[60]

The Gentiles regarded such measures as "unfair competition." Their response was the organization, in 1870, of a political party known as "Liberal." It was under the banner of this party that Sutherland made his debut in politics. In 1880 at the age of eighteen, he served as secretary of the party convention.[61] Some indication of the party's program is furnished by its Congressional candidate's letter accepting the nomination in 1876. "I desire," the aspirant wrote, "the establishment of the supremacy of law, freedom of thought, freedom of speech and freedom of action in Utah—to establish a system under which everyone may freely and fully exercise his own individuality, choose his own business, political, and social relations."[62] Sutherland, no doubt, subscribed wholeheartedly to these Spencerian objectives and did what he could for the party's success. In 1890 he was its candidate for mayor of Provo, but failed by something like a two-to-one margin.[63]

By that time the party had become distinctly less militant in its opposition to the Church. It had then only the single goal of delaying the admission of Utah to the

60 My account is drawn from Hamilton Gardner's "Cooperation Among the Mormons," *Quarterly Journal of Economics*, xxxi (1917), 461-503.

61 Jensen, *History of Provo*, p. 188.

62 R. W. Baskin, *Reminiscences of Early Utah*, Salt Lake City (1914), p. 25. Baskin has an excellent account of the rise of the Liberal party.

63 Jensen, *History of Provo*, p. 194.

Union until polygamy should be abolished. In this it was joined by a number of younger Mormons, among them Reed Smoot. The explanation of this change in policy lies, perhaps, in the change in the Church. After the death of Brigham Young in 1877, the cooperatives, with the assent of the hierarchy, began to lose something of their democratic, equalitarian character. Ownership was permitted to become centralized. Furthermore, under the new policy of laissez faire, the advantages of the cooperatives were made available to the Gentiles. As Bernard DeVoto says, "Israel had to make terms with finance" and hence developed "not in the direction of Rochdale, New Harmony, the Oneida community, Brook Farm, the United Order or the Kingdom of God—but in the direction of Standard Oil."[64] Obviously, nature was not to be cheated!

The lesson for Sutherland in the failure of these Mormon cooperative adventures was the inevitable triumph of natural forces which defied control. In yet another way Sutherland's life in Utah confirmed his individualistic leanings. Long before Sutherland's memory, Brigham Young had, by a rigorous control of the water supply, made large holdings of land unprofitable. In Utah, therefore, there was a widespread holding of land. One traveler reported that the economy was based on the general ownership of land, remarking, "All are proprietors; none are tenants."[65] Brigham Young had intervened, also, to place a ban on speculative enterprises, such as mining. The result was that Utah presented to Sutherland's eyes something approaching Jefferson's ideal of an agrarian democracy where each man was the master of his own vine and fig tree. The Mormons did not wait for the state to build schools but furnished their own with such effectiveness that there was less illiteracy than in Massachusetts.[66] In other ways, they seemed to demonstrate that the coercive meas-

[64] *Forays and Rebuttals*, Boston, Little, Brown and Company, 1936, p. 122.
[65] William E. Smythe, "Utah as an Industrial Object Lesson," *Atlantic Monthly*, LXXVIII (1896), 610.
[66] *ibid.*

ures of the state were unnecessary. They were infused with a passion for independence, and Sutherland frequently testified to their energy and thrift. Initiative had its due reward and idleness none at all. Brigham Young himself declared: "My experience has taught me, and it has become a principle with me, that it is never any benefit to give out and out, to man or woman, money, food, clothing or anything else if he is able-bodied and can work and earn what he needs, when there is anything on earth for him to do. To pursue a contrary course would ruin any community in the world."[67] A half century later the Church remembered these words and, with Sutherland's warm applause,[68] forbade acceptance by its members of government relief.[69] The result of Sutherland's contact with the Mormons was that they confirmed him in his Spencerian ideology. Where they appeared to challenge it, as for example, in the cooperatives, they were unsuccessful and, where guided by it, victorious in the face of all obstacles.

6.

In 1890 the Church issued its famous manifesto prohibiting the further contracting of polygamous marriages. The way was then clear for politics to assume a national pattern. The Liberal party, its mission accomplished, was soon disbanded. Sutherland promptly announced himself to be a Republican.[70] Two considerations were probably responsible for this choice. Coming as he did from England and with no antecedents in either party, Sutherland prized the record of the Republicans as the party of the Union. All through his political career he seemed to remember that the secessionists had been Democrats. The second reason was that the Republicans believed so strongly in a protective tariff. With its sugar, lead, and wool industries, Utah was peculiarly fertile ground for the protective idea.

[67] Quoted in the *New York Times*, August 7, 1936.
[68] Sutherland to Mrs. Jeanette A. Hyde, May 26, 1936.
[69] *New York Times*, October 3, 1936.
[70] Jensen, *History of Provo*, p. 197.

Already in 1888, along with Reed Smoot, Sutherland had organized the Harrison-Morton Republican Club of Central Utah. In 1892 he sought the Republican nomination for Congressional Delegate but failed by the slender margin of six votes. That same year he attended his first Republican National Convention as an alternate.

In 1893 Sutherland, seeking larger opportunities, moved from Provo to Salt Lake City, where he became a member of one of the leading law firms.[71] The rewards were immediate; in a short while, Sutherland's income rose to a figure of over $10,000 annually.[72] His growing stature in the profession received other confirmation. In 1894, he was one of the organizers of the Utah State Bar Association. The next year he was one of the speakers at the annual meeting.

The subject of this speech was "The Selection, Tenure, and Compensation of the Judiciary."[73] In addition to recommendations on each of these issues, it contained some interesting revelations of Sutherland's early conception of the nature of law and of the judicial function. To bolster his argument for an indeterminate tenure for the judiciary, Sutherland adduced a comparison of its task with that of the legislature. Legislators, he explained, must always be concerned with the "changing needs and views of the people" and should reflect these changes. A wholly different situation was said to obtain with the judiciary. "Judges," he amplified, "do not make laws, but declare them; the rules which govern their deliberations and decisions are to a large extent fixed and permanent, in no wise to be controlled by temporary considerations or policies." This being true, the judge of one era could easily satisfy the demands of another. Even so great a legislator as Daniel Webster "would stand aghast in the attempt to legislate for the people of the present day"; but an eminent jurist like Chancellor Kent could be transplanted with

---

[71] Others in the firm were Parley L. Williams and Waldemar Van Cott.
[72] Account book in Sutherland papers.
[73] 2 *Rep. Utah Bar Ass'n* 47 (1895).

ease. He would be able, merely "by reading the statutes which have been enacted since his death," to "serve the commonwealth quite as well as any of the present incumbents"![74]

The mission of the judiciary also came in for review. The judicial department was said to stand "as a shield to prevent the exercise of oppressive and arbitrary power on the part of the government itself, whose creature it is, against the citizen, though never so humble or insignificant. Its duty is to protect the individual against the unjust demands of society."[75] Since they had only to "declare and apply the law," courts often had "the solemn duty to disregard the wishes and sentiments of a majority of the people and declare in favor of the position of a single individual" as against the whole world.[76] Hence, the judicial department "is and should be the strongest" branch of the government.

7.

Sutherland's address, with its overweening concern for the protection of the minority, was not unlike hundreds of others delivered to lawyers in the closing years of the last century. Far beyond its actual contents, it is important as a reminder that Sutherland's formative years at the bar coincided with the development of a political creed by American lawyers openly and bitterly hostile to majority rule. This creed was essentially the Spencerian gospel of laissez faire but it was preached with a new intensity by such eminent lawyers as John Forrest Dillon, Joseph Choate, and John Randolph Tucker. Sutherland could not escape hearing this preaching by his seniors in the profession. The important fact is that he listened. In later years he was to quote "Mr. Tucker" as if he were unquestionable authority. Indeed, Tucker's personal influence on Sutherland is easily demonstrated. But Tucker is perhaps more important as a fair representative of the influence of the legal profession generally. In his works, one

[74] *ibid.*, p. 57.   [75] *ibid.*, p. 47.   [76] *ibid.*, p. 48.

can find a systematic expression of the ideas Sutherland daily met with in contacts with other lawyers.

Tucker, once president of the American Bar Association, was a professor of law at Washington and Lee University and a publicist of note. He was the author of a huge two-volume treatise on the Constitution.[77] His book reveals him to have been an orthodox Spencerian. Once more, happiness is held to be "the status wherein man is in harmony with self and the external world."[78] Interference with the liberty of another is an impious encroachment on rights which come from God, to whom alone the individual is responsible. The object of government is to achieve "the greatest good to each—consistent with the greatest good to all, and not the greatest good to the greatest number."[79] Paternalism in political agencies comes in for a most scathing excoriation, being based, as Tucker said, on falsehood and fraud. It would surely result in a plutocracy of the few and pauperism of the mass. Tucker asserted as his "cardinal canon of political science: Limit law-making to the defense of man-right, and of his self-use for self-development, without aid or hindrance from government."[80]

Tucker proposed to enforce adherence to this principle in the United States by means of an extreme federalism. He held the Constitution to be "not a social compact, but an interstate compact" between thirteen "free, sovereign and independent states," ordained and ratified by them in their corporate capacities.[81] In another place, Tucker denominated the Union "a confederacy by State Peoples." It was "artificial and derivative"; only the states were "natural and original." As such, they were "indivisible, indestructible, and impenetrable."[82]

With these conceptions of the origin of the Constitution and of the states, it was easy for Tucker to find that Calhoun's theory of concurrent majorities was in full force in

[77] John Randolph Tucker, *The Constitution of the United States*, Chicago, Callaghan and Company, 1899.
[78] *ibid.*, p. 21.   [79] *ibid.*, p. 55.   [80] *ibid.*, pp. 83-84.
[81] *ibid.*, p. 73.   [82] *ibid.*, p. 314.

the United States. This spectacle excited Tucker to the most extravagant laudation of the federal system. It was "an example in which the guards to the personal rights and liberties of the people are better defined and more effectual than under any system of government known among men." "How majestic," his rhapsody continued, "is this essential unity of the people's will and purpose through diverse and independent agencies for their expression! How true a unity is obtained by not taking the will of the whole without reference to the parts, but the will of each distinct part to attain the will of the whole! *How superior this to a government based on the majority of numbers! The government of the numerical majority is the mechanism of brute force: ours is the result of the triumph of the moral forces of intelligent popular will over brutal selfishness.*"[83]

On such a diet did Sutherland feed. It was no doubt rendered palatable by the marvelous compatibility existing between Tucker's conception of the Union and the idea of laissez faire. For when Tucker came to discuss the various powers granted Congress by the Constitution, he insisted that they were limited by those reserved to the states. For example, he bitterly attacked the notion that the general welfare clause was a substantive addition to Congressional power; and even if it were, he argued, it could not be used for "purposes which are within the exclusive province of the states."[84] His treatment of the commerce clause was along similar lines. In regard to it, he produced the following two controlling canons of interpretation:

1st. Commercial power to be necessary and proper while regulating commerce in its normal condition, must so regulate as not to destroy the essential reserved rights of the States. It is neither necessary nor proper for it to do so, but both unnecessary and improper. . . .

2nd. As long as the person or thing is in commercial *transitu* the State can not touch it, and the State must so exercise its power in respect to these as not to interfere with the essential rights of Congress to regulate commerce. But before transitus has

[83] *ibid.*, p. 101. Italics are mine.   [84] *ibid.*, pp. 476-479.

once begun, or having begun has ceased, congressional power does not attach and the State power is exclusive.[85]

What Tucker hinted at here, he explicitly developed elsewhere in his discussion of commerce as being principally transportation.[86] Furthermore, he drew a fine distinction between commerce and the *objects* of commerce, to which the power of the general government was held not to extend.[87] Yet another diminution of the grant was achieved by the theory that, since the purpose of the Constitution was the liberation of commerce from obstacles imposed by the states, the power to create new obstacles could not be attributed to the new government. Therefore, it must be predicted, Tucker declared, "that the courts will never hold any law of Congress, which prohibits, restricts, or ties interstate commerce, to be either necessary or proper as a regulation of commerce, but they must hold it to be a perversion of the fundamental principles of the constitution."[88]

These, then, were the theories of the Constitution current among Sutherland's companions at the bar as he was making his way to eminence in the legal profession. It can be seen that they beautifully complemented the teachings of Maeser and Cooley. And when after 1890, the Supreme Court of the United States, following years of resistance, made the lawyers' ideas its own, it must have seemed to the adoring Sutherland that their validity as eternal principles had been indisputably established.

8.

The development whereby the Court was won to the ideology of laissez faire and dual federalism roughly paralleled the first thirty-five years of Sutherland's life. It thus was an integral part of his education and must be considered, if only summarily. The major prophet on the Court of the new day was the renowned Stephen J. Field who was to wrest from John Marshall the record for

---

85 *ibid.*, p. 536. 86 *ibid.*, pp. 523ff.
87 *ibid.*, p. 526. 88 *ibid.*, p. 529.

tenure.[89] In the course of his long career as a Justice, Field achieved a spectacular triumph in persuading the Court to abandon its traditional tolerance for state legislative action. Field's substitute was a theory of supraconstitutional rights enforceable in the courts irrespective of popular majorities. It was first advanced by him, in 1871, in the *Legal Tender Cases*.[90] He was then speaking, it should be noted, for a minority.

For acts of flagrant injustice . . . there is no authority in any legislative body; even though not restrained by an express constitutional prohibition. For as there are unchangeable principles of right and morality without which society would be impossible, and men would be but wild beasts preying upon each other, so there are fundamental principles of eternal justice, upon the existence of which all constitutional government is founded, and without which government would be intolerable and hateful tyranny.[91]

Two years later the *Slaughter House Cases* [92] brought before the Justices, for the first time, the Fourteenth Amendment. The result was a decision announcing that, except in regard to recently liberated slaves, the states' legislative power remained unimpaired. In a noteworthy dissent,[93] Field protested that the rights of citizens were antecedent to the creation of a state and could not "be destroyed by its power." The due process clause of the Fourteenth Amendment, if constitutional provision were needed, was to be construed as a substantive limitation on the states. He developed his theory still further, again in dissent, in the *Munn* case[94] three years later. By liberty,

---

[89] An excellent and thoroughly readable biography is Carl Brent Swisher's *Stephen J. Field, Craftsman of the Law*, Washington, The Brookings Institution, 1940. See also Howard Jay Graham, "Justice Field and the Fourteenth Amendment," 52 *Yale L. J.* 852 (1943). On the general development of constitutional law in the last part of the century see Edward S. Corwin, "Social Planning Under the Constitution," *Am. Pol. Sci. Rev.*, xxvi (1932), 1, and Alpheus T. Mason, "The Conservative World of Mr. Justice Sutherland, 1883-1900," *Am. Pol. Sci. Rev.*, xxxii (1938), 443.

[90] 12 Wall. 457 (1871).   [91] *ibid.*, p. 670.
[92] 16 Wall. 36 (1873).   [93] *ibid.*, pp. 83-111.
[94] *Munn* v. *Illinois*, 94 U.S. 113 (1877).

Field said, something more was intended than "mere free-dom from physical restraint or the bounds of a prison." It meant freedom "to act in such manner, not inconsistent with the equal rights of others, as [one's] judgment may dictate for the promotion of his happiness; that is, to pursue such callings and avocations as may be most suit-able to develop [one's] capacities, and give to them their highest enjoyment."[95]

Field's great quarrel with his brethren was really over the question of judicial supremacy. Were judges bound to respect legislative determinations of reasonableness, as Waite had indicated in the *Munn* case? In the years im-mediately following that decision, it seemed that the an-swer would continue to be in the affirmative. Indeed, the situation was such that, as late as 1890, there was a de-mand for still further amendment of the Constitution to the end that property rights should be rendered secure from the threat of popular majorities.[96] But relief came quickly thereafter, and without formal amendment of the Constitution. In that very year, the first *Minnesota Rate* case[97] was decided. By this decision, the Court claimed for the judiciary the right to determine the ultimate rea-sonableness of utility rates. All possible doubt of the Court's intention to rule was erased in 1895 by the de-cisions rendered in *Pollock* v. *Farmers Loan & Trust Com-pany*,[98] *United States* v. *E. C. Knight Company*,[99] and *In re Debs*.[100]

In the first of these cases, the Court heard Joseph Choate assail the income tax as "communistic," and responded with the findings that it was a direct tax and therefore invalid unless apportioned. Justice Field made known the Court's fear that this assault on capital was only the be-

---

95 *ibid.*, p. 142.

96 Marshall, "A New Constitutional Amendment," 24 *Am. L. Rev.* 908 (1890).

97 *Chicago, M. & St. P. Ry.* v. *Minnesota*, 134 U.S. 418 (1890).

98 157 U.S. 429 (1895).

99 156 U.S. 1 (1895).

100 158 U.S. 564 (1895).

ginning, that it would be "but the stepping stone to others, larger and more sweeping, till our political contests will become a war of the poor against the rich, a war constantly growing in intensity and bitterness."[101]

Only three months before the *Pollock* case, the Court had occasion to declare that the activities of the Sugar Trust were not subject to the power of Congress. The result was the virtual nullification of the Sherman Act for more than a decade, and the curtailment of the commerce power to the point of impotence.

The *Debs* case supplied the business community with protection from interference originating in yet another quarter. There, in the absence of a statute authorizing such procedure, the Court approved the issuance of an injunction restraining Debs and the other leaders of the Pullman strike of 1894 from interfering, by either speech or act, with the operation of the railroads. Justice Brewer, speaking for the Court, declared that "the strong arm of the National Government could be put forth to brush away all obstructions to the *freedom* of interstate commerce."[102] The fact that the injunction had broken the strike was cited as proof of "the wisdom of the course pursued by the Government."[103] Private employers were not slow to take the hint, and the injunction was sped upon its notorious career in the "settlement" of labor disputes—a career which abated only with the Norris-LaGuardia Act in 1932.[104]

The result of the Court's vast extension of its powers was to endow it, in some quarters at least, with a prestige it had not enjoyed since the days of Marshall. More and more, the justices were called upon to determine the political destiny of the country. To all such invitations they responded with an alacrity which discouraged any doubt of their superior qualifications. The judges themselves,

[101] *Pollock* v. *Farmers Loan & Trust Co.*, 157 U.S. 429, 607, 15 Sup. Ct. 673, 39 L. Ed. 759 (1895).

[102] *In re Debs*, 158 U.S. 564, 582, 15 Sup. Ct. 900, 39 L. Ed. 1092 (1895). Italics are mine.

[103] *ibid.*, p. 598.

[104] 47 Stat. 70-73 (1932), 29 U.S.C. § 101-115 (1946).

perhaps a little intoxicated by their power and the homage paid them, were not inclined to be apologetic for the new state of affairs. When Justice Field retired in 1897, he unblushingly reminded his brethren that they constituted the "safeguard that keeps the whole mighty fabric of government from rushing to destruction."[105] And Justice Brewer, in 1893, could see no reason why judges should not govern. The great body of them, he asserted,

are as well versed in the affairs of life as any, and they who unravel all the mysteries of accounting between partners, settle the business of the largest corporations and extract all the truth from the mass of sciolistic verbiage that falls from the lips of expert witnesses in patent cases, will have no difficulty in determining what is right and wrong between employer and employees, and whether proposed rates of freight and fare are reasonable as between the public and owners; while as for speed, is there anything quicker than a writ of injunction?[106]

The wonders performed by the justices must have impressed Sutherland as he watched the course of constitutional development. In law school, he had been assured that the sound and enlightened view, the intellectually respectable view, was that of the minority. Now this minority had converted itself into a majority. What better proof was needed of the wisdom of his teachers? There is other evidence, considerably less speculative, that the Court of 1895 impressed itself on Sutherland's consciousness. His entire subsequent career confirms the fact. For him, as for the justices, popular government, unrestrained by judges, was unthinkable and sure to result in self-obliteration. He absorbed not only this Court's general outlook but its particular conception of federalism, liberty, and property. In 1909 he explicitly asserted his high opinion of the 1895 Court. Its members, he declared, "were as magnificently equipped in learning and ability as any who have sat in that august tribunal before or since";

105 168 U.S. 717 (1897). Field sagely concluded, "This negative power, the power of resistance, is the only safety of a popular government, and it is an additional assurance when the power is in such hands as yours."

106 Quoted by Alpheus T. Mason in *Brandeis, A Free Man's Life*, New York, Viking, 1946, p. 102.

moreover, if, in the *Pollock* case, they appeared to set at naught prior rulings of a hundred years, it was but the correction of a century of error.[107]

9.

On Utah's admission to the Union in 1896, Sutherland was elected to the first state legislature. There he served as chairman of the Senate Judiciary Committee. In this office he helped shape the institutions of the new state. He was active, too, in forwarding other legislation. Particularly notable was his advocacy of the eight-hour day for miners, the statute sustained by the Supreme Court in *Holden* v. *Hardy*.[108] If Sutherland's championship of this measure is surprising, his support of William Jennings Bryan in the year's presidential campaign is even more so. Sutherland later explained that his stand was occasioned solely by Bryan's views on the free coinage of silver, from which the people of Utah had much to gain.

The first phase of Sutherland's career may be said to have been brought to a close in 1900 when he first sought and won a national office. By that date, at the age of thirty-eight, he had become a well-established figure, both professionally and politically. In only eighteen years at the bar he had won for himself reputation and a reasonable financial competence. More important, he had amassed the intellectual resources on which he was to draw in the years ahead. There were, of course, details here and there to be filled in, but, by and large, his education was complete. Maeser, Cooley, Utah society, Bench and Bar, all had a part in the process. Had they allied themselves beforehand they could hardly have produced a more perfect harmony. And in this lay both the strength and the weakness of George Sutherland as he began a service of nearly forty years in the nation's highest councils.

[107] 44 *Cong. Rec.* 2096 (1909).

[108] 169 U.S. 366 (1898). Sutherland related his part in the adoption of the statute in the course of an address to the Senate in 1912. See 48 *Cong. Rec.* 6797 (1912).

2

MISGIVINGS, 1900-1912

In 1900, when he was thirty-eight, George Sutherland was named by the Republicans of Utah as their candidate for the state's lone Congressional seat. Sutherland, of course, was no stranger to the inner circle of the party, having been one of its founders in Utah and one of its leaders in the state legislature. There were other considerations, however, which weighed just as heavily in winning the nomination for him. At this time, the Utah electorate was markedly flexible, party affiliations not having settled into any fixed pattern. The two major parties were almost evenly matched. The personalities and abilities of the candidates, therefore, were of more than usual importance.

The Democratic candidate to succeed himself was Sutherland's old schoolmate and law partner, William H. King. In every way he was a formidable foe. He had earlier been a member of the legislature and a justice of the State Supreme Court. Thus, he was well known throughout Utah. In addition, he was an orator of great power and a communicant of the Mormon Church. Such political assets rendered his election almost a certainty in the view of close observers.[1]

Sutherland, however, had assets of his own. In the state legislature, he too had had an opportunity to demonstrate his abilities before a state-wide audience. Futhermore, he was well situated so far as the Church was concerned. As a non-Mormon, he stood to get the support of those who regularly opposed the Church. At the same time, he was sure to win the votes of many of the Faithful. He had attended a Mormon school and had many Mormon friends. Moreover, when he had opposed the Church, as in the days of the Liberal party, he had done so with moderation.

[1] *Salt Lake Telegram*, December 20, 1902.

He denounced polygamy but consistently fought against a ruthless prosecution of those devoted to the practice.

Sensing that Bryanism had reached and passed its peak, Sutherland very shrewdly sought in the campaign to tie his fortunes to those of McKinley and Roosevelt. He lost no opportunity to attack Bryan and the Democratic record in national affairs and to defend that of the Republicans. In particular, he dwelt on the wisdom of McKinley's decision to stay in the Philippines. The result would be, he proudly proclaimed, that we would thereby "continue to expand our trade until every ship that went to those islands would be filled with American goods, manned by American sailors and flying the American flag."[2]

In conducting his campaign, Sutherland had the active aid of the strongest men in the Republican party. Governor Heber M. Wells accompanied him on his tour of the state and was amazed at Sutherland's popularity. Men and women, he observed, "came to him at the end of meetings to shake hands with him, and to claim that they were schoolmates of his. I think I never saw a man who had as many schoolmates as the Hon. George Sutherland and the people everywhere seem to recognize in him a stalwart, able, respected, honest son of Utah."[3]

Another who gave Sutherland the strongest kind of support was Tom Fitch, a veteran Utah orator. The two frequently spoke from the same platform. Fitch seems to have had the responsibility of defending the Republican economic record and stating the party's social creed. In what was described as a "truly magnificent oration," Fitch met the Democratic charge that the Republicans had fostered the growing concentration of wealth to the disadvantage of the laboring man.[4] Fitch conceded that "economic changes often produce inconvenience and loss to individuals who may be temporarily deprived of employment." But, he said, this was to be borne because the GOP recognized that this Government is not "a Probate court," whose duty is was to act

2 *Salt Lake Tribune*, October 31, 1900.   3 *ibid.*   4 *ibid.*

as a guardian for weaklings, but a Republic where the race must be to the swift and the battle to the strong. It is a Government where equality of opportunity will be enforced, but never equality of result. . . . Let Rockefeller accumulate another one hundred millions, so long as he can do so lawfully. . . . We live in an age of light, we live in an advancing generation, and the retrogressive, whining, wealth-hating, labor-striking doctrines of Byranized Democracy are out of joint with the times.[5]

[5] *ibid.* Fitch's entire address is worthy of note because it is such an excellent example of what was then considered good political oratory. Consider the following attempt to persuade the laborer that he was really better off poor than rich: "Where is the tyranny of the wealth owners to be found? In what form does it manifest itself? In Europe a laborer takes off his hat when he meets a lord. In America a man keeps his hat on when he meets a millionaire, unless the millionaire salutes him first. In Europe the teamster turns out for the carriage with a coronet upon its panels. In America the multi-millionaire will lose a wheel if he does not turn out for the coalcart if the latter has the right of way.

"What, at last, do rich men obtain from life more than the poorest of us? Toil brings hunger, and hunger is a better sauce than any served at the Alta club. God gives his beloved as sweet sleep upon a cot as upon the downiest couch. Public libraries and galleries give the treasures of learning and art to the poorest. Music and drama can be enjoyed as well from the galleries as from the boxes. A trolley car gives a safer and smoother and swifter ride than a carriage drawn by horses. There are no reserved seats in nature's amphitheater. The ripple of the river, the verdure of the lawns, the shade of the trees and the perfume of the flowers belong to rich and poor. I stood the other evening upon the hill above my home and watched the burning sun dissolve in fret-work clouds of color that filled earth and air with glory, and then the gray lids of twilight fell upon the drowsy eyes of our inland sea, and the stars came out and the great temple lifted its beautiful spires to the darkening sky. God gives such visions of beauty alike to capitalist and pauper, and the poorest laborer equally with the multi-millionaire can find heaven in the prattle of his babies and the arms of the woman he loves."

Fitch's closing remarks are also worthy of being preserved: "For forty years I have helped to hold aloft the banner of Republicanism. Fortune has given to me neither poverty nor riches. The rewards of party service have passed me by. My whitened hairs admonish me that my ship is nearing its shore. It may be that I shall not participate in another Presidential campaign. Therefore would I say what may be a last word to the young, bright men and women who will help to guide the feet of my country along the aisles of the coming century, when I shall have journeyed on to my palace among the stars.

"I give to them the greeting of the gladiators of old to their emperor, 'Hail Caesar, we who are about to die, salute you!'

"Young men of America, the Republican party gives into your hands

The great event of the campaign came on election eve when the two candidates faced each other in the Salt Lake City theatre before an enthusiastic throng of several thousand. King supporters were massed on one side and those of Sutherland on the other. The Republican *Tribune* reported that the Democrats present contained a number of "vicious-tempered disturbers," who prevented Sutherland from finishing his address, despite his rival's plea for order. In what he was allowed to say, Sutherland assailed Bryan for relegating the silver issue to the background. As to the trusts, of which there had been much talk, he admitted their existence but called attention to the Sherman Act which had been passed by the Republicans. He called attention, too, to the party's attempt to secure a constitutional amendment on the subject. King responded with a charge that the Republicans had brought hard times, that they had not acted on the trusts, and that silver was an issue, however much his opponent might try to obscure the fact.[6] Aided partly, no doubt, by the great victory of the national ticket, Sutherland triumphed the next day by the slim margin of 241 votes out of a total of more than 90,000.[7]

2.

Over a year after his election, Sutherland arrived in Washington for the first session of the new Congress. He lost little time in calling on President Roosevelt "in the interest of his constituents." The new Congressman reported that McKinley's successor had adopted an innovation in the manner of his reception of callers.

Instead of admitting one at a time to his private office, the President comes out into the reception room and makes the rounds of his visitors, devoting a minute or two to each one. . . . There

---

the grandest heritage of the ages. I beseech you to preserve it and not ally our country with the fate of a party which for fifty years has never once been right upon any issue in American politics."

[6] *Salt Lake Tribune*, November 6, 1900.

[7] *ibid.*, November 8, 1900.

were fully 100 callers in the room and Mr. Roosevelt dispatched the business in a remarkably short time.[8]

Soon afterwards, Sutherland made the customary calls on the various departments, obtaining the promise of several new mail routes, additional funds to the amount of $50 a year for clerk hire in the post office at Nephi, and consideration of free delivery service at Provo.

Before leaving for the capital on November 13, 1901, Sutherland had given an interview to the Utah press in which he had listed the problems likely, in his opinion, to concern the new Congress. There was, first of all, the question of the disposition of arid lands held by the national government. Sutherland was for cession to the states. If this could not be accomplished, he wanted direct federal aid in building reservoirs, although it would "necessarily involve federal control." Secondly, Sutherland committed himself to the extension of the Chinese Exclusion Act, which was to expire within a year.

The Chinese laborers, who would naturally come to this country would be brought into unhealthy competition with our own laborers. We already have one race problem in the South with the negroes, and to open our doors to the unrestricted immigration of Mongolians would be to invite another and more serious race problem in the West.[9]

More important than either of these questions was that of maintaining "adequate" tariff protection for Utah's sugar crop. Sutherland attributed the "wonderful advancement" in the sugar industry to the Republican policy, which provided both bounty and tariff. As to the tariff, he said that "if the Republican party does not maintain it, it will be false to all its teachings." He warned that an "attempt will be made to remove the duty from Cuban sugar under the guise of reciprocity, but such a claim is a sham and a delusion. To permit admission under a reciprocity treaty with reference to such articles as we are capable of producing in sufficient quantities to supply our

[8] *Salt Lake Tribune*, November 26, 1901.
[9] *Salt Lake Tribune*, November 14, 1901.

own people, free of duty, is free trade pure and simple."[10]

Sutherland's fears proved to be well justified. In response to a widespread plea from people all over Cuba, the Administration sponsored a program of tariff reciprocity which proposed to lower the duty on raw sugar by twenty per cent. It was represented that the newly-liberated island was threatened with starvation unless some such relief was forthcoming. Mayors of practically all the island's cities, leaders of business and labor organizations, and the sugar planters combined to emphasize the desperate conditions.[11]

When a bill authorizing reciprocity reached the floor of the House, the Democrats, in a move aimed at the Sugar Trust, proposed the elimination of the differential duty on *refined* sugar so long as the reciprocity agreement was in force. A group of sixty-two Republicans, mainly from the sugar producing states, saw in this proposal an opportunity to kill the whole reciprocity program. They calculated, quite reasonably, that the bill could not pass the Republican Senate if it included this affront to eastern business interests. Accordingly, the sixty-two, Sutherland among them, forsook party regularity and, in a tumultuous session, joined with the Democrats to add the offensive provision.[12] The Republican leadership, observed *The Nation*, was "trampled upon . . . in a way quite unexampled in party history."[13]

The debate on the bill was bitter and marked with recriminations. The party leaders characterized the rebels as "juvenile Republicans" and "amateur statesmen." Sutherland, although a first termer, took the floor to respond on April 15, 1902. His address on the occasion showed him to be even then an effective antagonist with a ready supply of caustic wit at his command. Knowing that at one time some of the leaders themselves had opposed reciprocity, Sutherland answered their taunts by describing an amateur statesman as "a member of the House who

---

10 *ibid.*   11 35 *Cong. Rec.* 4201 (1902).
12 *ibid.*, p. 4419; *Deseret Evening News*, April 26, 1902.
13 *The Nation*, LXXIV (1902), 317.

has not been in the business long enough to have acquired the ability to be upon more than one side of the same question at the same session."[14] On the general merits of the bill, his speech was directed towards impeaching the testimony of those who had said it was necessary. In true Spencerian style, he found that the trouble really was that the Cuban growers were inefficient. It did not occur to him that the same might be said of American producers. Thus, in one breath, he could argue strenuously for the tariff and in the next, declare: "I submit that if that is true it is no part of the duty of the American Congress to make up the difference between good business ability and bad business ability. It is no part of the duty of the American Congress to equalize the difference between good business ability and bad business ability, even among our own people, let alone among the people of a foreign land."[15]

Sutherland's stand on this issue had important political consequences. It marked his earliest major disagreement with Theodore Roosevelt and prevented him from ever becoming an ardent follower of the zealous Colonel. Of course, the differing viewpoints of the two men must necessarily have resulted, sooner or later, in a parting of the ways, but their divergence might have been less complete had there been an initial period of cooperation. The most important result of this insurgency, however, was its effect on Utah politics and Sutherland's subsequent political fortunes. As will be seen, his stand upon this question gained Sutherland an issue on which to make his campaign for a seat in the United States Senate.

As a new member of Congress from a relatively unimportant state, Sutherland's committee assignments were not exciting. They included the Committee on Private Land Claims and the Committee on Irrigation.[16] In this latter post, his intimate knowledge of the water problem in the West enabled him to make a conspicuous contribution. The question of the disposal of the arid lands did come before the Congress, as he had predicted it would. Sutherland

14 35 *Cong. Rec.* 4204 (1902). 15 *ibid.*, p. 4204. 16 *ibid.*, p. 244.

proposed the solution which was finally adopted—the sale of the lands with the proceeds going into a special fund for the development of irrigation facilities.[17] It was further provided that the amount spent in each state should correspond to the money therein realized. Sutherland made a rather lengthy defense of the measure when it came before the House.[18] In this speech, he took occasion to narrate the epic story of the Mormon struggle with the desert. He vouched for the act's constitutionality, declaring that Congress, in the exercise of its powers, could select any unprohibited means, provided they were "reasonably adapted" to a legitimate end. He assured the lawmakers that the bill did not, with its power of eminent domain, place vested water rights in jeopardy as "it would be absolutely void and worthless if it did."[19] His efforts were successful and the act passed by a large majority.[20]

Sutherland was active also in the matter of Indian affairs and made a speech of some length in support of a measure to open to settlement the Uintah reservation in his state. While pleading for a just, and even a generous treatment of the Indian, he argued that the tribal system was "contrary to the genius of our civilization which is builded upon the idea of individual action and responsibility" and that therefore it must not be allowed to "stand in the way of homes and farms for fifty thousand citizens of the Republic."[21] Here, too, he was successful, but only after the Indians' friend in the White House had obtained a promise of additional legislation on their behalf.[22]

These legislative successes of Sutherland's in a body where seniority counts for so much are impressive. They are important now, however, chiefly as the initial step of his campaign for a seat in the Senate. At the time of his service in the House, from 1901 to 1903, Utah was represented in the upper chamber by Thomas Kearns, a Republican and Joseph L. Rawlins, a Democrat. Rawlins'

17 *ibid.*, p. 6977.   18 *ibid.*, pp. 6968-6971.
19 35 *Cong. Rec.* 6770 (1902).   20 *ibid.*, p. 6778.
21 *ibid.*, p. 1881.   22 *Salt Lake Herald*, May 22, 1902.

term was due to expire in 1903. Since it was almost certain that there would be a top-heavy Republican majority in the next legislature, this made likely the addition of another Republican to the Senate. Kearns, a multimillionaire mine owner, was the nominal leader of the party. He had been elected in 1901, but only after Reed Smoot, an Apostle of the Mormon Church, had withdrawn from the race. It was generally understood that Smoot could have had the place had he pushed his fight and just as generally believed that Kearns had promised to support him two years hence.[23]

Although this was still the understanding when the new Congressman went to Washington late in 1901 for his first session, Sutherland undoubtedly, even at that time, entertained the ambition of his own election to the Senate. He recognized Kearns as an obstacle to the realization of his hopes, just as the Senator saw in Sutherland a potential menace to his leadership. The split was in the open by the middle of December, the immediate cause being the distribution of patronage. On December 14, the *Salt Lake Herald* reported that there was "a breach" between the two over the question of the appointment of the United States marshal. Later, Kearns' support of the reciprocity program supplied an issue which rendered the dispute one over a question of policy and thus guaranteed its continuance.

Meanwhile, Sutherland made no formal announcement of his candidacy, but went steadily about the business of making friends for himself by energetically serving the people of Utah. He gained great applause from the Mormon people by writing an article for a Washington newspaper telling of their good qualities, asserting that polygamy was dying a natural death, and that the Church was no longer an issue in Utah politics.[24] Later he publicly opposed Smoot's candidacy on the ground that he was a high Church official. He was quick to explain that he did

<hr />

23 *Truth*, July 4, 1902; *Salt Lake Herald*, August 28, 1902.
24 *Washington Evening Times*, February 7, 1902.

so exclusively because Smoot's election would "bring more disastrous criticism and agitation respecting Utah and her people."[25]

Smoot was, at the same time, meeting with other difficulties. Senator Kearns, probably under White House pressure, had deserted him.[26] Yet Smoot was so strongly entrenched in Utah that it hardly seems likely that Kearns' disaffection could have kept him from the Senate, but it did influence him to seek a rapprochement with Sutherland. Once again it was a case of former schoolmates getting together. This was not very difficult to accomplish, since the two had few real differences of opinion. An agreement was made that each would continue to recruit legislators favorable to his cause, that the one getting the largest number of commitments should have the seat in 1903, and help the other oust Kearns himself in 1905.[27] The first election Smoot won with little difficulty. Sutherland did not stand for a second term in the House but stayed in Utah where he could prepare for the finish fight with Kearns.

This struggle over the senatorship assumed, in some respects, the shape of a contest between supporters and opponents of the administration of Theodore Roosevelt. Without doubt, Roosevelt had expressed himself as being opposed to Smoot in the earlier contest.[28] Furthermore he favored Senator Kearns with the greater share of the Utah patronage. This, perhaps, emboldened the Kearns paper, the *Salt Lake Herald*, to report that Sutherland's influence at the White House was a "minus quantity."

[25] Sutherland to unnamed friend, reprinted in *Salt Lake Herald*, June 12, 1902.

[26] *Goodwin's Weekly*, July 12, 1902; *Deseret News*, January 13, 1903. There seems to be no doubt that T. R. expressed a wish privately that Smoot be defeated. But, on the other hand, Mark Hanna seems to have befriended the Apostle. *Salt Lake Herald*, August 28, 1902.

[27] *Salt Lake Herald*, December 4, 1902, quoting *Washington Times* of unnamed date. Kearns' term was for only four years because the legislature could agree on his election only after two years of the regular term had elapsed.

[28] *Salt Lake Herald*, January 13, 1903.

T. R., however, was greatly offended at such a report and took the unusual step of suggesting that Sutherland bring the *Herald* correspondent to see him so that he might personally correct the erring journalist. This Roosevelt did the next day in the following terms: "Of course, you know the President does not give interviews, but I want to state to your paper upon the highest authority, that any story to the effect that there is a break between Mr. Sutherland and the administration is absolutely false. On the contrary there is no man in Congress for whom I have a higher regard than for Mr. Sutherland. The President has the highest regard for his ability and integrity, and his relations at the White House are of the most cordial character."[29]

This was extraordinary praise, indeed, for a first term Congressman and for one who had opposed the Administration on a major issue. But even its publication could not completely disassociate Sutherland from the group known to be only lukewarm to T. R. The situation was further beclouded by the proceedings at the Republican State Convention in Ogden on September 12, 1902. The Smoot-Sutherland combine contrived to prevent any endorsement of the Administration's reciprocity program but Sutherland won a great ovation by moving the amendment of the platform to urge the nomination of Roosevelt in 1904. This caused one journalist to report that Sutherland had thus, "by one of the smoothest little bunco games ever worked in Republican politics in this state, secured all the glory of swinging Utah into the Roosevelt column."[30]

But this is not all of the story. It was complicated still further by a curious happening involving one of Roosevelt's staunchest supporters, Albert J. Beveridge, the Senator from Indiana. Beveridge had been invited to the convention to present the customary eulogy of party accomplishment. The Smoot-Sutherland forces, however, were greatly afraid that his eloquence might persuade the

[29] *Ogden Standard*, July 9, 1902.
[30] *Salt Lake Herald*, September 12, 1902.

convention to endorse the Roosevelt tariff vagaries. With this in mind, they secured an order of business whereby Beveridge would be permitted to speak only after all of the business of the convention had been transacted. Beveridge, as might have been expected, was not exactly pleased with these arrangements which required him to sit around most of the day almost a forgotten man. In his subsequent wrangles with Sutherland in the Senate, he might often have remembered that day spent cooling his heels in Ogden, Utah.[31]

Out of office for the time being, Sutherland devoted the years 1903 and 1904 to his practice and to preparation for the final showdown with Kearns in 1905. They were years of success—and tragedy. For in June, 1903, his only son, Philip, died of typhoid fever while attending St. Paul's School in Concord, New Hampshire. Despite his heartbreak, Sutherland was able to voice "a deep and abiding conviction that some larger and better plan than my own is being fulfilled." Three months later he was writing, "Philip's memory—the recollection of his gentle yet manly life—is and will ever remain my dearest possession."[32]

The year 1904 soon came and in the elections of that year Sutherland, with the capable assistance of Reed Smoot, routed the Kearns forces. He became the unanimous choice of the Republican legislative caucus for the seat in the Senate held by Kearns and was elected in January, 1905. He was, of course, elated at this consummation of a four-year struggle. Addressing the caucus after his success, he remarked: "To be a member of the United States Senate is the most exalted position in the gift of the people of this State. I have no words to express my deep appreciation of the honor you have conferred upon me."[33]

The Utah press was, in general, commendatory. One paper saw in Sutherland's success "a flattering tribute to his political sagacity and courage, and his personal

[31] *ibid.*   [32] Notebook in the Sutherland papers.
[33] *Salt Lake Herald-Republican*, January 12, 1905.

popularity with the citizens of all sections of the State."[34] The Kearns organ, while conceding that Sutherland had assumed no obligation by which "a Senator should not be bound," interpreted the result as a demonstration of the power of the Mormon hierarchy.[35] This interpretation, whether accurate or not, was shared by even some of Sutherland's friends. E. B. Critchlow, one of the leading lawyers of Salt Lake City, remarked in a hearty and obviously sincere congratulatory letter: "Permit me to say again that on the theory that the Devil even is entitled to his due, the Church leaders are entitled to what little credit can be figured out for them in permitting the people of the State to send in you the man best equipped and best fitted for the high station of Senator."[36]

3.

Critchlow's letter can be better appreciated when it is recalled that he was at the time leading in the fight to persuade the Senate to unseat Reed Smoot because of his connections with the Mormon Church. It was in connection with this controversy that Sutherland delivered his first major speech in the Senate some two years later on January 22, 1907.[37] Smoot, it will be remembered, was one of the Twelve Apostles. The fight on him, emanating originally from a group of Utah Gentiles, was supported by numerous petitions presented to the Senate from the entire country. The National League of Women's Organizations urged "all true women who love our Republic, and who would guard the purity of its altars and its firesides, and the happiness of its daughters" to sign a memorial to Congress. Smoot's removal was demanded "for the protection of children unborn, whose right to legitimate parentage should be protected," and because his presence in the Senate was an "insult to every home and to every wo-

[34] *Goodwin's Weekly*, January 14, 1905.
[35] *Salt Lake Tribune*, March 5, 1905.
[36] E. B. Critchlow to Sutherland, January 12, 1905.
[37] 41 *Cong. Rec.* 1486 (1907).

man in our free and enlightened Republic."[38] After listening to this and similar appeals, the Committee on Privileges and Elections reported a resolution, on June 11, 1906, to bar Smoot from the Senate.[39]

There were four charges against Smoot. It was asserted that he was a practicing polygamist, having enjoyed connubial relations with as many as twelve of the sisters of the Church. A Presbyterian minister from Utah went up and down the country revealing the sordid details, giving names and explaining that none of the excess wives could be found because they had been "spirited away."[40] Again, it was said that in becoming a Mormon, Smoot had sworn to some strange oath requiring him never to cease importuning "high heaven for vengeance upon this nation for the blood of the prophets who have been slain."[41] Charges more likely to cause Smoot grave difficulty were that the Church had persisted in its belief in polygamy, despite the manifesto of 1890, and that it interfered in the political life of Utah to an insufferable extent.[42]

Sutherland was in a position to be of great influence in this matter. Had he turned on Smoot, the Apostle must surely have suffered defeat. He was urged from several quarters to do just that. One correspondent, an anonymous "friend," admonished him that this was the "flood" of his career, that if he but seized the opportunity, he might become a national hero by denouncing Smoot.[43] Of course the intimate relationship between the two men did not allow of the slightest inclination to such action and, as Sutherland showed in his detailed analysis of the charges, it was hardly warranted. He knew, on his own authority, that Smoot was not a polygamist and never had been. He could recall, too, that the Apostle had supported him for Mayor of Provo in 1890, when the sole issue was their party's opposition

---

[38] Poster of National League of Women's Organizations in Sutherland papers.

[39] 40 *Cong. Rec.* 8218 (1906).

[40] Related by Sutherland, 41 *Cong. Rec.* 1488 (1907).

[41] 40 *Cong. Rec.* 8219 (1906).

[42] *ibid.*   [43] Undated letter in Sutherland papers.

to plural marriages. And if a clincher were needed, even some of those who were now opposing Smoot specifically disavowed the polygamy charge. As to the oath, Sutherland pointed out that the testimony was so divergent as to its precise content that it could not possibly serve as a basis for expulsion. Smoot, himself, affirmed that it made no reference to the "nation" and Sutherland supposed, quite reasonably, that the whole thing was an innocent ceremonial suggested by a text in Revelation: "How long, O Lord, holy and true, dost Thou not judge and avenge our blood on them that dwell on the earth?"[44]

The more serious accusations, that the Mormons had treacherously persisted in their belief in polygamy and that they controlled Utah politics, were refuted by Sutherland with a comprehensive review of the whole question. He recalled the fact that, a quarter of a century previously, a great number of the younger Mormons, including Smoot himself, had joined the Liberal party, with the idea of ridding the Church of its peculiar institution. Their victory was won in 1890 with the manifesto of the Church forbidding polygamous marriages in the future. There seemed afterwards to be a tacit agreement not to disturb those homes founded on marriages contracted before 1890, if the Church would use its influence to enforce the manifesto. This had been faithfully done, Sutherland reported. Hence, Utah was now at peace and polygamy doomed to ultimate extinction. The remaining polygamists Sutherland staunchly defended as good, upright citizens and as pure in their motives as their accusers.[45] The final point, that of undue church interference in the affairs of state, was met by a recital of the wide divergences of opinion among the Mormons themselves and a witness to their character for independence and individual responsibility.[46]

The address accomplished its immediate object—Smoot's right to his seat was affirmed a few days later.[47] It ac-

[44] 41 *Cong. Rec.* 1490 (1907); the verse is from Rev. 6: 10.
[45] 41 *Cong. Rec.* 1492 (1907).   [46] *ibid.*, p. 1497.
[47] *ibid.*, p. 3429. The date was February 20, 1907.

complished other things as well. It solidified Sutherland's hold on the Utah electorate. It revealed to the Senate Sutherland's power as an advocate, his capacity for presenting his argument in a dignified, yet lucid, manner. There was, also, a hint of the biting satire with which he was later to flail his political opponents. Finally, it demonstrated, if only incidentally, something of the man's basic beliefs. The first was a notion of a "fundamental justice" which must bind each senator. Sutherland explained it as follows:

In one sense the power of this Senate to deal with the accused Senator is plenary. It may be exercised arbitrarily. In a legal sense, the Senate is not accountable to any other authority or tribunal for its action. Right or wrong, wise or unwise, just or unjust, its decision becomes the unappealable law of the case. But in another sense, and in a higher and a better and juster sense, its action is restricted by those considerations of fundamental justice which find an abiding place in the conscience of every just man.[48]

Another idea expressed was that on occasion the rights of one individual must be protected even though he stood alone against the world. The framers, Sutherland asserted,

intended that this great Senate should be a conservative force, a deliberative body, that should neither blindly follow nor impatiently reject the demands of the multitude. I can conceive of cases—cases involving questions of legislation, questions of political or governmental policy—where the demands of the people should not only be heeded, but should be obeyed. But I respectfully submit that this is a case where the *right* of one individual is more sacred than the mere *demand* of *all* the people.[49]

Most important of all, perhaps, was Sutherland's avowal of a sure faith in inevitable progress. The Mormon Church, he exclaimed,

like every other church and every other thing in the universe, is subject to the law of evolution. I am glad to believe that in some way I do not understand there is at the very heart of things some mighty power which silently and surely, if slowly, works for the exaltation and uplifting of all mankind. I am not religious in the

[48] *ibid.*, p. 1486.   [49] *ibid.*

ordinary acceptation of the term; I have no patience with mere forms or mere creeds or mere ceremonies; but I do believe with all the strength of my soul that "there is a power in the universe, not ourselves, which makes for righteousness." I am an optimist in all things. I do not believe that the world is growing worse. I feel sure it is getting better all the time.

I am no believer in the fall of man. Man has not fallen. He has risen and will rise. In the process of evolution he has so far progressed that he is able to stand erect and look upward . . . and so while he sees the heights he ascends them only with slow and toilsome effort. But he does ascend. . . .

There are occasional lapses, the goings forward and the slippings back, the fallings down and the risings up, and, thank God, the . . . ultimate triumph if the resolution be sound at the core.[50]

4.

In a legislative way, Sutherland's first great contribution in the Senate had to do with improving the administration of justice. The movement for such reform, which has not yet spent its force, was then in its infancy.[51] But it was not too early for Sutherland, always a procedural liberal, to realize the necessity for action. Soon after he took his seat in the Senate, he was appointed to the special Statutory Revision Committee which later grew into the Joint Congressional Committee on the Revision and Codification of the Laws.[52] The task before the Committee was a formidable one. There had been no general statutory revisal since 1878. In the years which had elapsed, two supplements to the Revised Statutes had been issued and, after them, three volumes of the Statutes at Large. The result was, in the words of the Committee, "an irregularity and confusion which . . . will hardly be found in the permanent laws of any other legislative body of modern times."[53]

The first efforts of the Committee to rectify this situa-

[50] *ibid.*, p. 1499.

[51] See Roscoe Pound, "A Generation of Improvement of the Administration of Justice," 22 *N. Y. U. L. Q. Rev.* 369 (1947).

[52] 40 *Cong. Rec.* 9472 (1906).

[53] *Report of the Special Joint Committee on the Revision of the Laws*, Sen. Rep. No. 10, 60th Cong., 1st Sess. 5 (1908).

tion were confined to the criminal laws. The result was a criminal code of 342 sections which "brought together all statutes and parts of statutes relating to the same subject, omitted redundant and obsolete enactments, made such alterations as seemed necessary to reconcile the contradictions, supply the omissions, and amend the imperfections of the original text," and finally, proposed such changes in the substance of the law as seemed advisable.[54] The code passed the Senate on February 26, 1908, with Sutherland assisting Senator Heyburn in its defense.[55] Final action by the House, however, did not come for over a year.[56] But even there Sutherland had a part in supplying the decisive stimulus. In January of 1909, some two months before the House acted, he published an article in the *North American Review* on the achievements of the code in which he outlined the reasons that made its enactment imperative.[57]

After presenting its criminal code, the Committee turned to the task of collecting and codifying the laws relating to the judicial establishment in the form of a Judicial Code. It was presented to the Senate in March 1910.[58] In addition to making the law accessible and understandable, this code included a long overdue institutional reform. It provided for the abolition of the old Circuit Courts, which had, with the passage of the Act providing for the Circuit Courts of Appeals, lost any justification they might once have had. Nevertheless, leading lawyers of the American Bar Association, Joseph H. Choate among them, opposed the change.[59] Despite this opposition, the useless court was abolished as Sutherland and his colleagues pressed for a judicial system in keeping with the times.

[54] *ibid.*, p. 6.
[55] 42 *Cong. Rec.* 2530 (1908).   [56] 43 *Cong. Rec.* 3791 (1909).
[57] "The Nation's First Penal Code," *North American Rev.*, CLXXXIX (January 1909), 107.
[58] 45 *Cong. Rec.* 2937 (1910).
[59] See 46 *Cong. Rec.* 298 (1910), where their memorial is reprinted. See also Felix Frankfurter, "The Business of the Supreme Court: A Study in the Federal Judicial System," 39 *Harv. L. Rev.* 325, 355 (1927).

Indeed, in matters of judicial administration, Sutherland was always one of the most enlightened and progressive men in the Senate. When he came to the Senate, the Supreme Court was being swamped with appeals from the District of Columbia which it had to accept. Some years before, the Court had been given discretionary jurisdiction of cases arising in the Circuits. The result was that lawyers brought their cases in the District of Columbia on the slightest pretext so that they might have access to the Supreme Court as a matter of right. Thus, the purpose of the discretionary jurisdiction act was thwarted. The Court's business was still too large for it to handle. Sutherland was quick to perceive the difficulty and it was he who introduced the bill which eventually brought relief to the Court.[60]

Another measure of tremendous importance in the administration of justice which Sutherland introduced was one providing for the delegation to the Supreme Court of the power to prescribe the rules of procedure in the federal courts.[61] Unfortunately, the passage of this bill was not effected until nearly twenty years after Sutherland left the Senate.[62] It might be added that he had a similar experience in his persistent effort to secure adequate salaries for the federal judiciary.[63]

5.

Sutherland, of course, could give his allegiance to the reform of the administration of justice without ever having to call in question any of the basic components of his political philosophy. It was not so in regard to the great program of social and political reform fostered by the Progressive movement, which coincided with his senatorial service. By any definition, the era of the Progressives was one of the most remarkable in our history. It was the era of trusts and trust busting, of corruption and investiga-

[60] 46 *Cong. Rec.* 2134 (1910). [61] 53 *Cong. Rec.* 452 (1916).
[62] 48 Stat. 1064 (1934), 28 U.S.C. §§ 723b and 723c (1940).
[63] 54 *Cong. Rec.* 731 (1917).

tion, of Morgan and McNamara, a period characterized by a popular unrest which gave expression to all the accumulated discontents and grievances of thirty-five years.

Far to the left were heard strident voices calling for the abolition of private property and the immediate institution of socialism. Others less radical insisted no less vehemently that government ownership and development of utilities and natural resources was the path of democracy's triumph in the twentieth century. Others thought more rigid controls of the corporations would suffice—controls which would shatter the great aggregations of wealth from which the country was said to be suffering..Even the rich and the conservative were not unaffected by the clamor. Stimulated by the prevailing mood of the day, many of them developed an unwonted awareness of the problems of the poor, and some, a creative sympathy. William Howard Taft is an excellent case in point. In 1894 he accepted so casually the prejudices of his class that he could even rejoice at the slaying of striking railroad workers.[64] Yet, fifteen years later as President he approved a vast program of workmen's compensation, a limited work week, and other measures designed to improve the conditions under which laborers toiled.

George Sutherland, too, felt the impact of the Progressive movement. As attempts to give legislative expression to the popular aspirations of the period came to be made, he sought a middle way. He was able to support a good deal of the Roosevelt program including such measures as the Employer's Liability Act,[65] the Pure Food and Drugs Act,[66] and the Hepburn Rate Bill.[67] Roosevelt's heresies on the tariff undoubtedly annoyed him as did, perhaps, the Colonel's more violent denunciation of the "malefactors of great wealth." But the President's will-

[64] Harry F. Pringle, *The Life and Times of William Howard Taft*, New York, Farrar and Rinehart, 1939, p. 128.

[65] 35 Stat. 65 (1908).

[66] 34 Stat. 768 (1906).

[67] 34 Stat. 584 (1906); for Sutherland's votes on these measures, see 42 *Cong. Rec.* 4550 (1908), 40 *Cong. Rec.* 2773 (1906), *ibid.*, p. 7088.

ingness to compromise and delay prevented any head-on collision which would have precipitated an open break. Moreover, the Roosevelt foreign policy, with its program of naval expansion and bold assertion of America's new position as a world power, found in Sutherland an enthusiastic supporter.[68] Accordingly, in the campaign of 1908 the Senator could speak of "the present splendid President" and unreservedly praise the Republican record.[69]

Sutherland's position in regard to Roosevelt in the 1908 election was indeed typical of that of a large section of the Republican party. The underlying conflict between the Progressives and the Old Guard had not yet been brought to the surface. For the purposes of the election, party unity was preserved by obscuring the issues. This unity, however, barely survived Taft's inauguration. The first act of the new President was to call the Congress into special session on March 15, 1909, for a revision of the tariff. This was in conformity with the Republican platform which had promised a new tariff act. While there had been nothing said as to which direction the revision was to take, the general assumption was that it was to be downward. Taft himself, never the most ardent protectionist, had explicitly avowed that understanding during the campaign. His message to the new Congress, however, contained no specific recommendations. Nevertheless, the House of Representatives very quickly passed a bill which distinctly pleased the low tariff men.[70]

There was to be an entirely different story in the Senate. That body was accustomed to leaving the final word on tariff matters to Senator Nelson W. Aldrich of Rhode Island. His preeminence was unchallenged, even by Theo-

[68] See 42 *Cong. Rec.* 5265 (1908), where Sutherland supported T. R.'s demand for two new battleships. "War is always possible," said Sutherland.

[69] *Salt Lake Herald*, September 16, 1908, in which is reprinted Sutherland's keynote address to the Utah State Republican Convention.

[70] 44 *Cong. Rec.* 1302 (1909); George E. Mowry, *Theodore Roosevelt and the Progressive Movement*, Madison, University of Wisconsin Press, 1946, pp. 46-47.

dore Roosevelt. As the embodiment of capitalist virtue, he ruled with a ruthless hand from his vantage point as chairman of the Committee on Finance. This committee, to which the House bill was immediately referred, proceeded to add 847 amendments, the majority of them designed to correct the misapprehension of the House as to the true nature of the promised revision.[71]

When the radically altered measure was reported to the Senate on April 19, 1909, there ensued "some of the greatest tariff debates in the history of the United States Congress."[72] A formidable group of senators, led by La-Follette, Beveridge, and Dolliver, subjected both the bill and Aldrich to the most scathing denunciation. Section by section the bill was analyzed and its comforts to the great business interests exposed. Despite this presumptuous and unprecedented opposition, Aldrich was able to hold his supporters in line, with the consequence that the bill appeared headed for approval in much the shape it had been brought to the floor.

However, the situation was suddenly complicated by a threat to the Old Guard of an entirely unexpected character. Senators Borah and Bailey, in the midst of the tariff debate, introduced a proposal for an income tax.[73] The Supreme Court had, of course, in the year 1895 pronounced such a tax unconstitutional, but the decision had been accompanied by strenuous dissents.[74] Furthermore, the changes in the personnel of the Court encouraged advocates of the tax to hope that a new measure would be sustained. Whether constitutional or not, the idea of an income tax had great support and there was doubt as to the possibility of successful resistance. The prospect of such a radical innovation frightened Aldrich even more than that of a reduction in duties and even to the extent that he was willing to reduce the rate on specific items in exchange for votes to throttle this "communistic" venture.[75]

[71] Mowry, *op. cit.*, pp. 48-52.
[72] *ibid.*, p. 53. [73] 44 *Cong. Rec.* 1351 (1909).
[74] *Pollock* v. *Farmers Loan & Trust Co.*, 158 U.S. 601 (1885).
[75] Mowry, *op. cit.*, p. 53.

At this juncture Sutherland came forth with a lengthy address designed to show that the Court in 1895 had reached the proper conclusion.[76] He had, all through the session, loyally supported Aldrich, not because of any slavish acceptance of dictation, but rather because of a strong conviction of the wisdom of the protective policy. In reply to a question posed by *Collier's* asking how it happened that he, a Western man, should have concurred with Aldrich 117 times and never have opposed him, Sutherland responded: "I am a Republican and a protectionist. . . . I am not a protectionist in spots. . . . Protection is a broad national policy and not a local policy in any sense of the word."[77]

In opposing the income tax, Sutherland gave the most intense consideration to the internal evidence offered by the Constitution and the opinions of the framers on the question. The specific point at issue was whether or not the tax was a "direct" one and as such subject to the necessity of apportionment. To resolve this question, Sutherland proposed four steps—an examination of the Constitution itself, an inquiry to determine "under what circumstances the written document was prepared," a consideration of the legislative construction, and finally a study of the conclusions of those "skilled in the mysteries and subtleties of language," specifically the courts.[78]

The wording alone of the pertinent clauses of the Constitution rendered the answer "perfectly clear" to Sutherland. After noting that the uniformity clause [79] speaks only of "duties, imposts, and excises," he argued that the apportionment clause applied to any levy which was neither a duty, impost, or an excise.[80] For this view he professed to find support in the proceedings of the convention and

[76] 44 *Cong. Rec.* 2080-2096 (1909).
[77] *Salt Lake Telegram*, August 31, 1909.
[78] 44 *Cong. Rec.* 2080 (1909).
[79] "The Congress shall have Power to lay and collect taxes, Duties, Imposts, and Excises . . . but all Duties, Imposts and Excises shall be uniform throughout the United States." *U.S. Const.* Art. I, § 8.
[80] 44 *Cong. Rec.* 2082 (1909).

accompanying circumstances. He attempted to show that the members of the convention believed that wealth was distributed roughly according to numbers, and that this conception was not confined in its application merely to real property, thereby rendering apportionment of any tax convenient.[81] Sutherland went on to distinguish the carriage tax sustained in *Hylton* v. *United States* [82] as a "use tax" and one not falling on the property itself.[83] Finally he called to his aid the opinion of the Court in the *Pollock* case. After delivering the estimate of the 1895 Court previously quoted, he assured the Senate that, if the ruling by the justices had "set aside the prior decisions of the Court for a hundred years, we may be sure that those judges did not do that for light or trivial reasons." After all, precedent was "only the opinion of a former traveller as to the location of the pathway. It is not the pathway itself. . . . We may question the opinion of the traveller . . . we can not question the pathway itself."[84]

The net effect of this maiden speech by Sutherland on a constitutional question is difficult to assess, since bargaining between Taft and Aldrich finally determined the fate of the proposed income tax.[85] That Sutherland should have been entrusted with the task of stating the Old Guard's case on this vital issue shows that the conservative forces already realized that a powerful ally was at hand. The speech served to warn the Progressives that Sutherland was a lawyer with all the materials of constitutional interpretation at his fingertips. It must have served, too, to bring Sutherland to the notice of President Taft as a possible court appointee, for in the following July, the rumor that Sutherland was destined for the Court began to circulate.[86]

[81] *ibid.*, p. 2084.   [82] 3 Dall. 171 (1796).

[83] 44 *Cong. Rec.* 2088 (1909).   [84] *ibid.*, p. 2096.

[85] Mowry, *op. cit.*, p. 58. The bargain was that Taft was to use his influence to head off the income tax if Aldrich would agree to the passage of a corporation tax.

[86] *Utah Independent*, July 22, 1909.

6.

The administration's confidence in Sutherland was underlined by his appointment, on January 20, 1910, to the joint Congressional committee to investigate the Interior Department and the charges hurled against its Secretary by the National Forester, Gifford Pinchot, and Lewis R. Glavis, one of its clerks.[87] Without going into the details of the controversy, it is sufficient to say here that the investigation quickly became a matter of burning interest, with the prestige of the Taft administration at stake. The committee's investigation centered around the explosive issue of the extent Ballinger, and through him Taft, had retreated from the conservation policies of Roosevelt. The hearings, in which Sutherland's future colleague on the Supreme Court, Louis D. Brandeis, played an important part as counsel for Glavis, developed a plain picture of government functioning as the adjunct of private interests. On the many procedural questions which had to be decided by the committee, there was always a partisan division, with Sutherland never straying from the path of party regularity. And when the committee's final vote was reached, he signed the majority report which exonerated Ballinger.

For his part in the exoneration of Ballinger, Sutherland was roundly excoriated by his political opponents in Utah as "a willing tool of the Guggenheim interests."[88] And while the inquiry was yet in progress, *Collier's* called attention to the fact that Sutherland's chief newspaper support in Utah came from a journal owned by one of the largest stockholders in the Utah Copper Company, a Guggenheim enterprise. The magazine reminded its readers that Sutherland "and his partners have been for years the premier corporation attorneys for Utah's big business

[87] 45 *Cong. Rec.* 836 (1910); for the best account of this controversy, see Alpheus T. Mason, *Bureaucracy Convicts Itself*, New York, Viking Press, 1941.
[88] *Ogden Standard*, October 19, 1916.

interests" and that therefore there was a particular demand, in his case, for "an impartiality which he has not so far shown."[89] Yet, it must be said in Sutherland's defense that however inadequate the government's policy on conservation, the testimony as to any moral turpitude on Ballinger's part was inconclusive.

7.

Sutherland's support of Ballinger, taken together with his opposition to tariff reform and the income tax, demonstrates that he was not to be swept off his balance by a popular clamor regardless of its volume. Yet this independence did not lead to an attitude of blind antagonism to all change. Sutherland's complaint was rather of the "mad spirit of impatience" which urged the abandonment of "the methodical habits of the past" and sent the country "careening after novel and untried things." It seemed to him that the Progressive cry was: "Get somewhere else than where you are—it matters not where—only, in God's name, let it be quickly!"[90]

Sutherland, while recognizing the necessity for change, demanded that it be orderly and deliberate. Thus, he told the Senate in 1911:

Mr. President, I am no standpatter. I am not in favor of standing still. No one who takes the slightest thought desires that we shall do that. Of course, we must advance, but we must at our peril distinguish between real progress and what amounts to a mere manifestation of the speed mania.

To illustrate his point, he continued:

Among the games of the ancient Greeks there was a running match in which each participant carried a lighted torch. The prize was awarded not to that one who crossed the line first, but to him who crossed the line first with his torch still burning. It is important that we should advance, but the vital thing it not that we should simply get somewhere—anywhere—quickly, but that we

[89] *Collier's Weekly*, May 21, 1910.
[90] 47 *Cong. Rec.* 2795 (1911).

should arrive at a definite goal with the torch of sanity and safety still ablaze.[91]

This was more than mere rhetoric. Sutherland did find measures to support which promised great benefits to the masses and at the same time did not seem to him likely to extinguish the torch. He vigorously supported acts establishing the eight-hour day for laborers employed by the United States,[92] the Children's Bureau,[93] the Postal Savings Banks,[94] and a system of workmen's compensation for interstate employees.[95] With respect to the last two, he had especially significant roles.

It may appear strange today, but it is none the less true, that the Postal Savings bill excited a good deal of opposition when it was presented to the Senate in 1910. It was denounced as an attack on the banking structure of the country and pictured as an encouragement of socialism, if indeed it was not the ogre itself.[96] Furthermore, it was declared to be unconstitutional.[97] In a long speech in the Senate on March 2, Sutherland rejected all these arguments.[98] He asserted that the government had a duty to provide banking facilities in those sparsely settled areas where such facilities did not exist.[99] Because the bill would thus put more money in circulation, he believed that its effects would be broadly beneficial.[100]

The main concern of his argument was to prove that the bill was constitutional. Sutherland may indeed have

[91] *ibid.*   [92] 37 Stat. 137 (1911).

[93] 37 Stat. 79 (1911). There were no recorded votes on these measures. Sutherland's support of them is related in the *Salt Lake Herald-Republican*, July 9, 1916.

[94] 36 Stat. 814 (1910).

[95] A full record of Sutherland's support of this measure would require considerable space. The most complete statement of his position can be found in the *Report of the Employers' Liability and Workmen's Compensation Commission*. Sen. Doc. No. 338, 62d Cong., 2d Sess. (1912).

[96] The opposition to this measure is recounted by Sutherland at 45 *Cong. Rec.* 2613 (1910); see also *ibid.*, p. 3564, where Congressman Adair reproduced the complaint of one of the banking fraternity.

[97] See the address of Senator Rayner of Maryland, 45 *Cong. Rec.* 1519 (1910).

[98] *ibid.*, pp. 2613-2620.   [99] *ibid.*, p. 2613.   [100] *ibid.*

had the additional purpose of furthering his ambibition of an appointment to the Supreme Court. He may have felt that it was necessary for him to allay suspicions aroused by his defense of the *Pollock* decision. Accordingly, he emphasized throughout his speech the necessity for a liberal interpretation of the Constitution. That instrument, the Senator asserted, "is not a fetish before which one must prostrate himself in fear and trembling."[101] The Constitution was made for the people, he said, "not they for the Constitution."[102] In regard to its interpretation, he laid down the following principles which he said were no longer open to dispute:

1. An Act of Congress is valid not only where it operates directly to carry into effect any of the specifically enumerated powers, but also where it can be seen in any degree, or under any circumstances, to promote the operation or efficiency of such power.

2. The specifically enumerated powers declare the ends which Congress is authorized to effectuate. The ends which Congress may lawfully attain are limited by the affirmative provisions of the Constitution. The means which may be adopted to attain the ends are unlimited except by the prohibitions of the Constitution.

Any means may be employed which are fairly and reasonably adapted to bring about the result. The extent to which such means conduce to the end—the degree of their efficiency—the closeness of the relationship between the means adopted and the end to be attained, are matters addressed exclusively to the judgment of Congress.

Whether the end sought to be attained is lawful is a matter of constitutional power and not of legislative discretion; but the lawfulness of the end being conceded, the choice of the means is a matter of legislative discretion and not of constitutional power.

3. The relation between the means and the end need not be direct and immediate.

4. If the law carries out any constitutional power, it is not rendered invalid because it also, to a greater or less extent accomplishes some other result which is wholly beyond the power of Congress to deal with as a separate and independent matter. And I cite *McCray* v. *United States* (195 U.S. 27).

---

[101] *ibid.*, p. 2614.   [102] *ibid.*, p. 2620.

5. While it is true that the Constitution continues to speak with its original words and meaning, their scope and application continually broaden so as to include new conditions, instrumentalities, and activities.[103]

As an illustration of the operation of these principles, Sutherland cited the history of the commerce clause in the courts.

The framers of the Constitution never dreamed that it would be expanded so as to include the multiplicity of things which it undeniably includes today. In the beginning the generally accepted meaning of the power was that it extended only to the interchange of commodities among the States. It was not regarded as applying to transportation or the instrumentalities of transportation except as such transportation and the instrumentalities thereof were connected with navigation. Transportation by land was only dimly, if at all, regarded as being included. Transportation by water was undoubtedly what the framers had chiefly in mind. Carriage by land was of the simplest possible character, requiring no regulation at the hands of the Federal Government and little, if any, regulation at the hands of any law-making power. But all this was changed by the advent of the railroad, by the invention of the telegraph and telephone. The power has been gradually extended until today it is recognized as embracing everything which is the subject of trade and every instrumentality and means by which trade among the States is carried on or facilitated. It is not unreasonable to look forward to the day when, with the perfection of aerial navigation, it will include the regulation of the aerial craft and the air itself, so far as may be necessary to regulate commercial intercourse among the States by this future method.[104]

Of considerably greater importance were Sutherland's strenuous efforts to secure the adoption of a workmen's compensation statute for employees of interstate carriers. On June 25, 1910, Congress, by joint resolution, authorized the appointment by the President of a commission to make a thorough investigation of the subject of employer's liability and workmen's compensation.[105] Sutherland was not appointed to the commission until the fol-

[103] *ibid.*, p. 2615.   [104] *ibid.*, p. 2620.   [105] 36 Stat. 884 (1910).

lowing April, but he was then immediately elected its chairman.[106] The other members at this time were Senator George E. Chamberlain of Oregon, Representative William G. Brantly of Georgia, Representative Reuben O. Moon of Pennsylvania, W. C. Brown, President of the New York Central Railroad, and D. G. Cease, editor of *The Railroad Trainman.* Hearings were held, off and on, from May 10 to December 11. The final report, containing a draft of a proposed statute and a justification of it, together with a transcript of the testimony taken, was submitted on February 2, 1912, to the President who, in turn, passed it on to Congress with the comment that the details of the bill had been "most admirably worked out," and with a strong plea that the Act be passed with all appropriate speed.[107]

In conducting the hearings, Sutherland took especial care to afford all interested parties an opportunity to present their views. Representatives of business, labor, and civic organizations were heard. The experiences of the states and of the various European countries were exhaustively considered. The Commission's inquiry into the constitutional issues was particularly thorough.[108] In 1911, workmen's compensation was by no means the commonplace it is today. Indeed, in March of that year, the highly regarded New York Court of Appeals had invalidated the New York statute, branding it as "plainly revolutionary."[109] Controversial as the whole question was, however, Sutherland's conduct of the investigation was generally applauded.[110] The *Springfield Republican* commented that the proposed bill furnished proof that "progressive legislation, in behalf of the toilers and demanded by the spirit of the age, can be secured without delays that become intolerable."[111]

[106] *Report of the Employers' Liability and Workmen's Compensation Commission,* p. 11.

[107] *ibid.,* pp. 5-8.   [108] *ibid.,* pp. 25-55.

[109] *Ives* v. *South Buffalo Railroad Co.,* 201 N.Y. 271, 285 (1911).

[110] *Literary Digest,* xliv (1912), 414, 1026; *The Survey,* xxviii (1912), 492.

[111] Quoted, *Literary Digest,* xliv (1912), 1026.

The report of the Commission, obviously Sutherland's handiwork, explained the proposed statute and outlined, with the help of a formidable array of statistics, the considerations that made it desirable. The harshness of the common law doctrines of assumption of risk, negligence, contributory negligence, and the fellow-servant rule was demonstrated. Statistics were presented which showed conclusively that while there were some large recoveries, the *average* amount allowed by the proposed bill would be far greater than under the old system. Furthermore, recovery would be far easier, the services of a lawyer being required only in special cases. Noteworthy features of Sutherland's measure were that it was compulsory, its remedies exclusive, and payments under it were to be periodical rather than in a lump sum.

A large section of the report was devoted to demonstrating that the bill was constitutional. Here Sutherland was confronted with the twin problem of showing that the compensation measure was a valid exercise of the commerce power and at the same time not a deprivation of due process. The difficulty over the commerce clause was virtually removed on January 15, 1912, by the decision of the Supreme Court in the Second Employers Liability Act case.[112] Once again, Sutherland emphasized that Congress was limited in its choice of the means of executing its powers only by the express prohibitions, provided, of course, they "are appropriate, plainly adapted to the end" and not violative of the "spirit of the Constitution."[113] He argued that this Act was a justifiable regulation of commerce in that it would promote safety on the railroads and make it possible for employees, with their minds relieved of anxiety, to render more efficient service.[114]

The due process clause offered a more substantial difficulty. It had been contended that to impose liability on the carriers, irrespective of fault, constituted "a naked

[112] *Mondou v. New York, N.H. and H. Ry.*, 223 U.S. 1 (1912).
[113] *Report of the Employers' Liability and Workmen's Compensation Commission*, p. 25.
[114] *ibid.*, p. 28.

transfer of the property of the employer to the employee or his dependents."[115] Sutherland met this objection by equating the power of Congress over interstate commerce with the police power held by the States. In that area, he said, "it is to be remembered . . . that the power of Congress to regulate interstate and foreign commerce is the full and complete power of sovereignty. It is all the power possessed by the State over such commerce before the Constitution was framed, and necessarily includes, by whatever name called, every power which the State possessed over the subject."[116] He found "singularly appropriate and convincing" Mr. Justice Holmes' assertion that the police power "may be put forth in aid of what is sanctioned by usage, or held by the prevailing morality or strong preponderant opinion to be greatly and immediately necessary to the public welfare."[117]

Finally, Sutherland argued that the due process clause did not sanctify the procedures of the common law. "The Constitution does not say that no person shall be deprived of his property, but that he shall not be so deprived without due process of law. The latter are the vital words. By them it was not intended to erect a wall against changes in the common law or against the adoption of new principles to meet new conditions."[118] And in a word of warning, he added: "If this phrase could be now so construed as to prevent the adoption of a law, which the almost universal sentiment of modern society regards as just and reasonable, it would amount to not a bulwark against injustice, but an impregnable wall against the advance of justice as developed by the enlightened minds of mankind."[119]

When the bill came to the Senate floor, Sutherland was the leader in its defense.[120] It met rather determined resistance from some Southern members, notably Smith of Georgia. It was Smith's contention that the awards allowed

[115] *ibid.*, p. 30.   [116] *ibid.*, p. 32.

[117] *ibid.*, p. 35, quoting from *Noble State Bank* v. *Haskell*, 219 U.S. 104, 111 (1911).

[118] *ibid.*, p. 36.   [119] *ibid.*   [120] 48 *Cong. Rec.* 4406ff. (1912).

were generally inadequate. He petulantly demanded to know if Sutherland thought a foot worth only some $2500, a question which the Utah senator showed to be a little wide of the real issue by reminding Smith that the bill's purpose was to make certain some recovery in any event.[121] The measure was finally passed by the Senate on May 6, 1912, and sent to the House.[122] There it was referred to the Judiciary Committee, which failed to report it back to the floor before the end of the session.[123]

Despite this disappointing conclusion, there was some comfort for Sutherland and more to come later. President Taft established a system of compensation for Canal Zone employees in accordance with a provision of the Panama Canal Act of August 24, 1912.[124] In doing so, he freely drew from the materials collected by Sutherland. The significance of this move was well stated by Henry L. Stimson, the Secretary of War. "This measure," he said, "for the first time brings the Federal Government abreast of the most advanced thought and experience of other countries."[125] Finally, when the United States adopted a statute for itself in September 1916,[126] the work of Sutherland and his commission may be said to have, in large measure, rendered it possible.

It seemed likely, in December 1912, that Sutherland was destined to have still further opportunity to demonstrate his abilities in the field of labor legislation. In August of that year Congress, in response to wide popular demand, provided for the creation of a body to investigate the entire labor problem.[127] The investigation was to cover a period of three years and was liberally provided with funds. To direct it the recently defeated president chose his reliable supporter from Utah. Taft named as associate members of the new commission George B. Chandler, a member of the Connecticut legislature, Charles S. Barret of Georgia, president of the Farmers

---

[121] *ibid.*, p. 4407.   [122] *ibid.*, p. 5959.   [123] *ibid.*, p. 6099.
[124] 37 Stat. 560 (1912).   [125] *The Survey*, xxix (1912), 114.
[126] 39 Stat. 742 (1916).   [127] 37 Stat. 415 (1912).

Union, representing the public; Frederick A. Delano, a railroad executive, Adolph Lewisohn, a mine owner and philanthropist, F. C. Schweatman of St. Louis, an electrical engineer, representing capital; A. B. Garretson of the Order of Railway Conductors, John B. Lennon, treasurer of the American Federation of Labor, and James O'Connell, vice president of the Federation, representing Labor. When the personnel of the commission was announced, there was an immediate protest from those who had urged its establishment in the first place.[128] Some of its members were acknowledged to be "men of ability and distinction," but the failure of the president to name a woman or a trained economist or social worker, plus the fact that industrial unionists were not represented, was said to make the commission's success highly unlikely.[129] In only a single instance, however, was Sutherland singled out for condemnation. The *Independent* called him nothing more than "a superficial student of the problems of industry."[130] But his appointment was considered adequate by the liberal *Survey*, which recalled the good work he had done for the compensation proposal.[131] The appointments were to fail of confirmation, however, irrespective of their merits, since the Democrats, anticipating Wilson's inauguration, refused to allow consideration of over 1300 Taft selections.[132]

Sutherland's advocacy of the compensation bill can best be accounted for by attributing it to the influence of the Progressive movement on his thinking. It furnishes convincing evidence that he, too, was earnestly solicitous of improving the lot of the submerged classes and that in doing so he was not always rendered powerless by the dictates of a political theory. As he himself declared in 1913—again in support of a compensation program:

[128] *The Survey*, xxix (1912), 492.   [129] *ibid.*
[130] *The Independent*, lxxiv (1913), 381.
[131] *The Survey*, xxix (1912), 381.
[132] *New York Times*, January 30, 1912; *ibid.*, March 4, 1913.

There is a growing feeling that the individualistic theory has been pushed with too much stress upon the dry logic of its doctrines and too little regard for their practical operation from the humanitarian point of view. We are discovering that we can not always regulate our economic and social relations by scientific formulae, because a good many people perversely insist upon being fed and clothed and comforted by the practical rule of thumb rather than by the exact rules of logic.[133]

This, one is tempted to remark, is Sutherland speaking when he was in possession of facts which stubbornly refused to accord to the Spencerian dialectic. On one other notable occasion, he found himself confronted by a similar situation. Sometime, around 1910 presumably, his attention was drawn to the plight of American seamen by Andrew Furuseth, the president of the Seamen's Union. By all accounts, Furuseth, a Norwegian immigrant, was an arresting figure. What might well serve as a description of Sutherland's first meeting with him is the following account left by another Senator:

One morning in December, 1909, there came into my office in the Capitol building, a tall, bony, slightly stooped man with a face bespeaking superior intelligence and lofty character.

He wanted to interest me in the cause of the American sailor....

I asked him to tell me about it. Sitting on the edge of the chair, his body thrust forward, a great soul speaking through his face, the set purpose of his life shining in his eyes, he told me the story of the sailor's wrongs.

... He was a master of his subject. His mind worked with the precision of a Corliss engine. He was logical, terse, quaint, and fervid with conviction.[134]

The great burden of Furuseth's complaint was that, under the law as it then stood, seamen could be imprisoned for a refusal to work.[135] The Thirteenth Amendment notwithstanding, they were not free men. This condition was

---

[133] "Compulsory Workmen's Compensation Law," Sen. Doc. No. 131, 63d Cong., 1st Sess. 11 (1913). This was an address delivered to the International Association of Casualty and Surety Underwriters.

[134] Robert M. LaFollette, writing in *The Survey*, xxxiv (1917), 116.

[135] See *Robertson* v. *Baldwin*, 165 U.S. 275 (1897); also 1 Stat. 131, § 7 (1790) and Rev. Stat. 4598 (1875).

finally righted by the Seamen's Act of 1915.[136] In addition, the Act undertook generally to improve the conditions under which seamen lived. Sutherland's part in securing this legislation has been graphically related by Furuseth. When the seamen's wrong was called to the Senator's attention, said their leader, he became "from that moment an earnest champion of legislation which would restore to us our rights as men and to the travelling public such increased safety as the law could provide. There was nothing that he could do that he did not gladly do. There was no time that he was not ready with encouragement and advice and any action that would advance the legislation."

In conclusion, there was the following warm tribute by Furuseth to Sutherland: "I learned to know a lover of freedom, a man who understands thoroughly what freedom means, and a man who, in the protection of freedom to all men, regardless of their station in life, may be trusted and relied upon under all possible conditions."[137]

Plainly, Sutherland was willing on an occasion to invoke the power of the state in behalf of social improvement. His own summary of the limits to which this was permissible speaks best for him. Writing to Samuel Gompers, he said:

I have always favored laws which had for their object the substantive betterment of workers, such as those which enforce proper sanitary conditions, safety appliances and machinery, adequate, and as far as possible automatic compensation for injuries, and so on. I have also favored, and still favor, by legislation the eight-hour day in industries such as mining, smelting, and other industries where long employment is injurious to health. In addition to this, I am in favor of an eight-hour day in all the mechanical industries where the same set of muscles are continuously employed, or where the strain and attention is continuously required about the work. But whether the eight-hour day should be compelled by legislation, or brought about by the efforts of the employees, aided by public sentiment, is a matter about which I am in serious doubt.

[136] 38 Stat. 1164 (1915).
[137] Furuseth to D. O. Jacobs, published in *Utah Labor News*, August 5, 1916.

The State is justified in stepping in where its police activities are involved, as they are involved in the cases I have mentioned. If the State undertakes to go further and interfere in the relations of employees, while in many instances and perhaps for a time that interference might result in the betterment of conditions from the point of view of the workman, there is grave danger that it may be utilized in other instances and in the course of time, to his positive detriment.

Whenever you concede the power of the State to interfere in such matter, you have effectually conceded it whether the results be good or evil. For example, if we once undertook by legislation to fix wages, they may be at first fixed at a high sum, but under this concession they may sometimes be fixed at a very inadequate sum.[138]

This letter, with its painful searching, on the one hand, for excuses to justify state intervention and, on the other, with its evident doubt in the theoretical wisdom of such intervention, reflects the fundamental dilemma faced by Sutherland during the Progressive era. Fact and theory were battling for the mastery of his mind. It was really an unequal struggle, for the conservative ideology had been Sutherland's intellectual meat and drink since he was a mere lad. Thus, when he was seeking to reduce by law the hazards faced by the worker and to ameliorate—again by law—the wretched conditions in the nation's ships, he was, at the same time bewailing "the mania for passing laws on every conceivable subject."[139]

8.

A cursory reading of Sutherland's speech to the Senate on July 11, 1911, reveals how staunchly, in spite of his liberal flirtations, he held to the conservative faith. The Progressives, interested as they were in a social readjustment, largely centered their efforts to secure this in a program of institutional and political reform. Their anal-

[138] Sutherland to Samuel Gompers, January 15, 1916.

[139] *Milwaukee Journal*, October 14, 1911, in an interview Sutherland gave to the press while in the city to investigate the election of Isaac Stephenson to the Senate.

ysis of the situation convinced them that most of the injustices from which men suffered arose from the fact that the people no longer ruled in America. Legislators, it was charged, were oblivious of the popular will once they had been elected. The lack of faith in the traditional democratic processes was well exemplified by the cynical remark of a Colorado labor leader: "What is the use of your ballots anyway? You might as well tear them up and throw them in the gutter."[140]

The Progressives were still more dismayed when they surveyed the nation's judiciary and its work. For two decades they witnessed the spectacle of the rich escaping an income tax only because five members of the Supreme Court so willed it. They saw in 1908 with the *Lochner* case [141] a ban imposed by the justices on all social legislation that did not strike them as reasonable or necessary, and in 1911 they beheld invalidation of a workmen's compensation act by the New York Court of Appeals.[142] Indeed, it seemed to Theodore Roosevelt that the course of the judiciary had been one calculated "almost to bar the path to industrial, economic, and social reform."[143] The result of this dissatisfaction with the operation of the institutions of American democracy was the proposal of a set of devices to guarantee the triumph of the will of the people as voiced by a majority at the polls. The underlying theory was that the Interests had gained control of the Government because the people had the right only of *choosing representatives*. If, it was reasoned, the people could decide directly on the big questions of the day, and if they could retire recalcitrant officials, then government by interest could be prevented and the general welfare would always triumph. The judiciary was not to be exempt

---

[140] Ray Stannard Baker, "The Reign of Lawlessness," in Willard Thorp (and others), *American Issues*, New York, J. B. Lippincott Co., 1941, I, p. 855.

[141] *Lochner* v. *New York*, 198 U.S. 45 (1904).

[142] *Ives* v. *South Buffalo Railroad Co.*, 201 N.Y. 271 (1911).

[143] Roosevelt to Herbert Croly, February 29, 1912, quoted in Mowry, *op. cit.*, p. 215.

nor were the products of their learning, for the people were to be given the opportunity to recall the erroneous decisions of wayward judges. These proposals for the initiative, referendum, and recall seemed to Sutherland to promise nothing but anarchy and chaos, where emotionalism and sentiment were sure to prevail. He often 'asserted his belief that ultimately the people should rule,[144] but he believed, too, that they should be protected from their own weaknesses. The issue therefore was to just what extent the will of the people should prevail.

In July of 1911 the question became of immediate practical importance to the Senate with the introduction of bills providing for the admission to the Union of Arizona and New Mexico. The constitutions proposed for the new states contained clauses authorizing these radical innovations. This fact prompted Sutherland to make the most noteworthy address, perhaps, of his entire senatorial career.[145] The press accorded it the prominence of a major utterance. Its entire text was printed in many newspapers and there were editorial comments and excerpts in countless others. The *Washington Post* observed: "It has been many a day since the Senate has been so interested in a speech," and this despite the stifling heat.[146] To the *Pittsburgh Gazette Times* it was "a masterly exposé,"[147] and to the *Philadelphia Inquirer* the speech "was one of the wittiest and, at the same time, one of the most sensible that has been heard in the Senate in a long time."[148] The Senate, itself, seems to have had some inkling of what was to come, for there was a full attendance, many Representatives also being present.[149]

The first paragraph indicates the tone of the speech:

[144] See e.g., "The Law and the People," Sen. Doc. No. 328, 63d Cong., 2d Sess. 7 (1913); "The Courts and the Constitution," Sen. Doc. No. 970, 62d Cong., 3d Sess. 10 (1912).

[145] 47 *Cong. Rec.* 2793-2803 (1911).

[146] July 12, 1911.

[147] July 17, 1911.

[148] July 17, 1911.

[149] *Washington Post*, July 12, 1911.

During the last few years, the United States of America has become the field of operation for an amiable band of insurgent soothsayers, who have been going up and down the land indulging in cabalistic utterances respecting the initiative, the referendum, the recall, and the divers and sundry other ingenious devices for realizing the millennium by the ready and simple method of voting it out of its present state of incubation. They direct our attention to the clouds flying above the far western horizon, upon which the flaming finger of the Oregon sun has traced, in radiant and opalescent tints, glowing pathways and shining minarets, stately temples and castles and palaces, pinnacles of gold and caves of purple, and they tell us that these are the visual signs which mark the exact location of the new and improved political Jerusalem, where the wicked officeholders cease from troubling and the weary voters do all the work. They bid us join them in an airy pilgrimage to this scene of pure delight, and assure us that here, high above all selfish and mundane things, is the land flowing with milk and honey, where every bird is a songster, where the exquisite and perfect flowers of political purity are in perpetual bloom, where every prospect pleases and only the standpatter is vile, where all the laws are perfect and corruption and wickedness are forgotten legends.[150]

Sutherland went on to denounce the objectionable proposals as leading to the "ultimate destruction of our republican institutions." He held up to savage ridicule the notion that the "average man" was qualified to determine the issues of high politics.

The individual fallibility of the average man will at once be conceded, but there are some people who seem to imagine that there is some mysterious virtue in mere numbers; that ten men are necessarily more intelligent, more moral, and more honest than one man; that by adding together a thousand individuals none of whom has even gone beyond the multiplication tables, some strange and weird transmutation results by which the combined mass is enabled to work out the most difficult problem in Euclid with the utmost accuracy.[151]

The task of government, he insisted, demanded the application of specialized judgment which could be the

[150] 47 *Cong. Rec.* 2793 (1911).   [151] *ibid.*, p. 2797.

property of only a few. With some manifestation of impatience, he declared:

Those who are so intemperately appealing to the people to take over the direct management of their government, with its multiplicity of detail and difficulty, the successful operation of which demands concentration of effort and thoroughness of application, are preparing the way for future mischief. They are advocating a political creed alluring to the imagination, but utterly impossible of successful realization, and which, if adopted, will lead us more and more into the domain of the impracticable, with political chaos or political despotism as the ultimate result.[152]

Sutherland further prophesied that legislators would be driven to yield their legitimate prerogative "of deliberation and independent judgment as to what is wisest and best and become mere recording agents."[153] The executive officers, he warned, will become "less and less self-reliant men and more and more automatic machines."[154]

Especially obnoxious to Sutherland was the provision for the recall of judges. This proposal, he said, rested on the delusion that the judge, like a congressman or an executive, represents a constituency. This notion he declared to be utter nonsense. "What is a constituent," he asked. "He is a person for whom another acts. A constituent implies as a necessary corollary, a representative who speaks for him." But, Sutherland announced,

A judge has no constituents; he is only in a restricted sense a representative officer at all. The people who select him can with propriety make known their wishes only through the laws which they enact. The judge is the mouthpiece of the *law*. His constituents are the *statutes* duly made and provided. If his decisions are wrong, the remedy is to appeal to the high court—not to the people. . . . The judge represents no constituents, speaks for no policy save the public policy of the law. If he be not utterly forsworn, he must at all hazards put the rights of a single individual above the wishes of *all* the people. He has no master but the compelling forces of his own conscience.[155]

152 *ibid.*, p. 2803.   153 *ibid.*
154 *ibid.*   155 *ibid.*, p. 2802.

There was a further fallacy, Sutherland declared, in the proposals for complete popular rule. Such an idea was antithetical to the notion of constitutional government. Constitutions were made, he explained, not merely for the purpose of restricting the representatives of the people but also to prevent "hasty, ill-considered, and unjust action on the part of the majority of the people themselves." He continued:

> The written constitution is the shelter and the bulwark of what might otherwise be a helpless minority. Tyranny is no less hateful in the hands of the people than in the hands of the despot, and the oppression of the minority by the majority is tyranny no less than is the arbitrary oppression of the king. The forward march of democracy will be of little avail if in the end it rescue us from the absolutism of the king only to hand us over to the absolutism of the majority.[156]

Distressed as he was by the current radical tendencies, Sutherland closed with these hopeful words:

> My sure confidence rests in the saving grace of the sober second thought of the American people, for, in the last analysis, we are a practical and conservative people, sometimes, it is true, dreaming with our head in the clouds, but always awakening to the realizing sense that we must walk with our feet upon the earth. Sometimes the haunting spell of the darkness is upon us, but in the end the night goes, "the dawn comes, the cock crows, the ghost vanishes"; we open our eyes and all the uneasy and terrifying visions disappear in the light which fills the east with the glowing promise of another morning.[157]

When Sutherland delivered this speech on July 11, 1911, the Progressive revolt against the Administration had already reached a point where there was an open attempt to deny Taft the customary renomination. The candidacy of Robert M. LaFollette was in full swing and, by February of the next year, Colonel Roosevelt acknowledged that he was receptive.[158] In this situation Sutherland naturally supported his friend in the White House. He

156 *ibid.*, p. 2799.   157 *ibid.*, p. 2803.
158 See Mowry, *op. cit.*, Chapters 6 and 7.

was a delegate to the tempestuous convention in Chicago and on the critical vote on the seating of contested delegations, he delivered Utah's support to Taft. After the choices of the convention were formally determined, Sutherland was selected to notify Sherman, the Vice-Presidential nominee, of the party's action. This he did in ceremonies held at Utica, New York, on August 21. There he delivered a scorching attack on Roosevelt and the Progressives. The "Bull Moosers" were in Sutherland's view guilty of "intellectual surrender," "blind and benighted idolatry," and most abject "self-abnegation." It seemed to him that the great question of the campaign was whether "the government is to be given over to the chaos of disorganization."[159]

Sutherland's most elaborate effort of the campaign, however, was not delivered under the auspices of a political party but as an address to the American Bar Association at its meeting at Milwaukee in August.[160] Theodore Roosevelt, by his insistent attacks on the judiciary and the trend of their decisions, had raised the issue of the place of the courts in a democracy. Sutherland interpreted Roosevelt's onslaught as not only an attack on the courts but an assault on the Constitution as well. Accordingly, he chose to speak to his brother lawyers on the subject, "The Courts and the Constitution."

The Constitution, he emphasized, was not designed to give effect to "the passing whims and caprices and fleeting emotions of the constantly changing numerical majority."[161] The problem facing the framers, he said, "was that of devising a form of government by which the *sober and deliberate* will of the people might be effectuated."[162] In Sutherland's view, this had been accomplished, first by providing for representatives to do the real work of governing, and second by the creation of "three separate and

---

[159] *New York Times*, August 22, 1912.
[160] "The Courts and the Constitution," Sen. Doc. No. 970, 62d Cong., 3d Sess. 10 (1912).
[161] *ibid.*, p. 4.　　　　　　　　[162] *ibid.*

distinct departments," each with its "appropriate powers" and each without "any authority to invade the domain of the others."[163]

Sutherland quoted John Randolph Tucker to prove that this arrangement constituted a contract between the forty-eight states. From this, he reasoned that the interpretation of the Constitution could not be altered so long as a majority in one state dissented.

While the Constitution may be amended . . . against the wish or protest of a minority by the concurrence of three-fourths of all the States, it may not be *construed* by a majority of the people, however preponderating, so as to bind the minority, however small, but such binding construction, when the question arises in a justiciable controversy, can be made only by the court which in the contemplation of the Constitution is the duly established official arbiter for that purpose.[164]

The judgment of the people, therefore, on constitutional questions could not be followed, for at the polls "men are not measured but counted."[165] And this was all to the good according to Sutherland because its effect would be to "preclude sudden and ill-considered determinations based upon transitory passion or emotion."[166] There was thus available an influence "to steady the public thought against inconsiderate and precipitate action."[167] The reformers to the contrary, there was an imperative need for such an influence because there could "be no greater delusion than to suppose that by putting a ballot into the hands of a voter you thereby put wisdom into his head."[168]

Sutherland was not unmindful in this address of the problems faced by people of the United States in 1912. In his analysis, the liberty of the individual had been achieved. "The new struggle and the new aim," he remarked, "is for his betterment. . . . The great and growing cause which must engage the thoughtful attention of statesmen is that of the social welfare."[169]

163 *ibid.*   164 *ibid.*, p. 9.   165 *ibid.*, p. 10.
166 *ibid.*, p. 11.   167 *ibid.*   168 *ibid.*, p. 13.
169 *ibid.*

The Senator insisted that this could be accomplished under the Constitution in due time. Skilled draftsmanship, he pointed out, could have saved many statutes which were properly overthrown. For those rare occasions when the judges did make mistakes, the remedy was not "to coerce by popular pressure a different ruling," but to wait patiently for the inevitable retirement of the offenders. "If the judges in office can not be persuaded of their error by the general voice of reason, new judges will eventually take their places, and in the long run the popular view, if founded upon sound premises, will prevail. If not so founded it should not prevail."[170]

In the election, Taft went down to a crushing defeat. But Sutherland was successful in persuading Utah not to desert the President—a considerable feat when it is remembered that there was a similar result in only one other state.

Taft's failure in 1912 had important results for his staunch Utah supporter other than the more obvious ones. As remarked before, the Progressive movement presented Sutherland with a dilemma. The dilemma was founded in the contradictions between a cherished theory of government and the necessity forced on him as a member of the majority party to govern. The majority could not but notice, and to some extent be guided by, the demands of the hour. Under this pressure, Sutherland on occasion, during the Roosevelt and Taft years, perceived the necessity for state action in modern society. This pressure continued to exert an influence on him, in some degree, even when he was a minority Senator. But once out of public elective office, all inducement to question the extreme theories of Spencerian individualism was removed. Sutherland was then entirely free to follow his speculative inclinations. Thus, when a new Republican President proclaimed the restoration of "normalcy," the pupil of Maeser and Cooley, the student of Spencer and Tucker, knew that really his doubts had been unfounded and that he had been right all along. But that is a story for another chapter.

[170] *ibid.*, p. 10.

3

CONSECRATION, 1912-1922

THE return of the Democrats to power under Woodrow Wilson on March 4, 1913, brought George Sutherland face to face with a new program of reform. From the first he was in opposition, and, however much he may have been convinced that the Republicans were the only party with the capacity to govern, his opposition was considerably more fundamental than that of a mere partisan. To Sutherland, who knew his early works well, Wilson was a turncoat—a man who, because of his political amibitions, had abandoned his earlier sound beliefs for the visionary schemes of the Progressives.[1] Furthermore, the new President not only had unsound ideas. Still worse, he knew how to make them effective.

Wilson's political abilities were spectacularly demonstrated in the first few months of his presidency when he forced through Congress the legislative implementation of the promised "New Freedom." One of the most important bills passed was the Underwood Tariff Act, which, among other things, removed the duty from sugar entirely. This, of course, touched Sutherland on one of his tenderest spots. To him it seemed provable that the prosperity of the country was due to the policy of protection more than to any other single factor. This prosperity, he conceded, was only the indirect result of the tariff, the first aim of which admittedly was to make production profitable, thereby creating a demand for labor.[2]

This, of course, had been said many times before. Sutherland's argument against the Underwood bill was more concerned with the manner in which the reduction in the rates was being driven through Congress. He saw in Wilson's vigorous demonstration of the possibilities of the presidency a threat not merely to the country's economy

[1] 47 *Cong. Rec.* 2798 (1911).   [2] 50 *Cong. Rec.* 4296 (1913).

but even to the Constitution. The principle of the separation of powers had "been set aside as though it were a meaningless platitude worthy of no man's respect."[3] The Democrats, he asserted, had become a mere "mechanical assemblage of cogs and wheels, turning out legislation in response to the demand of the executive." "Congress no longer legislates," he mourned, "it has sunk to the level of an automaton." The Senator continued with this bitter indictment:

> The President does not tender advice. He issues orders to the caucus, and to the caucus each member surrenders his opinions, his judgment, and his political conscience, not in the interest of the Republic, nor for the welfare of the people, but in order that the fetish of party solidarity may be maintained. The members of the majority on the floor of the Senate do not deliberate; they listen and obey. A few months ago the wheels of the Democratic machine were turning smoothly in the direction of a duty on wool and a continuing duty on sugar, but the hand of the master was placed on the reverse lever, and immediately every one of you, to a wheel, revolved in the opposite direction. Some of you mildly and some of you vehemently protested. Some of you did not relish the notion of crushing your constituents, who were following the vehicle in the trusting belief that you were going forward instead of coming back; but you went back, nevertheless, and in your ignominious flight to the rear, as you swept over and past these protesting victims of misplaced confidence, your voices were lifted in mournful unison to the mystic but familiar words of the old ballad:
>
> > I hear a voice you can not hear,
> > Which says I must not stay;
> > I see a hand you can not see,
> > Which beckons me away.[4]

Sutherland renewed his attack on Wilson's methods with even greater intensity fourteen months later. The occasion was the appearance before the Senate of a bill to authorize the United States to subscribe to the capital stock of a corporation, which was "to purchase, construct, equip,

---

[3] *ibid.*, p. 4297.

[4] *ibid.* Sutherland also opposed the Federal Reserve Act about this same time. See 51 *Cong. Rec.* 1488 (1913).

maintain and operate" a fleet of merchant vessels. "The present administration," he declared, "came into power nearly two years ago . . . and yet, during that entire time, I will defy any man to point to a single act of important legislation, outside of the appropriation bills, which has been originated in Congress. . . ."[5] He continued:

We have fallen upon evil times when this great body, representing the majesty and power and strength of a hundred millions of the most intelligent and freest people that the world has ever seen, will not resent the attempt of the President of the United States to tell them what they should and what they should not do.[6]

Sutherland had something to say, too, on the substantive provisions of this bill. He saw at issue "the fundamental principle upon which this government was established, namely, that it is a civil government and not a business organization."[7] The bill raised for him the possibility of a bureaucracy so large that the people would be powerless.[8] Moreover, it was entirely unconstitutional, being "a socialistic experiment entirely outside the purposes of the Federal Government."[9]

The Senator was equally vehement in his rejection of the Act establishing the Federal Trade Commission. Congress, he argued, had no general regulatory power over corporations just because they happened to be engaged in interstate commerce; and he quoted with approval an author who asserted that the power did not attach until transportation had begun.[10] The wide subpoena powers of the Commission were severely condemned as violative of the Fourth Amendment, as was the wide discretion given the Commission to determine what it conceived to be unfair competition.[11] Sutherland then advanced his view of the wise solution of the corporation problem, the existence of which he was quick to admit. He would have the govern-

[5] 52 *Cong. Rec.* 2621 (1914).
[6] *ibid.*, p. 2623.   [7] *ibid.*   [8] *ibid.*, p. 2624.   [9] *ibid.*, p. 2628.
[10] 51 *Cong. Rec.* 12806-12807 (1914). The author quoted was Thomas C. Spelling.
[11] *ibid.*, p. 12809.

ment make combinations exceeding a certain size unprofitable by a judicious use of its taxing power. He was confident that the Court would not inquire into the purposes of Congress, "if the law itself upon its face be under some power of the Constitution."[12]

Another measure sponsored by the Wilson administration which Sutherland strenuously opposed was the Clayton Anti-trust Act. What particularly excited him was the effort to exempt labor unions from the operation of the Sherman Act. The *Danbury Hatter's* case,[13] decided in 1908, had engendered a suspicion that any nation-wide strike would run afoul of the Act. The Clayton Act was hailed by labor leaders as removing this threat. It asserted that "the labor of a human being is not a commodity or article of commerce."[14] Further, it provided that the anti-trust laws were not to be construed "to forbid the exercise and operation of labor, agricultural, or horticultural organizations . . . or to forbid or restrain individual members of such organizations from lawfully carrying out the legitimate subjects thereof, nor shall such organizations, or the members thereof, be held or construed to be illegal combinations or conspiracies in restraint of trade, under the anti-trust laws."[15]

Sutherland was not recorded as voting on the Clayton bill but there is no doubt that he was opposed to it. He said as much on several occasions.[16] Furthermore, some time before the passage of the Act, there was before the Senate a proviso to an appropriation bill which raised the question of labor's status under the Sherman law. This proviso read as follows:

[12] *ibid.*, p. 12983. On Sutherland's later attitude towards a statute which had the appearance of legality, see *Macallen* v. *Massachusetts*, 279 U.S. 620 (1929).

[13] *Loewe* v. *Lawlor*, 208 U.S. 274 (1908).

[14] 38 Stat. 730, § 6 (1914), 15 U.S.C. § 17 (1940).

[15] *ibid.*

[16] See, e.g., "Superfluous Government," an address delivered to the Cleveland Chamber of Commerce on December 8, 1914, printed in pamphlet form.

That no part of this money shall be spent in the prosecution of any organization or individual for entering into any combination or agreement having in view the increasing of wages, shortening of hours, or bettering the conditions of labor, or for any act done in furtherance thereof, not in itself unlawful.[17]

Sutherland's reaction to this language was emphatic—and highly prophetic of his interpretation of the Sherman Act when he later became a member of the Supreme Court. This provision, he told the Senate, "is either an unnecessary and useless thing or it is a vicious thing—one or the other. If this provision means only that a labor organization shall not be prosecuted under the anti-trust law for any legitimate attempt by a combination or contract or otherwise to increase the wages of its members or to shorten the hours or better the conditions of labor, then it is a needless thing, because labor organizations have that right now. . . . The anti-trust law does not reach such a combination because labor is not an article of commerce. . . . I have never heard it seriously doubted. I do not recall any decision of a court which has held the contrary."[18]

But while he was sure that labor might organize and strike under the law as it then stood, he was equally certain that it could not do so "for the purpose and with the effect of restraining interstate commerce." That, he declared, was held by the law to be an evil thing. If, he continued, "it is an evil thing, if it is wrong to restrain trade among the states of this union, what difference does it make who commits the wrong? Is it not as great a wrong for a number of working men to combine to violate the anti-trust law as it is for a number of capitalists or a number of manufacturers to do the same thing?"[19]

In his view, therefore, if the proviso meant anything it meant that the personality of the actor rather than the quality of his acts was to determine criminality. Such eclecticism on the part of the law appalled the Senator.

17 51 *Cong. Rec.* 11802-11803 (1914).   18 *ibid.*, p. 11803.
19 *ibid.*, p. 11804. *Cf.* Sutherland's opinion for the Court in *Bedford Cut Stone Co.* v. *Journeymen Stone Cutters' Ass'n*, 274 U.S. 37 (1927).

He sharply concluded: "I hope that I never will be able to get my own consent to vote for so utterly indefensible a piece of class legislation as this proviso would write into the law of the land."[20]

2.

In his assaults on the Wilson administration, Sutherland must have derived considerable encouragement from the adulation accorded him by the conservative community at this time. He was now definitely a national figure. Honors and recognition came with increasing frequency. In 1913, Columbia University awarded him an honorary degree. The citation read:

> George Sutherland—United States Senator from Utah, profoundly versed in the law and polity of the Constitution; contributing with patient and scholarly statesmanship to the preparation and enactment of the judicial code of the United States; a chief influence as chairman of the Commission appointed by the President of the United States upon Workmen's Compensation in drafting the well-considered bill which stood the exhaustive scrutiny of the Houses of Congress; earnest believer in American civil liberty and its powerful expositor and defender.[21]

In this same year, Sutherland delivered two addresses which confirmed the fact that he had by then come to be something of a national public orator. The first was before the International Association of Casualty and Surety Underwriters at its meeting in Quebec in July. His subject was, appropriately, workmen's compensation. Essentially, the address added little to what Sutherland had earlier said on the subject. It is of interest now as perhaps his last convincing expression of a healthy relativism in regard to law and legislation. His opening remarks, evidently suggested by a perusal of the writings of Justice Holmes, were:

> Conditions produce opinions which, when sufficiently potential, find expression as law. Changed opinions naturally result from

[20] *51 Cong. Rec.* 11804 (1914).
[21] *New York Times*, June 5, 1913.

changed conditions, and as conditions are never at a standstill it follows that the law of one generation never quite satisfies the sentiment of the generations which follow. It is the business of the lawmaker to determine—and sometimes determine at his official peril—out of a multitude of opinions that from time to time develop which of them are sufficiently substantial to be given statutory expression.[22]

A wholly different tone pervaded the Senator's speech the following December to the Pennsylvania Society of New York. He had been invited at the suggestion of ex-President Taft, who told his friends in the Society that Sutherland was "the one man in the country" they should try to secure for the occasion.[23] His subject, this time, was "The Law and the People."

His address was a pointed defense of the conservative approach to politics. He confessed that it was necessary for him "to plead guilty to being a little bit conservative."[24] Conservatism, he explained by way of justification, was a "habit of thought which induces the individual who has it to propound certain disturbing and exasperating inquiries respecting terminal facilities before he journeys to unfamiliar places."[25] Furthermore, the conservative trust in the past was not wholly baseless. Surely, said Sutherland,

out of the infinitely varied experiences of mankind—the long, long wanderings through the night of barbarism, the slow deliverance from the shackles of feudalism, the passionate struggles against arbitrary power, the stern destruction of despotic governments, the bloody restoration of order out of confusion, the pathetic alternation of success and failure in the efforts at self-government—some lessons of final wisdom have been learned, some monuments of deathless truth have been lifted up against which no challenge of time or circumstance can ever again prevail. If from all the painful struggles of the past, where so much that was temporary has been lost, nothing of permanence has been

22 "Compulsory Workmen's Compensation Law," Sen. Doc. No. 131, 63d Cong., 1st Sess. 3 (1913).

23 H. P. Davison to Sutherland, October 15, 1913.

24 "The Law and the People," Sen. Doc. No. 328, 63d Cong., 2d Sess. 3 (1913).

25 *ibid.*, pp. 3-4.

gained; if from all the strivings for order without oppression and justice without discrimination no fixed and immutable principles have been established, then indeed are we vain pursuers of shadows which come and go in endless and unmeaning procession.[26]

Sutherland, however, was unwilling to admit that the processes of history had been so futile.

Some things have become finalities. From it there has emerged at least this one basic principle, without which popular government is builded not upon the rock which endures but upon the dissolving quicksands into which all the democracies of antiquity have disappeared: That liberty to be secure must rest upon a foundation of preestablished law, administered by upright, impartial, and independent judges, to the end that there shall be a government of laws and not of men.[27]

The key point of this analysis is the role assigned to the judges. They alone could guarantee liberty. Accordingly, they, unlike mere politicians, were selected for their "learning, ability, and impartiality." Their "patient and thorough-going processes" were contrasted to the "superficial methods of the hustings." Majorities, Sutherland pointed out, could be unwise and even unjust. They had been responsible for the "frenzied story of the crusades, the black records of witchcraft and slavery, to say nothing of many minor and less harmful mistakes and delusions."[28]

Thus, the universality of an opinion could never be accepted as a conclusive test of its truth or justice. "The opinions of a few men of high character and attainments, intelligently selected from almost any community, will ordinarily be a far safer guide to follow than the opinions of many men chosen at random."[29] The great hope of the United States, therefore, must be in the courts. There, judges, "stainless as virtue and incorruptible as the everlasting truth," would be found fully capable of the high task of *"compelling* justice between the rich and the

[26] *ibid.,* p. 5.   [27] *ibid.*   [28] *ibid.,* p. 3.   [29] *ibid.,* p. 7.

poor, the powerful and the weak, the multitude and the man. . . ."[30]

In the succeeding years, Sutherland was more and more often called on for addresses at scattered points over the nation. In 1914 and 1915 he was heard by the Cleveland Chamber of Commerce, the Missouri Bar Association, the Manufacturing Jewelers' Association, and the Beacon Society of Boston. On all these occasions he was accorded the most laudatory introductions, being almost regularly designated the "ablest lawyer" in the Senate. Furthermore, he seems to have pleased his audiences, for he regularly won tremendous applause.[31]

His address at Cleveland,[32] delivered December 8, 1914, is representative of what he had to say in these years. It, like the others, was a blistering attack on the extension of governmental activity. The title given to it, "Superfluous Government," was highly descriptive. The Senator was sure that of all the laws receiving the imprimatur of legislators throughout the country, twenty-five per cent were "wholly bad," twenty-five per cent had "no real excuse for existence," and another twenty-five per cent were of "doubtful wisdom." "We are creating," he lamented, "an army of official agents, governmental bureaus and all sorts of Commissions to pry into our affairs, smell out our shortcomings and tell us what we may and what we may not do."[33] This great welter of what seemed to him "unwise or unworkable or unnecessary" legislation led him to suggest, if only facetiously, that the legislators who voted for it should be incarcerated. "Certainly," he concluded, "no jail could be utilized to better advantage."[34]

Sutherland was particularly distressed by the new tendencies because he believed a far better corrective was available. His idea was that "business and social morality in the main and in the long run thrive and grow in response

---

[30] ibid., p. 8.

[31] There are numerous letters in the Sutherland papers requesting reprints of these addresses. Some business men ordered them by the hundreds to distribute over the country.

[32] "Superfluous Government" (1914).   [33] ibid., p. 3.   [34] ibid., p. 4.

to public sentiment far more than in response to statutory compulsion."[35] Therefore, he was certain that "individual conduct should be left to be regulated and governed by moral restraint rather than by statutory enactment, unless it can be clearly shown that interference by legislative enactment is necessary for the preservation of the rights of others or for the protection of society as a whole."[36] Such a procedure was demonstrably preferable because any statute, being perforce "rigid" and "inelastic," could be "only measurably successful." The wise course was to resist the effort "to make everybody perfect by legislation," and to guard against encouraging the "idle and profligate" by social welfare legislation stimulated by an "excess of sentiment." The conclusion, seemingly inevitable, was that government "must not be allowed to wander too far from the sphere of its normal and traditional functions or interfere overmuch with the liberty of the individual to work out his destiny here and his salvation hereafter in his own way."[37]

3.

Sutherland's hostility to governmental action had the natural result of restricting the area in which he could excel as a lawmaker. By his own deliberate decision, he isolated himself from the dominant current of activity of the day. His record during the Wilson years, however, was not entirely a negative one. As already noted, during these years he fought for an improved procedure in the courts, for justice to the seamen, and, of course, for workmen's compensation. In other matters, where his individualistic theory was not brought into question, he proved himself capable of constructive statesmanship. Thus, he urged on at least two occasions the passage of an act which would indemnify those who served prison sentences as a result of convictions later proved to be erroneous.[38] And although he had been

---

35 *ibid.*, p. 9. 36 *ibid.*, p. 6. 37 *ibid.*

38 49 *Cong. Rec.* 356 (1912); 50 *Cong Rec.* 128 (1914). Here again, Sutherland was years in advance of his time. Congress finally adopted such a statute in 1938. See 52 Stat. 438 (1938), 18 U.S.C. §§ 729-732 (1940).

deprived of the chairmanship of the Industrial Relations Commission, he supported, against Democratic opposition, liberal appropriations for the Commission's study.[39]

The Senator's most significant contribution had to do with the woman's suffrage Amendment to the Constitution. So long as he was a member of the Senate, Sutherland seems to have been the acknowledged leader of the forces fighting in behalf of the women. He introduced the Amendment in 1915 and it was known by his name.[40] He lost no opportunity to further the cause. He spoke at memorial services for a militant suffragist. He received delegations from various women's organizations, counseling them as to their tactics and providing them good copy. The women, for their part, acknowledged that he was their "powerful ally" and praised him for his "generous help and support."[41] Charles E. Hughes also recognized Sutherland's eminence in this matter. In 1916, when he was a candidate for the Presidency, he revealed his support of the Amendment by the tactic of a telegram to his Utah supporter.[42] The Amendment did not emerge from Congress until Sutherland had been retired, but it is clear that his support was in large measure responsible for the speed with which final success came.

Sutherland's support of the Amendment was to him an act of simple justice. "Any argument which I may use to justify my own right to vote," he declared, "justifies the right of my wife, sister, mother, and daughter to exercise the same right."[43] The only possible objection, he thought, was that voting was a matter for the states to regulate. But since the Constitution provided for its own change, and since once before the nation had acted on the suffrage question, he felt that all doubt must yield to the tremendous popular demand for women to participate in the electoral process.[44]

[39] 51 *Cong. Rec.* 11686 (1914).   [40] 53 *Cong. Rec.* 75 (1915).
[41] *The Suffragist*, March 7, 1914; *ibid.*, November 4, 1915.
[42] *New York Times*, August 2, 1916.
[43] 53 *Cong. Rec.* 11318 (1916).   [44] *ibid.*, p. 11319.

4.

One of Sutherland's chief interests during the Wilson years was in the field of foreign policy. There, because of his membership on the Senate Foreign Relations Committee, his views were of more than ordinary importance. He had long been the advocate of a vigorous diplomacy which strongly, and even belligerently, called always for an assertion of American rights. It was therefore to be expected that Wilson's cautious, sometimes pacifistic, approach excited in him only contempt and disgust. He was appalled that the President should ask, in early 1914, for the abandonment of the exemption from tolls accorded American coastwise shipping in the Panama Canal. Great Britain had denied that the United States had any right to make such an exemption under the Hay-Pauncefote Treaty, which stipulated that the Canal was to be open to "all nations" on equal terms. Rather than argue the point, the President asked that the exemption be removed. His thought was that "we ought to reverse our action without raising the question whether we were right or wrong, and so once more deserve our reputation for generosity."[45]

This proposal filled Sutherland with indignation. In language so bitter that it is difficult to understand today, he branded the President's proposal as without precedent and "utterly subversive of every consideration of self-respect."[46] Congress, he argued, was not at liberty to surrender any American rights. Sutherland was willing for the matter to be arbitrated. Characteristically, he thought that it could be left in full confidence to a tribunal of judges. Such a tribunal, even if it should be exclusively English or exclusively American, was sure to render a "just and righteous determination."[47]

[45] 51 *Cong. Rec.* 8730 (1914).   [46] *ibid.*, p. 8731.

[47] *ibid.*, p. 8737. Another noteworthy demonstration of Sutherland's faith in judges took place in the Senate on December 7, 1916. The Senate was considering a bill to allow the President to appoint a new district judge whenever he found that an incumbent was unable to do all the work of the district. Sutherland strenuously objected on the ground that the

The lengths to which Sutherland was willing to go in defense of what seemed to him American rights were eloquently put by him in a speech to the Senate on March 7, 1916.[48] The suggestion had been made, following the *Lusitania* and other disasters, that American citizens be officially advised to forbear from traveling on belligerent merchant vessels armed for defense. The reasoning was that since the submarine itself had so little defensive power, torpedo assaults without warnings on such vessels must now be considered to be fully consistent with international law—and this in spite of the fact that, until the advent of the submarine, the right of merchantmen to arm for defense had never been doubted. Sutherland brusquely rejected the idea that the law had changed. His view was that the "new weapon must yield to the law and not that the law must yield to the new weapon."[49] Therefore, since American citizens were within their rights in traveling on armed merchantmen, he demanded that the government sustain that position

at whatever cost or consequence. A nation that will not resent a flagrant and illegal attack upon the lives of its own citizens is only less detestable than a man who will not fight for his wife and children. . . . I would rather have war with all its sacrifices and suffering than that this nation, with its long history of heroism and glory, should play the poltroon when confronted by a supreme national duty, because it places a greater value upon its ease than upon its honor.[50]

He continued with this interesting bit of political philosophy:

---

bill was an invalid delegation of power to the President to create an office. But even if it were not, the President was not the man to determine the need for a new judge. Sutherland's explanation was: "I think it preferable, if we are going to abdicate our power at all, that some *responsible judicial officer, like the Chief Justice,* shall certify the facts, and that upon such certification the President shall act, than to allow it to be done upon the *mere opinion of the President.* . . ." 54 *Cong. Rec.* 93 (1916). The italics are mine.

[48] 53 *Cong. Rec.* 3660-3664 (1916).

[49] *ibid.,* p. 366.   [50] *ibid.,* p. 3662.

Such a policy is not in keeping with American traditions or spirit. It is the duty of a self-respecting nation to stand, and to stand firmly for the rights of every citizen however humble against foreign aggression from any source however powerful. *That is what the federal government is for, since the state in which the citizens live protects him in his domestic rights.*[51]

Accordingly, the Senator called for an abandonment of Wilson's "policy of retreat and scuttle—the policy, that among other things, has ordered our people to abandon their rights in Mexico and that has made us flee our plain duty in the Philippines." His prescription was as follows: "Instead of forever telling our citizens to run, I should like for once to hear sombody bid them stand, with the assurance that their government will stand with them. Instead of warning our own people to *exercise* their rights at their peril, I would like to see issued a warning to other people to *interfere* with these rights at *their* peril."[52]

This speech was particularly well received by the press of the country. The *Grand Rapids News* remarked: "As a keynoter of American patriotism, Senator Sutherland must be handed the palm. His words burn into the very soul of every man who heard them. . . . To read the Senator's speech takes one back to the days of real statesmen."[53]

The *New York Sun* was equally complimentary. Its comment was: "A wind of sanity blew through the Senate when the junior Utah Senator, George Sutherland, read a carefully prepared speech upon submarine warfare and the foreign policy of the administration. Since the sixty-fourth Congress assembled there has been no utterance about the war more logical, lucid and courageous. It was virile with a healthy inspiring patriotism; eloquent without being oratorical, in short a notable speech."[54]

5.

How much an article of faith was Sutherland's insistence on a strong assertion of American rights is revealed by his

---

[51] *ibid.* The italics are mine.   [52] *ibid.*
[53] *Grand Rapids News*, March 24, 1916.   [54] March 9, 1916.

stand in the 1916 campaign when he sought for himself a third term in the Senate. He had been advised to be gentle in his treatment of Wilson, who was highly favored in the West just then because "he kept us out of the war." But Sutherland, even though such a tactic might conceivably have won the election for him, refused to compromise on such an issue. Its appeal was to him one of "cheap emotionalism and sentiment." The campaign, of course, raised other issues as well. Sutherland's opponent was his antagonist of other days, William H. King, who well knew how to exploit the new situation resulting from the Seventeenth Amendment.

In their attacks on Sutherland, King and his adherents pulled no punches. Sometimes, indeed, they displayed scant regard for the truth. The following represents the type of argument made:

Do you know that George Sutherland does not have a home or a freehold in Utah; that his property in this state consists of a few portable law books, and that his only interest in and attachment to the commonwealth is to make it a constituency to keep him in the United States Senate?

Do you know that George Sutherland sheepishly followed Aldrich, the bellwether of the reactionaries in his votes in the Senate upon the schedules of the repudiated Payne-Aldrich Tariff?

Do you know that George Sutherland, as a member of the congressional committee to investigate the Ballinger case, was a servile partisan of Ballinger, the tool of the Guggenheims in his schemes to exploit the coal and mineral resources of Alaska?

Do you know that George Sutherland opposed the enactment of the federal statute which abolishes the fellow servant rule and the doctrine of assumption of risk. . . ?

Do you know that George Sutherland, as a state Senator in the first legislature of Utah insisted that the statute which limits the time of service in mines and smelters to eight hours was unconstitutional. . . ?

Do you know that George Sutherland, had he been in attendance, would have voted against the Adamson bill to establish the eight hour standard as a measure of a day's work; and that Sutherland claims that the eight hour law is unconstitutional. . . ?

Do you know that George Sutherland voted against the Underwood Tariff?

Do you know that George Sutherland voted against the Federal Reserve Act?

Do you know that George Sutherland voted against the act to repeal the tolls exemption clause of the Panama Canal Law?

Do you know that George Sutherland voted against the Federal Trade Commission Act?

Do you know that George Sutherland voted against the Merchant Marine Law. . . ?

Do you know that George Sutherland thinks he belongs to that ultra-respectable class which believes it has a proprietary interest in the government of the country; that Sutherland does not represent the people, but is rather the servant of this class and is therefore incompetent to fairly or properly interpret the real needs and aspirations of the people as United States Senator from Utah?[55]

Sutherland was by no means helpless before onslaughts such as this, nor was he in the position of having to repel them alone. The leaders of organized labor sprang to his defense. Andrew Furuseth wrote to friends in Salt Lake City that he "would think it a great national loss, a real national misfortune, to lose Senator Sutherland from the United States Senate."[56] Samuel Gompers, the president of the American Federation, wrote his followers in Utah:

I take pleasure in saying that Senator Sutherland has been, not only sympathetic, but very helpful in the passage of many measures through the United States Senate which the organizations of Labor have urged for enactment, such as the railroad men's Hours of Service law; the Employers' Liability law; the popular election of United States Senators; legislation in behalf of children; the right of petition; the literacy test contained in the Immigration bills; eight hour legislation and Industrial Education and Vocational Trade Training measures. . . .

During the historic contest in the United States Senate on the Seamen's bill by Senator LaFollette, Senator Sutherland rendered exceptional service. . . . He is one of the members of the United

[55] *Ogden Standard,* October 19, 1916.
[56] Furuseth to D. O. Jacobs, published in *Utah Labor News,* August 5, 1916.

States Senate whom we always feel free to approach and solicit his assistance. . . .[57]

From neighboring Idaho, William E. Borah uttered a strong plea for his colleague's reelection. "George Sutherland stands second to none," he said. "His is one of the most constructive minds in the Senate. . . . Some of the ablest speeches I have heard in the Senate, since I have been there, have been those of George Sutherland."[58] But it was all to no avail. Wilson and King won Utah by comfortable margins, although King's was considerably less than Wilson's.

Sutherland's defeat did not embitter him. Indeed, he later regarded it as one of the most fortunate occurrences of his life—on a par with his election to the Senate in the first place.[59] He was extremely disappointed, however, that Utah and the West had gone for Wilson. To Senator Clark of Wyoming, he wrote: "I am not a bit sorry or unhappy over my own defeat, although I will confess my vanity received a wound or two. . . . I am disgusted over the way the entire West behaved. The voters, and particularly the women, were stampeded like a lot of frightened cattle over a false and maudlin appeal to their emotions."[60]

Letters offering consolation and expressing regret poured in from many colleagues and friends. Nicholas

[57] Samuel Gompers to O. E. Asbridge, June 30, 1916.

[58] *Logan Republican*, November 4, 1916.

[59] "It was my good fortune to serve some years in the legislative branch of the government. And I should like to pause here long enough to say that for that great opportunity I shall never cease to feel grateful to the people of my state. Indeed, I may say that I am under a debt of gratitude to them for two things, first for having given me fourteen priceless years in the house of representatives and the senate of the United States, and then, gently but firmly, and I sometimes think with unnecessary emphasis, having retired me to private life. I am quite serious in saying that, because while I would not take for the fourteen years experience I had in the house and senate any sum of money that could be named, the opportunity that has come during the last five years to improve upon the salary of a senator has been very far from unwelcome." Sutherland to Utah State Bar Association, 20 Rep. Utah State Bar Ass'n 63 (1924).

[60] Sutherland to Clarence D. Clark, November 20, 1916.

Murray Butler mourned: "Of all the bad news that comes from various parts of the country nothing has given me more personal disappointment. . . . I can not see what a constituency is thinking of when it fails to keep in the Senate, as long as he is willing to stay there, a statesman of your experience, high capacity and vision."[61] William E. Borah was certain that the Senate would "often have cause to regret the absence of your wise and patriotic counsel."[62] But, as has been said before, Sutherland was not downcast, remarking, "I have the feeling of one who is just beginning life anew."[63]

In twelve years in the Senate, Sutherland had become a national figure. He had come from a comparatively unimportant state, and he had been in opposition to the dominant ideas and personalities of the time. Although few men have been less concerned with the pursuit of popular acclaim,[64] Sutherland received his share and more. Besides the degree at Columbia already mentioned, one was awarded him by the University of Michigan in 1917. Newspapers referred to him as "one of the real leaders of the Senate,"[65] and often praised his "exquisite English" and the lucidity and vigor of his intellect.[66] The *Cincinnati Enquirer* suggested even that he "might someday be elected President of the United States but for the prohibitive detail that he is of British and not American birth,"[67] and the general counsel of the Southern Railway wrote that he often found himself wishing that Sutherland was "charged with the chief responsibilty of our government."[68] Most extreme, perhaps, were the remarks of Peter

[61] Butler to Sutherland, November 8, 1916.
[62] Borah to Sutherland, November 13, 1916.
[63] Sutherland to George Hansen, March 8, 1917.
[64] "Public men with only a small fraction of Senator Sutherland's vision, philosophy, wit, eloquence, common sense, equipose and learning are more widely known nationally than himself, lacking as he does, in roar, egotism and the advertising instinct." *Cincinnati Enquirer*, August 13, 1916.
[65] *New York Herald Tribune*, January 31, 1916.
[66] *Pittsburgh Gazette Times*, June 9, 1913.
[67] August 13, 1916.
[68] Alfred P. Thom to Sutherland, December 28, 1914.

W. Meldrim, a Georgia Democrat, and former president of the American Bar Association, who told a Utah reporter: "I do not believe that I am stating more than the general belief when I say that Sutherland is considered in Washington as being the ablest man in the United States Senate. There are those who will say, of course, 'What about Root,' when this statement is made. But in any argument that results from this thought, I always find the final decision is that of all the leaders of the Senate your Sutherland stands out as the ablest of them all."[69]

6.

On leaving the Senate, Sutherland opened offices for the practice of law in Washington. He did so under the most favorable circumstances, for the preceding autumn he had been elected president of the American Bar Association. This, in itself, was quite an achievement for Sutherland had been a member of the Association only one year at the time of his election. That the presidency should go to a member of such short and belated connection aroused, quite naturally, some protest. John H. Wigmore, dean of the Northwestern University Law School, circulated a four page memorandum, which had as its burden the idea that service in the Association, not the political arena, should determine the recipients of its honors. The Dean disclaimed any wish "to disparage the signal eminence of Senator Sutherland. I am told, and believe," he continued, "that he ranks as the leading constitutional lawyer in the Federal Senate. His work as chairman of the Senate Committee on Workmen's Compensation and his work on the Judiciary Committee have marked him as a wise and constructive statesman."[70] Indeed Wigmore's words were so laudatory of Sutherland all the way through, and he had so little to say for the other contender, Walter George Smith of Philadelphia, that the net effect of his appeal might well have been to add to Sutherland's vote. His

[69] *Ogden Examiner*, August 30, 1915.
[70] The memorandum is in the Sutherland papers.

triumph was a source of much pleasure to Sutherland. "It was," he confided to a friend, "a greater honor than being elected to the Senate, because nothing influences that organization [the A.B.A.] except the belief that they are doing the right thing."[71]

As president of the Association, Sutherland took his duties seriously, facilitating such help to the war effort as the Association could give, improving the *Journal*, and promoting the work of the Association generally. His term's climactic moment came with his delivery of the presidential address before the annual meeting at Saratoga Springs on September 4, 1917. His subject was "Private Rights and Government Control." The address was largely an elaboration of the one delivered at Cleveland. It opened with an interpretation of politics reminiscent of Burke and Mill. Since the beginnings of organized society, Sutherland declared, "two desires, in a measure conflicting with one another, have been at work striving for supremacy: First, the desire of the individual to control and regulate his own activities in such a way as to promote what he conceives to be his *own* good, and second, the desire of society to curtail the activities of the individual in such a way as to promote what it conceives to be the *common* good. The operation of the first of these we call liberty, and that of the second we call authority. Throughout all history mankind has oscillated, like some huge pendulum, between these two, sometimes swinging too far in one direction, and sometimes, in the rebound, too far in the opposite direction."[72]

[71] Sutherland to George Hansen, December 31, 1916.

[72] "Private Rights and Government Control," 42 *A.B.A. Rep.* 197 (1917). *Cf.* Mill, *On Liberty*, New York, Oxford University Press, 1942, p. 1; and Burke's: "To make a government requires no great prudence. Settle the seat of power; teach obedience; and the work is done. To give freedom is still more easy. It is not necessary to guide; it only requires to let go the rein. But to form a *free government*; that is to temper together these opposite elements of liberty and restraint in one consistent work, requires much thought, deep reflection, a sagacious, powerful and combining mind." *Reflections on the Revolution in France* (Everyman's Ed.), p. 242; also, Hobbes: "For in a way beset with those that contend,

Sutherland did not long leave his hearers in doubt as to where the great danger then lay. In spite of the fact that the "moral plane" of the business community was higher than ever before, its "voluntary code . . . finer in tone," nevertheless, the business community was "beset and bedeviled with vexatious statutes, prying commissions, and governmental intermeddling of all sorts."[73] There were, of course, times when it was necessary to choose "between the liberty of the citizen and the supposed good of the community." But always, Sutherland said, "doubts should be resolved in favor of the liberty of the individual."[74] Thus, whenever government enlarged its role to something more than mere police activity, it had "the burden of showing clearly the necessity for so doing."[75]

Sutherland's concern for individual liberty was more than mere window dressing which concealed an excessive tenderness for men of great wealth. This was strikingly revealed when in the course of his remarks he sought to show that the proper task of government was not to engage in business, but to *regulate* it. "Regulation," he went on to explain, "is naturally and necessarily a matter for the government *since it is unthinkable that one individual should have the power to regulate the activities of another*."[76] Nothing that follows gives any indication that he realized at all the extent to which, in the America of his day, some men *were* regulating the lives of others. The result was that he could also oppose regulation by government as utterly superfluous.

In addition to being unnecessary, and therefore evil, the governmental activity to which Sutherland was objecting bore in his mind the further stigma of being, at best, of doubtful constitutionality. The Federal Trade Com-

---

on one side for too great Liberty, and on the other side for too much Authority, 'tis hard to passe between the points of both unwounded." Letter to Francis Godolphin, April 15, 1651, reprinted in Thomas Hobbes, *Leviathan* (Everyman's Ed.), at p. xl.

[73] "Private Rights and Government Control," *supra*, note 72, p. 198.
[74] *ibid.*, p. 202.   [75] *ibid.*, p. 200.   [76] *ibid.*, p. 210.

mission, for example, had been given power to deal with matters in no way related to interstate commerce. He saw in the creation of such commissions an undermining of "the fundamental principle upon which our form of government depends, namely, that it is an empire of laws and not of men."[77] How different was this from the plan of the Fathers! They were men, said Sutherland, "jealous to the last degree of individual rights and liberties." Their "effort was to abridge rather than to extend the powers of government."[78] The lodging of power in the multitude had rendered such an aim more to be desired than ever. The following words "of wisdom and of power," written by Laboulaye, were borrowed by the orator to summarize his thoughts:

The more democratic a people is, the more it is necessary that the individual be strong and his property sacred. We are a nation of sovereigns, and everything that weakens the individual tends toward demagogy, that is, toward disorder and ruin; whereas everything that fortifies the individual tends toward democracy, that is the reign of reason and the Evangel. A free country is a country where each citizen is absolute master of his conscience, his person, and his goods. If the day ever comes when individual rights are swallowed up by those of the general interest, that day will see the end of Washington's handiwork. We will be a mob and we will have a master.[79]

7.

Although out of office after 1917, Sutherland continued to see much of Washington officialdom. As a lawyer, his opportunities for cultivating the acquaintance of the justices of the Supreme Court were undoubtedly much more frequent. From appearances, one of his most intimate friends was the awe-inspiring Chief Justice, Edward Douglas White. It was a regular thing for the two to be seen strolling homeward together in the late afternoon.[80] Sutherland saw the justices in court, also. The most notable

[77] *ibid.*, p. 204.   [78] *ibid.*, p. 210.   [79] *ibid.*, p. 213.
[80] Writer's interview with Justice Owen J. Roberts, May 14, 1947.

case he argued before them was that of *New York Trust Company* v. *Eisner*,[81] in which the Court sustained the validity of a tax on "the transfer of the net estate of every decedent." Sutherland, in challenging the tax for the Trust Company, had an almost impossible task because a highly similar levy had already been upheld in *Knowlton* v. *Moore*.[82] The only difference was that in the earlier case the burden had fallen directly on the legatee.

As counsel, Sutherland's only recourse was to "distinguish" the two cases and to call up the specter of an invasion of the rights of the states. "The taxing power of the United States," he declared, "can not constitutionally be so exercised as to amount to a usurpation of any sovereign power belonging to the states."[83] In the case at bar, he asserted, the state's power to regulate descent and distribution was being interfered with because, unlike the situation in *Knowlton* v. *Moore*, the tax was on the actual "processes" of the state.[84] He also urged that the statute, because of its varying rates, produced "gross and capricious inequalities,"[85] and that it was a direct tax and therefore must be apportioned.[86] Despite the many citations supplied to support these arguments, the Court was not convinced. Speaking through Mr. Justice Holmes, it replied: "The statement of the constitutional objections urged imports on its face a distinction that, if correct, evidently has escaped this court. . . . Upon this point a page of history is worth a volume of logic."[87]

In December of 1918, at the urgent importuning of his friend President Butler, Sutherland delivered the Blumenthal Lectures at Columbia. He chose the general topic, "The Constitution and World Affairs," a subject which was particularly pertinent then since the Armistice had only recently been signed. At this particular moment there

---

[81] 256 U.S. 345 (1921); 65 L. Ed. 964. Since the argument is printed only in the Lawyers Edition, I shall use it as a reference in the notes that follow.

[82] 178 U.S. 41 (1899).

[83] 65 L. Ed. 964, 966 (1921).

[84] *ibid.*, p. 965.

[85] *ibid.*, p. 969.

[86] *ibid.*, p. 971.

[87] *ibid.*, pp. 982-983.

was more or less general agreement on the necessity of America joining other nations in an effort to abolish war. In his series of lectures, Sutherland seems to have been friendly to the idea. He acknowledged that the war had brought to us a new relationship to other nations. A great task that confronted us, therefore, was to "find but not to make" new meanings in the Constitution. More important, however, as Sutherland told his hearers, was the recognition of the fact that the government had authority in the field of foreign affairs independently of the Constitution. President Butler, and many others, were enthusiastic in their praise of Sutherland's treatment of this highly controversial question. "Nothing that has taken place at Columbia in many years," Butler wrote, "has aroused so great an intellectual interest as your discussion."[88]

8.

Although he took no official role, Sutherland continued during these years his active participation in the affairs of the Republican party. Indeed, in the election of 1920, as confidential adviser to Warren G. Harding, he was one of the key figures. His acquaintance with Harding dated back to the time when they served together in the Senate, and such was their friendship that Sutherland was an early Harding man. He must have been, too, one of the

[88] Butler to Sutherland, December 24, 1918. The Lectures were printed in book form. See George Sutherland, *The Constitution and World Affairs*, New York, Columbia University Press, 1919. The following list of people in New York for whom Sutherland requested tickets to the Lectures is interesting as a catalogue of his friends in that city: Hon. Theodore E. Burton, Miss Grace C. Burton, A. B. Leach, W. E. Fulcher, J. B. Cobb, William P. Gilmour, James Fletcher, Jr., T. Staples Fuller, Lieut. H. A. Johnston, James Payne, Duncan Phillips, Arthur Turnbull, George B. Post, William C. Squire, 3d, Lieut. A. Robert Elmore, Miss Annie B. Jennings, Mrs. H. C. Auchinschloss, Miss Nellie S. Brown, Joseph S. Auerbach, Charles A. Boston, Julius Henry Cohen, Chauncey M. Depew, Lindley H. Garrison, William D. Guthrie, Charles E. Hughes, Elihu Root, Francis Lynde Stetson, Henry W. Taft, George W. Wickersham, Charles Thaddeus Terry, Everett P. Wheeler, Alton D. Parker, Charles D. Hilles, Gilbert H. Montague, Lewis H. Rowe, Hon. E. A. Armstrong, Samuel Untermeyer.

first to pick Harding as the eventual winner of the nomination, for in April he was writing Dean Bates of the University of Michigan Law School: "Of the avowed candidates, I should not be surprised if Harding has the best of the situation. He and his managers have been very discreet in the conduct of his campaign. They have antagonized none of the other candidates and he is quite sure, in my judgment, to draw strength from all the other forces when it is discovered that none of them has sufficient strength to win."[89]

As is well known, this proved to be a shrewd prognostication. After the convention, Harding quickly sought Sutherland's aid, writing, "I need you, and need you greatly, and I wish you would arrange to come to me as soon as you can and stay with me as long as your affairs permit."[90] Sutherland responded by becoming one of the retinue at Marion, and thereafter occupied such a prominent place on the Front Porch that he came to be known as Harding's "Colonel House."[91] In his advice to the candidate Sutherland insisted that Harding stay at Marion. Late in July, he gently but firmly advised the candidate that letting the people get a look at him would not help matters. He wrote from California:

I see that some people are insisting that you should make a "swing around the circle." There is, of course, a very natural desire on the part of people generally to see and hear a Presidential candidate. Quite a number have said to me, "Harding ought to come out to the Coast; the people want to see him." But I invariably find, upon further talk, that the wish is based upon the desire to see and hear you rather than on the conviction that it will aid in the election. My own judgment is the same as it was when I saw you, that better results will follow the front porch campaign with an occasional set speech somewhere, than will follow a spectacular tour of the country. Everything indicates that today the country is with us, that we have only to sit tight to be sure of winning.[92]

[89] Sutherland to Bates, April 26, 1920.
[90] Harding to Sutherland, August 8, 1920.
[91] *New York Times*, September 10, 1922.
[92] Sutherland to Harding, July 29, 1920.

That Harding did sit tight and that that was sufficient is familiar history. The great victory won by the Republicans was attributed to Sutherland.[93] Sutherland himself believed it to be the inevitable consequence of "Democratic incompetence, executive autocracy and the attempt to *compel* us to participate in European affairs."[94] As to the last of these, Sutherland's advice to the President-elect is of special interest, showing, as it does, the attitude of the inner circle of the Republican party on this question immediately after the election. He wrote:

We must proceed with the utmost caution in the work of instituting any new world relationship. We occupy a position of tremendous strategic value; we are the dominating power of this hemisphere; three thousand miles of water separate us from Europe and five thousand miles of water separate us from Asia; our leadership of all America is unchallenged; we haven't a military rival north or south, and we should never allow ourselves to be beguiled into any arrangement which will *permit* Europe to meddle in the affairs of this continent or compel us to meddle in the affairs of Europe.[95]

Whatever the cause of the Republican triumph, it was to Sutherland "the most joyous thing that ever happened."[96] Several factors, no doubt, contributed to his rapture, but none more so than the realization that the Progressive dragon had, at long last, been slain. For nearly three decades America had been, it seemed, in the throes of a political frenzy which threatened to engulf all that Sutherland held dear. But he could not believe that this was the norm or that it reflected the "sober and deliberate" choice of the American people. Years before he had prophesied that the "terrifying visions" and "haunting spells" would some day yield to the sun of a glorious

[93] "I congratulate you heartily on all that happened. I believe that the magnificent way in which Senator Harding conducted himself during the entire campaign was largely due to your guidance and advice, and I believe that the world in general gives you credit for this." Jules S. Bache to Sutherland, November 5, 1920.

[94] Sutherland to Harding, November 10, 1920.

[95] *ibid.*   [96] *ibid.*

new morning. And now his theory had been verified. Warren G. Harding was a man whom Sutherland knew could
be trusted. The world really was "getting better all the
time."

Sutherland's eminence in the new Administration was
immediately recognized. Mark Sullivan identified him as
Harding's most trusted adviser "in the field of thought
and policy."[97] He described him as "a man of unusual
ability and high-mindedness. I think," he continued, "that
anyone who would consult the accepted leaders of the legal
world . . . would be told that Mr. Sutherland is one of the
two or three best lawyers in America."[98] There were many
other reports assigning Sutherland to high place in the
government. It was considered a certainty that he would
be either Secretary of State or Attorney General. And
it seems probable that he could have had either position for
the asking.

For the time being, Sutherland refused to accept any
permanent assignment. He did, however, undertake special
missions for the President. In April, 1921, for example,
he investigated a strike of railway workers in Missouri.[99]
Later he served in an advisory capacity to the American
delegation to the Washington Conference.[100] And in the
summer of 1922, he appeared as counsel for the United
States in the Norwegian shipping case before the arbitra-
tion tribunal at The Hague.[101]

Despite this activity and the necessity of giving some
attention to his personal affairs, Sutherland found time
to address the New York State Bar Association in 1921.
This address, entitled "Principle or Expedient," is of
particular interest today, revealing as it does the state of
his thinking only a little over a year before his appointment to the Supreme Court.[102] In his earlier addresses,
particularly in those made before he went out of office,

[97] *New York Evening Post*, November 6, 1920.
[98] *ibid.*   [99] Sutherland to Harding, May 2, 1921.
[100] *New York Times*, November 2, 1921.
[101] See Sen. Doc. No. 288, 67th Cong., 4th Sess. (1922).
[102] "Principle or Expedient," 44 *N.Y. State Bar Ass'n Rep.* 263 (1921).

Sutherland had been willing to concede that the social welfare must henceforward be the concern of statesmen and be promoted, in certain ways, by government. In his remarks to the New York lawyers, however, there is no hint that he had retained even an ash of this idea. Earlier he had inveighed against the evils of a great concentration of wealth and proposed that it be prevented by a rigorous taxing policy. But now he declared that a redistribution of wealth could not be accomplished "without the consent of those whose property would be depleted." And that this is so, Sutherland continued, "is one of the great blessings of our constitutional heritage, and one to be guarded with the utmost jealousy; for if the hand of power shall ever be permitted to take from A and give to B merely because A has much and B has little, we shall have taken the first step upon that unhappy path which leads from a republic where every man may rise in proportion to his energy and ability, to a commune where energy and sloth, ability and ignorance, occupy in common the same dead level of individual despair. Any attempt to fix a limit to personal acquisition is filled with danger. . . ."[103]

Even the recent Republican triumph did not restrain Sutherland from warning that the growth of the Presidential office threatened "the stability of the principle of departmental independence," or from identifying as "our chief danger . . . the growing extension of vaguely conferred powers in the hands of administrative bodies." As for governmental regulation of the economy, Sutherland expressed the "very firm conviction" that there had already been too much. The mild postwar effort at price control drew his fierce denunciation. "It had been proved by centuries of experience," he said, "under all conceivable circumstances . . . that government should confine its activities, as a general rule, to preserving a free market and preventing fraud."[104] There were, he explained, "certain fundamental social and economic laws which are beyond the power, and certain underlying governmental

[103] *ibid.*, pp. 278-279.   [104] *ibid.*, p. 264.

principles, which are beyond the right of official control, and any attempt to interfere with their operation inevitably ends in confusion, if not disaster. These laws and principles may be compared with the forces of nature whose movements are entirely outside the scope of human power."[105]

Throughout his speech, Sutherland supported the Spencerian theory of adaptation as the only really efficient social corrective. Truth is discovered slowly and only after a "lingering period of inconvenience and suffering."

As we grow in intelligence the consequences which follow good or bad conduct more and more control our behavior. In our dealings with one another we are not controlled by statute law which visits an infraction of its terms by *punishment* more or less uncertain, more or less delayed, and more or less severe, half so often as we are by the unwritten moral law the violation of which imposes certain definite, unpleasant *consequences* upon the violator, which . . . promote repentance and reformation more surely than a statutory penalty.[106]

Once more Sutherland indicated his abiding suspicion of any particular popular majority. Because they yielded so frequently to the "desire of the moment," majorities could not be trusted. Indeed, the people were really the chief offenders in the attack on the old established landmarks. Sutherland sadly elaborated:

It is one of the anomalies of representative government that it is often the people who have themselves established the principle who most strenuously demand its violation. With painstaking care they limit the power of their official representatives by specific constitutional provisions, and then not infrequently turn their best energies in the direction of having the limitations disregarded and abuse those most who most faithfully follow their permanent will and reject their temporary fancies.[107]

But whatever the abuse, even though it be inspired by a "unanimous sentiment," judges must uphold the Constitution "under all conditions and at all times." Only in this way could the republic be preserved. For "self-govern-

<hr>

[105] *ibid.*, p. 268.   [106] *ibid.*, pp. 280-281.   [107] *ibid.*, p. 268.

ment, if it means anything, means the exercise of sufficient self restraint on the part of the people to uphold their own fundamental law against every temptation to subvert it. . . . Only thus can we preserve the character of our institutions as a government of laws and prevent their degeneration into a chaos of fleeting and fickle emotion."

These were the views, in 1921, of a lawyer speaking to lawyers. The next year their expounder was to be a judge who could, with the aid of his brethren, require any citizen of the United States to listen and take heed.

9.

Looking back on Sutherland's career, there is a temptation to say that fate intended him for the Supreme Court. When, finally, he was appointed on September 5, 1922, it was something of an anticlimax, so often had his "manifest destiny" been thwarted. Sutherland had been a senator only a year or two when it began to be bruited about that a seat on the Court was his goal and that he desired it "above all earthly rewards." The inauguration of Taft seemed to bode well for his prospects, since the two men shared substantially the same views on judicial problems.[108] Sutherland's appointment by Taft seemed all the more likely when stories began to filter out of Washington that the President considered the Senator "ideally" fitted for the bench and the Senate's "greatest constitutional lawyer."[109] Taft might well have appointed him, too, had not the vacancy caused by the death of Chief Justice Fuller late in November 1910 arisen after the elections of that year. From the first it was conceded that the President would appoint a Western man to the place. It soon narrowed down to a choice between Sutherland and Judge Willis Van Devanter of the Eighth Circuit Court of Appeals. At one point, a Utah paper, under a New York date line, reported that information had reached that city,

108 "Our views are much alike and it is important that they prevail." Taft to Sutherland, July 2, 1921.
109 *Utah Independent*, July 22, 1909.

"from a source that renders it impossible to doubt its accuracy," that Taft had decided on Sutherland.[110] The appointment of Van Devanter came the next day, however, indicating, if the above information was accurate, that Taft changed his mind at the last minute. There were three reasons which probably influenced him in favor of Van Devanter. The first centered around the thumping victories of the Democrats and Progressives in the still recent off-year election. Sutherland, as a loyal Administration supporter, was now needed more than ever in the Senate, and, contrariwise, the Progressives were not to be antagonized unless this proved unavoidable. In this respect Van Devanter filled the order nicely, as little was known of his political opinions. Last of all, Taft, having once been a Circuit judge himself, was anxious to make service on that court a steppingstone to the supreme tribunal.

Two other vacancies occurred in the remainder of Taft's term, but although Sutherland was mentioned as a likely nominee on both occasions, his chances were greatly lessened by the fact that a Western man had been so recently appointed. Furthermore, the Progressives were then more rampant than ever and publicly warned against the appointment of Sutherland.[111] The Wilson victories, of course, removed Sutherland's name from consideration for the ensuing eight years.

Those eight years, however, saw the strengthening of Sutherland's claim to an appointment with his rise to eminence in the Bar Association and as a public orator. The return of the Republicans to power could not have happened, as has been seen, under circumstances more favorable for the fulfillment of Sutherland's ambition. Besides being the new President's most trusted adviser, he was the architect of victory. Indeed, it seems probable that Sutherland, even before the inauguration, had been assured by Harding of an appointment. This explains his

---

110 *Salt Lake Herald-Republican*, December 12, 1910.

111 See the *Pittsburgh Sun*, November 10, 1911; *Detroit News*, November 8, 1911; *Portland Oregonian*, January 4, 1912.

resolute refusal to allow his friends to urge him for a place in the new cabinet, any position of which would almost certainly have been his for the asking. This view is further buttressed by a letter written to Sutherland only a few days after the election by one of Harding's confidantes at Marion. "I have gathered a pretty definite impression," Judson Welliver wrote, "that you are not going to be a member of the cabinet and that you will be the first appointee to the Supreme Bench. I can say quite honestly that I do not believe anybody in the entire party could have commanded so many expressions of approval as I have heard in your behalf."[112]

Sutherland almost certainly would have been the first appointee, had the vacancy not been in the Chief Justiceship. When the incumbent Chief Justice, Edward Douglas White, died in May 1921, Sutherland was considered as a very likely successor. Proffers of support came from both Democratic and Republican friends, but they were not encouraged.[113] William Howard Taft, anxiously awaiting the call in New Haven, was on tenterhooks lest it should go to his old supporter.[114] But Taft prevailed and Sutherland was again passed over, although it does not appear to have disturbed him at all. In July Taft, realizing Sutherland's great claim to the appointment, wrote almost apologetically: "I look forward to having you on the bench with me. I know, as you do, that the President intends to put you there."[115] Fourteen months later, September 5, 1922, when John H. Clarke resigned to work for world peace, Sutherland's hour came. He was appointed and confirmed, without discussion, on the day of Clarke's resignation.[116]

To a country hastening "back to normalcy" the appoint-

[112] Judson Welliver to Sutherland, December 10, 1920.

[113] Senator Charles S. Thomas (Dem. Colo.) to Sutherland, June 11, 1921; H. T. Newcomb to Sutherland, June 2, 1921.

[114] Harry F. Pringle, *The Life and Times of William Howard Taft*, New York, Farrar and Rinehart, 1939, pp. 958-959.

[115] Taft to Sutherland, July 2, 1921.

[116] 63 *Cong. Rec.* 12169 (1922).

ment was welcome. The *New York Times* described Sutherland as "eminently fit,"[117] and the *Oakland Tribune* was sure of "general approval."[118] Messages of congratulation poured in. "I do not know when a judicial appointment has given more general and justifiable satisfaction to the Bar," wrote William M. Chadbourne of New York. "Such appointments," he continued, "make us rejoice that under the Constitution the Supreme Court is the balance wheel of our system of government."[119] Justice McReynolds wrote that he was "delighted";[120] Harlan F. Stone, later a colleague, thought the appointment justified "my lifelong allegiance to the Republican party";[121] James M. Beck "rejoiced";[122] and Nicholas Murray Butler was similarly happy.[123] Only John H. Clarke, the retiring Justice, struck a sour note. He assured the new appointee he was beginning a "dog's life."[124]

[117] September 6, 1922.
[118] September 6, 1922.
[119] Chadbourne to Sutherland, October 3, 1922.
[120] McReynolds to Sutherland, September 5, 1922.
[121] Stone to Sutherland, September 11, 1922.
[122] Beck to Sutherland, September 29, 1922.
[123] Butler to Sutherland, September 25, 1922.
[124] Clarke to Sutherland, October 4, 1922.

4

APPLICATION, 1922-1930

THE Supreme Court, when Sutherland became a member in 1922, was soon, with the appointments of Butler, Sanford, and Stone, to achieve a stability of personnel which was to endure until 1930.[1] There was, in this period, very little of the personal asperity which had been present in other days. "The meetings are pleasanter than I have ever known them," Holmes wrote to Pollock shortly after Sutherland's elevation. This happy condition he ascribed "largely to the C. J. but also to the disappearance of men with the habit of our older generation, that regarded a difference of opinion as a cockfight, and often left a good deal to be desired in point of manners."[2] The compliment to Sutherland implied in these remarks was well deserved. His deep respect for the Court as an institution engendered a corresponding esteem for its members, rendering it easy for him to work harmoniously with them. Even in the sharp struggles of later years he retained this attitude, insisting to the end that minority views, however forceful, should be set forth "always . . . in terms which . . . do not offend the proprieties or impugn the good faith of those who think otherwise."[3]

In addition, there was the fact of Sutherland's long previous acquaintance with most of the other members. He had been intimate with Taft for something over fifteen years and Van Devanter he had known for an even longer period. Since his views seldom crossed those of McReynolds, there was not the danger of unpleasantness there

[1] Pierce Butler succeeded Mr. Justice Day on January 23, 1923; Edmund Terry Sanford succeeded Mr. Justice Pitney on February 19, 1923; Harlan Fiske Stone succeeded Mr. Justice McKenna on March 2, 1925.

[2] *Holmes-Pollock Letters*, Cambridge, Harvard University Press, 1941, II, pp. 113-114.

[3] Dissenting, *West Coast Hotel Co.* v. *Parrish*, 300 U.S. 379, 402 (1937).

which others suffered. With Butler, Sutherland is said to have developed a close friendship and one which grew as the years passed.[4] Nor was the situation radically different so far as it concerned the three justices whom Sutherland met so often in dissent. Stone's friendly feeling has already been noted. Holmes, aristocratic and skeptical to the core, could hardly have been expected to be warmly sympathetic with the newcomer who appealed so often to absolutes. Yet their relationship, if not intimate, was decidedly an amiable one. For this, undoubtedly, Holmes' appreciation of his colleague's considerable abilities as a raconteur was largely responsible. Indeed, Justice Roberts relates that it was a regular thing for Holmes, on his entry into the conference room, to make for Sutherland, and bending over so low that their heads were almost touching, longingly plead: "Sutherland, J., tell me a story." Justice Roberts adds that this entreaty was unfailingly honored to the accompaniment of roars of judicial laughter.[5] More serious was the following note penciled by Holmes to Sutherland in May 1925: "You are not feeling well. My cases are all written and if I can help you by taking some of yours I shall be glad to do so." To appreciate the magnanimity of this gesture one has only to recall the eagerness with which Holmes looked forward to periods of leisure.

With Brandeis, the crusader and advocate of reform, it might have been supposed that Sutherland's relations would be difficult. Their first meeting, occasioned by the Ballinger-Pinchot controversy, took place in the highly-charged atmosphere of partisan conflict with the two on opposing sides.[6] An even more embarrassing circumstance

[4] Writer's interview with Justice Owen J. Roberts, May 14, 1947.
[5] *ibid.*

[6] Conservation had been the issue on which Sutherland and Brandeis first opposed each other in 1910. Oddly enough, out of this very same issue arose their initial disagreement on the Court. The case was *United States* v. *Oregon Lumber Co.*, 260 U.S. 290 (1922), in which the new Justice rendered one of his first opinions. The question involved was the right of the government to recover damages for deceit from purchasers of public lands who had made false representations to induce the sale. The

was Sutherland's pronouncement, by his adverse vote on Brandeis' confirmation, that the "people's attorney" was unfit for the bench.[7] But these affairs seem to have reflected only the differences of opinion between two honest men. It is recorded that in 1921 Sutherland was the Judge's dinner guest, eating, as his approving host exclaimed, "like an expert."[8] Nor was this cordial friendship disturbed by their later disagreements on the Court. Each was often heard to affirm his respect for the other and, almost in the same breath, his regret at his friend's ideas.[9]

In the years that Taft was Chief Justice the business of the Supreme Court was rarely reported on the front pages of the newspapers. Nevertheless, cases of the highest moment were continually being heard and decided. They included in their range the classic problems of American constitutional law—the nature and extent of political authority, federalism, the separation of powers. On each of these questions George Sutherland had important things to say. Accordingly, his contribution to the work of the Taft Court will be considered under these three heads.

---

defendants argued that a prior unsuccessful suit by the government to have the sale set aside constituted an election of remedies which barred the subsequent action. This view Sutherland was willing to accept since it seemed to him that the government by the second suit was violating the maxim that one shall not be "twice vexed" for the same cause. The public interest in the matter led Brandeis to argue that the doctrine of election did not apply.

[7] 53 *Cong. Rec.* 9032 (1916).

[8] Alpheus T. Mason, *Brandeis, A Free Man's Life*, New York, Viking, 1946, p. 537.

[9] Writer's interview with Justice Owen J. Roberts, May 14, 1947. The picture given here of Sutherland's relationship with his colleagues is corroborated by Chief Justice Stone in his remarks at the memorial proceedings in honor of Sutherland, December 18, 1944. Stone remarked: "With [Chief Justice Taft] and with Justice Van Devanter and Justice Butler, the newly appointed Justice shared substantially common views of law, government, and public policy and in them especially he found congenial companions. But his relations with all of his associates were characterized by a personal regard and esteem which found their source in mutual respect and derived their strength from common devotion to the institution which they served. This friendly relationship with his colleagues rose above all differences of opinion. . . ." 323 U.S. xviii (1944)

APPLICATION

2.

In the more than a century and a half since the Constitution was framed, the idea that there are limits to political authority has been perhaps the most persistent and distinctive characteristic of American thinking on public affairs. This notion quickly made its appearance in judicial literature. Justice Chase, in the early case of *Calder* v. *Bull*,[10] announced: "I can not subscribe to the omnipotence of a state legislature, or that it is absolute without control; although its authority should not be expressly restrained by the constitution or the fundamental law of the state. The people of the United States erected their constitutions or forms of government, to promote the general welfare, to secure the blessings of liberty; and to protect their persons and property from violence. The purposes for which men enter into society will determine the nature and foundations of legislative power. The nature and ends of legislative power will limit the exercise of it. . . ."

John Marshall, too, made appeal to "the general principles which are common to our free institutions" in seeking "some limits to the legislative power."[11] Chase and Marshall, however, did not have available to them a due process of law clause with a substantive content which authorized the Court to intervene and impose its notions on errant legislators. That was a later development and one not assured of success until 1890. But twelve years before, Justice Miller had taken judicial notice of the "strange misconception" prevalent the country over that the due process clause gave to the courts a general authority to sit in judgment on the propriety of legislative actions.[12] History tells us that this "misconception," in the course of its career, became more respectable. By the time of Sutherland's accession to the bench, it was an accepted commonplace, providing him, in his very first term of court, with the materials for one of his most notable decisions.

[10] 3 Dall. 386, 387-388 (1798).
[11] *Fletcher* v. *Peck*, 6 Cranch 87, 135 (1810).
[12] *Davidson* v. *New Orleans*, 96 U.S. 97 (1878).

The case was *Adkins* v. *The Children's Hospital*,[13] which arose out of the Congressional Act of September 19, 1918.[14] By this statute, Congress provided for a board of three members with authority to fix minimum wages for women in the District of Columbia when, after notice and hearing, it should appear necessary. The wage was to be sufficient to supply "the necessary cost of living to any women workers to maintain them in good health and to protect their morals." There were two applications for an injunction to restrain the enforcement of the Act, one, understandably, from an employer, and one, also, from a certain Willie A. Lyons, a hotel employee who had been discharged from what she regarded as a satisfactory position because of the penalties threatened by the statute unless her wages were raised. Both employer and employee sought the protection of the due process clause of the Fifth Amendment, asserting a deprivation of liberty and property. The District Court, after dismissing the bills, was reversed by the Court of Appeals, following which the board carried the cases to the Supreme Court. This final tribunal, with Justice Brandeis not sitting, decided by a vote of five to three that the law was unconstitutional.

The fact that the statute was assailed by one of its supposed beneficiaries has a significance which, although generally overlooked, is of the highest importance. For whatever suspicions are generated by Willie Lyons' plea that she be allowed to work for $35 a month and two meals a day, there could have been no shrewder appeal to the sympathy of George Sutherland. The express pronouncement of the statute was that women were to be treated differently by the law than men. Such discrimination had been denounced by both John Stuart Mill and Herbert Spencer as an anomalous survival from a barbarous past. And Sutherland, doubtless moved by their words, had battled against it throughout his political career. Indeed, in 1916, when arguing before the Senate for woman's suf-

[13] 261 U.S. 525 (1923).   [14] 40 Stat. 960 (1918).

frage, Sutherland developed the same argument he was later to make in the *Adkins* case. He then said: "A division along a geographical line is not greatly more arbitrary than the existing separation of voters from nonvoters by the line of sex. Such a division is purely artificial, and is certain to disappear, just as the other superstitions which in the past have denied women equal opportunities for education, equality of legal status—including the right of contract and to hold property—and all the other unjust and intolerant denials of equality have disappeared, or are disappearing from our laws and customs."[15]

Accordingly, instead of seeing anything progressive in the challenged enactment, Sutherland viewed it as a reversion to an unsavory past. In his view, it was based on injustice, intolerance, and discredited superstition. Moreover, the statute appeared to flout the whole historical process, reviving, as it did, a discrimination marked by the Spencerian dialectic for certain destruction. Yet, for all this, it was no simple task to demonstrate the Act's illegality. According to orthodox doctrine, the prior decisions of the Court were higher authorities than the writings of any mere philosopher. And in *Muller* v. *Oregon*,[16] the Court in an opinion fashioned by a judge of the most intense laissez-faire convictions had approved the state's decision to constitute women a special class in the matter of the number of hours they might labor. But fifteen years had elapsed since that decision, and, as Sutherland explained, conditions had changed.

The ancient inequality of the sexes, otherwise than physical, has continued "with diminishing intensity." In view of the great—not to say revolutionary—changes which have taken place since that utterance, in the contractual, political, and civil status of women, culminating in the Nineteenth Amendment, it is not unreasonable to say that these differences have come now almost, if not quite, to the vanishing point. In this aspect of the matter, while the physical differences must be recognized in appropriate

[15] 53 *Cong. Rec.* 11318 (1916).
[16] 208 U.S. 412 (1908). The opinion was by Justice Brewer.

cases, and legislation fixing hours or conditions of work may properly take them into account, we can not accept the doctrine that women of mature age, *sui juris*, require or may be subjected to restrictions upon their liberty of contract which could not lawfully be imposed in the case of men under similar circumstances. To do so would be to ignore all the implications to be drawn from the present day trend of legislation, as well as that of common thought and usage, by which woman is accorded emancipation from the old doctrine that she must be given special protection or be subjected to special restraint in her contractual and civil relationships.[17]

The "joker" in all this, of course, is the assumption that freedom of contract was available for the male section of the citizenry. This difficulty had been attended to in an earlier part of the opinion. Almost at the beginning of the discussion Sutherland, while conceding that freedom of contract was "subject to a great variety of restraints," had declared that such freedom was *"nevertheless, the general rule and restraint the exception; and the exercise of legislative authority to abridge it can be justified only by the existence of exceptional circumstances."*[18]

To sustain this proposition, Sutherland could point to no provision of the Constitution but only to scattered pronouncements of the Court itself. The most notable of these was the *Lochner* case,[19] tarnished by years of evasion and criticism, but still never expressly overruled. Justice Peckham there had stated that legislative prescriptions dealing with the employment of "grown and intelligent men . . . are mere meddlesome interferences with the rights of the individual."[20] Hence, they could not be upheld unless the Court considered them reasonable and even necessary for the protection of the public. Governmental restrictions were presumably illegal until proved otherwise.

Faced with the necessity of justifying statutory enactments, lawyers such as Louis D. Brandeis patiently began to educate the Court to an understanding of conditions in

---

[17] *Adkins* v. *The Children's Hospital, supra* note 13, p. 553.
[18] *ibid.*, p. 546. The italics are mine.
[19] *Lochner* v. *New York*, 198 U.S. 45 (1904).   [20] *ibid.*, p. 61.

a modern industrial society. The result was that numerous statutes regulating the contract of employment were sustained,[21] and finally in *Bunting* v. *Oregon*,[22] the Court seemed to call on the opponents of the maximum hours law there considered to prove its *invalidity*. By virtue of Sutherland's Spencerian edict, however, regulation of any sort was once more "exceptional" and not to be easily tolerated.

Sutherland went further. He indicated that there were some regulations which could not be sustained, however justified. The statute here, he pointed out, prescribed the fixing of a wage. To him, this was an interference with "the heart of the contract" which could be allowed under no circumstances. In other words, there was at the center of business and social life a hard core which government could never penetrate. In this view, the many approvals of the minimum wage collected in the brief of Felix Frankfurter were entirely irrelevant. Sutherland stated that he had found them "interesting but only mildly persuasive" and, as he explained, "our own reading has disclosed a large number to the contrary." In any event, such evidence could "reflect no legitimate light" on the legality of a minimum wage. "The elucidation of that question," he tartly remarked, "cannot be aided by a counting of heads."[23]

But this was not all. It was bad enough for government to seek to regulate "the heart of the contract." To Sutherland, it was even worse for it to attempt to do so in the manner the statute prescribed. The statute had taken as a basis for the minimum wage a sum necessary to protect the health and morals of a woman worker. It had said nothing of the *value* of the service rendered. The anguished Justice thought this tantamount to confiscation and slavery.

[21] See the cases cited by Chief Justice Taft and Justice Holmes in their dissents in the present case.

[22] 243 U.S. 426 (1916). Mr. Justice McKenna remarked (p. 437): "We can not know all the conditions that impelled the law or its particular form. . . . But we need not cast about for reasons for the legislative judgment. We are not required to be sure of the precise reasons for its exercise or be convinced of the wisdom of its exercise."

[23] *Adkins* v. *The Children's Hospital, supra* note 13, p. 560.

APPLICATION

The *ethical* right of every worker, man or women, to a living wage may be conceded . . . but the fallacy of the proposed method of attaining it is that it assumes that every employer is bound at all events to furnish it. The moral requirement in every contract of employment, viz., that the amount to be paid and the service to be rendered shall bear to each other some relation of just equivalence, is completely ignored.—In principle, there can be no difference between the case of selling labor and selling goods. If one goes to the butcher, the baker or grocer to buy food, he is morally entitled to obtain the worth of his money but he is not entitled to more. If what he gets is worth what he pays he is not justified in demanding more simply because he needs more. A statute requiring an employer to pay in money, to pay at prescribed and regular intervals, to pay the value of the services rendered, even to pay with fair relation to the extent of the benefit obtained, would be understandable. But a statute which prescribes payment without regard to any of these things is so clearly the product of a naked, arbitrary exercise of power that it can not be allowed to stand under the Constitution of the United States.[24]

As a matter of fact, Sutherland was ready to assert that it was really quite impossible, in addition to being unconstitutional, for any board to determine the wage necessary for the preservation of health and morals. His atomistic view of society, his conviction that individuals were alike only in their will to be different, led him to reject in advance any such generalization. As he stated it: "The inquiry in respect of the necessary cost of living and of the income necessary to preserve health and morals, presents an individual and not a composite question, and must be answered for each individual considered by herself and not by a general formula prescribed by a statutory bureau."[25]

Taken at its face value, Sutherland's opinion could only be interpreted as asserting that under the Constitution it was impossible to attempt the solution of certain modern

[24] *ibid.*, pp. 558-559. But see *Murphy* v. *Sardell*, 269 U.S. 530 (1925) where a statute prescribing payment in relation to the value of the services rendered was overthrown.

[25] *Adkins* v. *The Children's Hospital*, *supra* note 13, p. 556.

social problems by legislation. It was true that the Justice conceded a power to government in the peripheral areas, provided it was shown to be desirable. But the "heart of the contract" remained untouchable. Therefore, regulation must necessarily be partial and inadequate. To which George Sutherland might well have responded that total government is not the instrument of free men. Nor could he allow to go unchallenged the suggestion that opposition to the statute connoted any lack of zeal for the general welfare. He, too, was seeking this end and in the only manner which allowed for sure and safe advancement. His own final rejoinder speaks best for him: "To sustain the individual freedom of action contemplated by the Constitution is not to strike down the common good but to exalt it; for surely the good of society as a whole can not be better served than by the preservation of the liberties of its constituent members."[26]

Basically, the decision in the *Adkins* case was an attack on the very idea of government. As such it was not allowed to go unopposed. Both the Chief Justice and Mr. Justice Holmes filed dissents. The latter asserted his usual reluctance to interfere with the dictates of a majority where the only objection was to be found within the "vague contours" of the due process clause. The Chief Justice could see no difference in principle between fixing wages and limiting hours. One was simply "the multiplier and the other the multiplicand." He confessed his surprise, too, at Sutherland's use of the *Lochner* case, which he had supposed had been "overruled *sub silentio*."

Outside the Court, restraint was cast to the winds, and comments of ominous character appeared. "The brutality of the majority decision can beget nothing but wrath," snarled the *American Federationist*.[27] "To buy the labor of a woman is now like buying pigs' feet in a butcher shop,"

---

[26] *ibid.*, p. 561.

[27] *The American Federationist,* **xxx** (1923), 400. This journal's comment also makes clear that much of labor's resentment of the decision arose from the fact that the opinion treated labor as if it were an article of commerce, thus coming within the scope of the Sherman Law.

mourned Samuel Gompers. "All progressive men and women must resent the language used by the Court. . . . It demeans humanity," he continued.[28] Elsewhere the opinion was described as a "calamity"[29] and as "setting the clock back many years."[30] Even the *New York Times* confessed itself to be a bit puzzled, although it was quick to commend Sutherland for his "conscientiousness and courage" in rendering a decision which he must have known would be unpopular.[31] And there were other less reserved laudatory comments, one from the Justice's old friend, Andrew Furuseth, the seamen's leader, who gave what may well have been Sutherland's own response to all the criticism: "Those who have enjoyed freedom a long time can not understand the real meaning of bondage, and are likely to hold out their hands for shackles."[32]

With the *Adkins* case, the country fully realized for the first time the extent of the new appointee's willingness to abide by the consequences of the unending struggle between man and man without a benevolent government to intervene on the side of the weaker party. This same philosophy was apparent in two other, but less dramatic, cases, decided the same term. The first was that of *Arkansas Natural Gas Company* v. *Arkansas Railroad Commission*,[33] where the utility was protesting the *lack* of power in the Commission to revise an earlier contract then found to be burdensome. In dismissing the suit, Sutherland could find no obligation in the state to interfere with natural processes and relieve a party of the penalties of an "improvident undertaking." Similarly, in *Georgia Railroad & Power Company* v. *Decatur*,[34] he refused to upset a contract even though it was argued that its continuance would result in confisca-

---

[28] *New York Times*, April 11, 1923.

[29] *ibid.*, April 12, 1923, quoting Mary Anderson of the Department of Labor.

[30] *American Labor Legislation Review,* XIII (1923), 137, quoting the *New York Globe.*

[31] *New York Times*, April 11, 1923.

[32] Furuseth to Sutherland, May 5, 1923.

[33] 261 U.S. 379 (1923).   [34] 262 U.S. 432 (1923).

tion. In the earlier decision, a wide tolerance of legislative action was avowed and this was repeated in two more opinions produced at the next term of court.[35] The last of these, *Radice* v. *New York*, raised echoes of the *Adkins* case. The statute under attack prohibited the employment of women between the hours of 10 P.M. and 6 A.M. in restaurants located in large cities. Here Sutherland easily found it possible to believe that there were facts existing which could justify the regulation. Impervious as he had been to any factual argument the year before, he was now able to state: "Where the constitutional validity of a statute depends upon the existence of facts, courts must be cautious about reaching a conclusion respecting them contrary to that reached in the legislature; and if the question of what the facts establish be a fairly debatable one, it is not permissible for the judge to set up his opinion in respect of it against the opinion of the lawmaker."[36]

When, it may be asked of Sutherland, does the validity of a statute depend on the existence of facts? Certainly not in such a case as that of the minimum wage. The answer suggested there was that, as to questions of constitutional power, *fact* can never be decisive. And the declaration just quoted does not negate this. For Sutherland was ready to admit all along that working conditions were subject to legislative governance. Accordingly, his inquiry in the *Radice* case was directed only toward ascertaining whether the regulations were reasonable. The surrounding circumstances were, of course, relevant to such an inquiry.

Yet there are at least two cases in which the presence of a particular condition was for Sutherland decisive of the issue of power. The first was that of *Euclid* v. *Ambler*,[37] decided November 22, 1926. In this case, the Court had before it a zoning statute passed by the village of Euclid, a suburb of Cleveland. Alfred McCormack, once Mr. Justice Stone's law clerk, relates that Sutherland was originally

---

[35] *Packard* v. *Banton*, 264 U.S. 140 (1924); *Radice* v. *New York*, 264 U.S. 292 (1924).

[36] *Radice* v. *New York*, p. 294.   [37] 272 U.S. 365 (1926).

convinced of the act's illegality and was actually preparing an opinion asserting that conclusion when Stone prevailed on him to change his mind.[38] Clearly, the statute was a novel exertion of political authority to curb individual freedom. As such it was rejected by Van Devanter, Butler, and McReynolds. How, then, could Sutherland have supported it? The answer to this question is a twofold one involving Herbert Spencer and Judge Cooley. Spencer had said that the growth of numbers was responsible for the existence of the state at all. Hence, in a political context, overpopulation is no ordinary fact but one of an ultimate character, capable of justifying political power. The statute, accordingly, could not be considered unreasonable if the alleged congestion actually existed.

More decisive, perhaps, was the influence of Cooley. The opinion makes clear that Sutherland saw in the zoning act not the deprivation of property, but its enhancement. A distinction observed by Cooley long before was therefore pertinent. It pointed out "the line between what would be a clear invasion of right on the one hand, and regulations not lessening the value of the right" on the other.[39] On this basis the common law had allowed the abatement of nuisances, and the forbidden industrial plants would approximate nuisances in a residential area such as Euclid. The result of the statute, then, was beneficial to property, and grounded as it was on the ultimate fact of overcrowding, it could not be set aside. But when, as in *Nectow* v. *Cambridge*,[40] neither of these reeds was available for support, a similar measure was unhesitatingly pronounced invalid.

The decision in *Euclid* v. *Ambler* marked only a temporary cessation of the struggle between Sutherland and the liberal justices which had begun with the *Adkins* case. It was resumed with a fierce intensity in 1927 in *Tyson* v. *Banton*.[41] The New York legislature had forbidden the

[38] Alfred McCormack, "A Law Clerk's Recollections," 46 *Col. L. Rev.* 710, 712 (1946).

[39] See Constitutional Limitations (7th ed.), p. 855, quoting from *Vanderbilt* v. *Adams*, 7 Cow. 349, 351.

[40] 277 U.S. 183 (1928).   [41] 273 U.S. 418 (1927).

resale of theatre tickets at a price greater than fifty cents in excess of the original cost. Tyson, a ticket broker, sought to enjoin the statute's enforcement with the customary allegation that his business was not "affected with a public interest," and thus was not amenable to regulation. The question of what businesses were of this class had been repeatedly before the Court since 1875. In that year the Court had affirmed the validity of a statute setting the price for storage in grain elevators.[42] Unfortunately, the accompanying opinion was susceptible of two distinct interpretations. One facet of this ambiguity grew out of the Court's reliance on a hitherto little-noticed passage from a work of Lord Hale's, written two hundred years previously, stating that businesses "affected with a public interest" could be made the subject of regulation. Laissez-faire judges subsequently drew from this the inference that there were some businesses not so affected, and, further, that the difference so indicated was absolute.

To others, however, this interpretation appeared to have been contradicted by the Court's broad assertion that property became "clothed with a public interest when used in a manner to make it of public consequence, and affect the community at large." Hence, it was possible to regard the case either as authority for the proposition that regulation could be achieved whenever the public interest, as voiced by the legislature, demanded it, or as setting up a closed category of activities subject to legislative direction, and totally eliminating the others. By 1923, if not before, the Court had made it clear that it considered the restrictive reading the proper one, thereby adopting a view which Sutherland had heard Cooley develop when the parent case was scarcely five years old and one which the Justice now eagerly embraced.[43]

His task, then, in the *Tyson* case, was to discover if the business involved was one of those "affected with a public

[42] *Munn* v. *Illinois*, 94 U.S. 113 (1877).

[43] See *Wolff Packing Co.* v. *Industrial Court*, 262 U.S. 522 (1923). For a history of the entire development see Walton Hale Hamilton, "Affectation with a Public Interest," 39 *Yale L. J.* 1089 (1930).

interest." In pursuit of the answer, Sutherland began by converting the brokerage business to that of entertainment by the simple process of declaring it to be "a mere appendage of the theatre." As such, he said, it was "in no legal sense a public utility."[44] Just as in the *Adkins* case the necessary minimum wage had been an "individual" question, so here it was said that "sales of theatre tickets ... are not interdependent transactions, but stand both in form and effect separate and apart from each other, 'terminating in their effect with the instances.' "[45] Accordingly, the public had no interest in the sales and the act must fall. "It may be true," Sutherland conceded, "that among the Greeks amusement and instruction of the people through the drama was one of the duties of government. But," he added, "certainly no such duty devolves upon any American government."[46]

In response to this holding, Holmes and Stone filed vigorous dissents, each with the concurrence of Brandeis, and there was also a separate dissent by Sanford. That of Holmes was particularly forthright in its denunciation of the use of "apologetic phrases" when uttered in regard to the "general power of the legislature to make a part of the community uncomfortable by a change."[47] Stone, for his part, challenged the Court's finding that this was a price-fixing statute at all, pointing out that the theatre was still able to ask whatever price it pleased. And, perhaps because he had lived in New York, he was able to see a definite need for the act.

A somewhat similar case, *Ribnik* v. *McBride*,[48] followed the next year when a New Jersey statute regulating the charges of employment agencies for their services was under review. Speaking for a majority, Sutherland approached this case as if the earlier one had foreclosed the issue. In spite of the fact that he had there treated Tyson as an integral part of the theatre and paid scant heed to

[44] *Tyson* v. *Banton, supra* note 41, p. 440.
[45] *ibid.*, p. 440.   [46] *ibid.*, p. 441.
[47] *ibid.*, p. 445.   [48] 277 U.S. 350 (1928).

the circumstance that he was a broker, the Justice now argued that what had been decided was that brokers generally were immune from price regulation. On broader grounds, he entered a stern denial that such a concept as the general welfare could be relied on to validate price control. It runs as follows:

> An employment agency is essentially a private business. . . . Of course, anything which substantially interferes with employment is a matter of public concern, but in the same sense that interference with the procurement of food and housing and fuel are of public concern. The public is deeply interested in all these things. The welfare of its constituent members depends upon them. The interest of the public in a matter of employment is not different in quality or character from its interest in the other things enumerated; but in none of them is the interest that "public interest" which the law contemplates as the basis for legislative price control.[49]

From this the conclusion must inevitably be drawn that, except for the few businesses operating under franchises, price fixing, regardless of how appropriate or necessary, was absolutely forbidden. The "heart of the contract" was to be governed by private desires rather than public necessities. The concession that the peripheral area could be controlled was really not of much help, for, as Stone pointed out and as the case of the employment agencies well illustrates, price control appeared oftentimes as the sole "appropriate and effective remedy."[50] Of course, it so appeared only to believers in government. Sutherland knew with Herbert Spencer that such appearances were illusory. Adaptation was the answer in the case of a man seeking a job just as it had been for the pioneer in his struggle against the wilderness.

[49] *ibid.*, p. 357.

[50] *ibid.*, p. 374. The *Ribnik* case was followed by *Williams* v. *Standard Oil Co.*, 278 U.S. 235 (1929), where an attempt to fix the price of gasoline was overthrown. Sutherland again spoke for the Court. Stone and Brandeis yielded to the extent of concurring in the result, but Holmes remained adamant. The *Ribnik* case was overruled in *Olsen* v. *Nebraska*, 313 U.S. 236 (1941).

APPLICATION

Attempts at price fixing were not the only regulatory statutes to fall before Sutherland's notion of limited political authority during the Taft era. In November 1928, he was the author of the Court's opinion invalidating a Pennsylvania law requiring the owners of drug stores, or owners of stock in corporations which operated them, to be registered pharmacists.[51] The avowed reason for this holding was that such a law had not been shown to be necessary to protect the public health. The Justice was explicit. After citing various protections in the Pennsylvania statutes, he concluded that the State had enough legislation on the subject and that the public health was "amply safeguarded" without further legislative exertion.[52]

The cases thus far considered demonstrate quite plainly that as a judge Sutherland's conception of the legitimate ambit of state interference was the same that it had always been. Other opinions make clear that even where he recognized the existence of authority, he encompassed its exercise with some rigid procedural demands. First of all, there had to be an exact equality before the law, an equality which acted as a "universal solvent" on all distinctions of every kind. Just how effective this solvent was in Sutherland's hands may be gathered from a glance at *Louisville Gas & Electric Company* v. *Coleman*,[53] decided April 30, 1928. The State of Kentucky had levied a tax on the registration of all mortgages in which the maturity period was over five years. Holmes, Brandeis, Stone, and Sanford were willing to sustain the exaction on the ground that all taxes had "to be laid by general rules" and that a line had to be drawn somewhere. In his opinion, Brandeis went into the economics of the situation, showing that short term borrowers were ordinarily at a disadvantage and that an obvious inequality existed between them and borrowers for a longer time. He therefore concluded that the lawmakers had good reason for exempting them from the incidence of the tax.

[51] *Liggett Co.* v. *Baldridge*, 278 U.S. 101 (1928).
[52] *ibid.*, p. 113.   [53] 277 U.S. 32 (1928).

Sutherland, speaking for the Court, rejected these arguments as inconclusive. For him the inequality to which Brandeis had alluded was as nothing to that of the statute:

Certainly one who is secured by the state in the priority of his lien for a period of less than five years enjoys a privilege which in kind and character fairly can not be distinguished from one who enjoys a like privilege for a longer period of time. The former reasonably may be required to pay proportionately less than the latter; but to exact, as the price of a privilege which, for obvious reasons, neither can safely forego, a tax from the latter not imposed in any degree upon the former, produces an obvious and gross inequality.[54]

That this inequality in the law, and not the social and economic conditions which evoked the law, was paramount in Sutherland's mind appears even more clearly with the next sentence when he posed an utter improbability as proof of his point: "If the state, upon the same classification, had reversed the process and taxed indebtedness maturing within a shorter period than five years, and exempted such as matured in a longer period, the inequality probably would be readily conceded, but the constitutional infirmity, though more strikingly apparent, would have been the same."

An even more extreme illustration of Sutherland's insistence on equality before the law is found in a case coming a year later, *Frost* v. *Corporation Commission*.[55] Oklahoma had, by a series of enactments, declared the cotton ginning business to be a public utility and had limited participation in it to those issued licenses by the State Corporation Commission on a showing of public convenience and necessity. It was provided, however, that in the case of a gin which was "to be run cooperatively" the license was to issue automatically if the petition was accompanied by 100 signatures. Acting under this statute, the Commission granted a license to a cooperative ginning company, whereupon Frost sought to have it canceled by the courts. Frost was himself a ginner in the locality of the proposed new gin

[54] *ibid.*, p. 39.   [55] 278 U.S. 515 (1930).

and he was operating under a license issued as a result of a showing by him of public convenience and necessity. It was this that produced his complaint, which was, specifically, that the same standards which had been required of him were not required of the cooperative. The case might have been disposed of, as Justices Stone and Brandeis suggested in their dissents, on the ground that Frost was not in a position to assail the statute. His was not the appeal of an unsuccessful applicant who stood on a parity with the cooperative. *Frost had his license.* But this did not satisfy Sutherland. To him the subsequent granting of a license to another on terms less rigorous than those originally obtaining, subjected Frost, albeit retroactively, to an unequal treatment by the law. And this inequality was not rendered any more palatable by a social policy favorable to cooperatives. Between them and the single ginner, there were in the eyes of Sutherland and his law, "no real or substantial differences."[56] They, therefore, were to be accorded exactly similar treatment.

If Sutherland demanded that the law follow unvaryingly the principle of equality, he further required that it be *rational*, both in statement and application. Thus, he looked for, in the case of presumptions imposed by law, a *reasonable* relation between the proved fact and the ultimate one to be presumed. He found such a relation in an act of Congress which created a presumption that opium found in one's possession had been smuggled into the country.[57] But it was not so in the case of *Ferrey* v. *Ramsey*.[58] There, the Court had under review a Kansas law which made bank directors liable for deposits to which they had assented after the bank had become insolvent. Both this assent and knowledge of the insolvency were imputed by statute to the directors. In the present case, the testimony showed that one director of the bank in question was so ill at the time deposits sued on were made that he could not possibly have given his assent or had

---

[56] *ibid.*, p. 525.   [57] *Yee Hem* v. *United States*, 268 U.S. 178 (1925).
[58] 277 U.S. 88 (1928).

knowledge of the condition of the bank. Yet this presented no insuperable difficulty to Justice Holmes since he was of the opinion that the directors could have been made liable in every case had the legislators so willed, and not merely when they had "assented" to a deposit. For him, it was therefore a question of brute power.

Quite characteristically, Sutherland took a different view. Not choosing to argue Holmes' broad assertion of power, he pointed out that, at any rate, the legislature had not exercised it. On the narrower question, he conceded that "the state may provide that proof of one fact shall be *prima facie* evidence of another." He insisted, however, that "this can be done consistently with the due process clause of the Fourteenth Amendment only where there is a rational relation between the two facts. . . . To me, it seems clear that there is no rational relation between the fact of insolvency and the fact here presumed, namely, assent to the reception of a particular deposit."[59]

The manner in which the state exercised its acknowledged powers was subjected to still another restriction by Sutherland in *Frost & Frost Trucking Company* v. *Railroad Commission*.[60] In that case, he in effect declared that even where the existence of power was unquestioned, it had to be exerted in such a way as not to come in conflict with personal rights in adjoining areas. The State of California had denied the use of its highways—a measure concededly within its authority—to all carriers for hire, public and private, not operating under a license and a rate schedule approved by the Commission. The plaintiff was a "private" carrier, who contracted for the charges on each movement. He resisted the statute on the ground that it converted him to a public carrier without his consent. Mr. Justice Holmes, speaking only for himself and Mr. Justice Brandeis, answered with a quotation from *Packard* v. *Banton*,[61] one of Sutherland's earlier opinions. There,

---

[59] *ibid.*, p. 96. [60] 271 U.S. 583 (1926).

[61] 264 U.S. 140 (1924). Sutherland there wrote an opinion sustaining a New York requirement that taxicab companies carry collision insurance.

Sutherland himself had alluded to the distinction between activities engaged in as a matter of right and those carried on by sufferance of the government. In respect to this latter situation, he had written, "The power to exclude altogether generally includes the lesser power to condition and may justify a degree of regulation not admissible in the former."[62]

In the present case, however, the Justice insisted that the state was attaching to the grant of its favors an unconstitutional condition, which the right of the state to withhold the use of its highways altogether could not excuse. The condition was unconstitutional because it had the effect of "compelling a private carrier to assume against his will the duties and burdens of a common carrier."[63] When it was suggested that Mr. Frost had not been compelled to do anything and might pursue some other occupation if such responsibilities did not appeal to him, Sutherland dismissed the idea as too brutal to expect sanction in an American court. In his view, Frost was confronted with

a choice between the rock and the whirlpool . . . an option to forego a privilege which may be vital to his livelihood or submit to a requirement which may constitute an intolerable burden. . . .

It is inconceivable [he concluded] that guaranties embedded in the Constitution of the United States may thus be manipulated out of existence.[64]

This case makes clear, in a way that others do not, Sutherland's conception of political authority. For him there was no general power of government, but a number of powers, the merger of which was never intended by the Constitution. They were as brooklets which could not be allowed to overflow and occupy the ground in between. That intermediate area was reserved for Mr. Frost and the American people as an unassailable refuge from the whirlpools which were ever threatening to engulf the liberties of free men.

[62] ibid., p. 145.
[63] Frost and Frost Trucking Co. v. Railroad Commission, supra note 61, p. 593.
[64] ibid., pp. 593-594.

3.

The limitations on political power was only one of the problems considered by George Sutherland and his colleagues when William Howard Taft was their leader. In these years, as at all times in its history, much of the Court's most important business arose out of its peculiar relation to the federal system. The nature of this relation has varied from period to period. By and large, it has been determined by the prevailing attitude toward the larger question—the nature of federalism itself. Here the justices have generally followed one or the other of two competing theories.

The first, in point of time, was that of *national* federalism. Under it, the elements of national power were traced, not to the states, but to the people. The general government, therefore, exercised its power independently of its effects on the states. As for the states, they were forced to be content with such powers as remained after those of the general government had been generously construed. In this view, the Supreme Court was an arm of the central authority itself, and owed no particular duty to the states.[65]

The second theory was that of *dual* federalism. It rejected the notion of national supremacy and substituted therefor the idea of two separate and distinct spheres of government, the state supreme in one and the nation in the other. The great task of the judges, so they thought, was to guard against ugly conflicts between the two. Justice Brewer gave a classic exposition of this theory in *South Carolina* v. *United States* when he declared:

We have in this republic a dual system of government—national and state—each operating within the same territory and upon the same persons, and yet working without collision, because their functions are different. There are certain matters over which the national government has absolute control, and no action of the state can interfere therewith, and there are others in which the

[65] *McCulloch* v. *Maryland*, 4 Wheat. 316 (1819); *Gibbons* v. *Ogden*, 9 Wheat. 1 (1824); *Martin* v. *Hunter's Lessee*, 1 Wheat. 304 (1816).

state is supreme, and in respect to them the national government is powerless. To preserve the even balance between these two governments, and hold each in its separate sphere, is the peculiar duty of all courts; preeminently of this. . . .[66]

For sixty years before these words were written, and for half as long afterwards, the idea they represent was triumphant in skirmish after skirmish with its older competitor. While not uniformly so, the decisions of the Supreme Court generally displayed a vigilant concern for the rights of the state. And neither in earlier times nor today has this concern ever been wholly absent from our judicial literature. The chief nationalist of all, John Marshall, conceded on more than one occasion the dual nature of the Union,[67] and just a short time ago Mr. Justice Douglas was reminding us that the Constitution presupposes vigorous and active states.[68]

It was Sutherland's fortune to live his life in the period when the idea of dual supremacy was winning its greatest victories. Seven years after his birth the Court announced: "The preservation of the states, and the maintenance of their governments, are as much within the design and care of the Constitution as the preservation and the maintenance of the National Government. The Constitution, in all its provisions, looks to an indestructible Union composed of indestructible states."[69]

Yet, even the nationalist can accept this statement. Indeed, in 1937, Mr. Justice Roberts observed that similar notions had achieved "universal recognition."[70] The central point of difference between the two theories is to be found elsewhere, principally in the idea that the powers reserved to the states by the Tenth Amendment constitute an independent limitation on the positive grants to the general government contained in the Constitution. Congress, so the dual federalists argued, could not exercise its acknowl-

[66] 199 U.S. 437, 448 (1905).
[67] See e.g., *Willson* v. *Blackbird Creek Marsh Co.*, 2 Pet. 245 (1829).
[68] Dissenting in *New York* v. *United States*, 326 U.S. 572 (1946).
[69] *Texas* v. *White*, 7 Wall. 700, 725 (1869).
[70] Dissenting in *Brush* v. *Commissioner*, 300 U.S. 352, 374 (1937).

edged power in such a way as to interfere with those reserved to the states.

In recent years, comment on this view of national power has emphasized its close relationship with the idea of laissez faire. And this is undeniably proper. Great segments of political authority have been made to disappear simply by hurling them into the chasm separating the two sovereignties in the eyes of the dual supremacists. But emphasis, too, should be placed on the genuine appeal of decentralization to men who certainly can not be pictured as enemies of government. Behind them stands a venerable conviction that government is most successful when subject to the intimate scrutiny and participation of the people.

It can not be claimed that Sutherland's affinity for dual federalism was unrelated to his general hostility to legislative power. Yet it ought not to be forgotten that the benefits of local authority and direction were very real to him and capable of exercising an attraction on their own account. Long before coming to the Court, he had voiced the opinion that: "In the framework of our political institutions nothing . . . is wiser than the dual system of government, under which matters which concern . . . the states as political units are left to the state governments. The state government can deal with its local problems far more wisely than the government at Washington, from which the problems are remote."[71]

Sutherland had substantial basis in his own experience for this conclusion. Conditions in Utah could not be duplicated anywhere else in the world. For example, it was exceedingly difficult, if not impossible, for outsiders to know just how to dispose of the problem of polygamy. The vast distance lying between Provo and Washington could easily have stimulated the feeling that it was impossible for the distant government to prescribe wisely for the people of Utah.

[71] "Superfluous Government," an address delivered by Sutherland to the Cleveland Chamber of Commerce, December 8, 1914, and printed in pamphlet form. The reference is to page 8.

In the final analysis, it was not only the gain to be derived from dual federalism that made Sutherland its advocate; and this is true whether the gain be conceived of in terms of governmental inaction or decentralization. Sutherland was a dual federalist because of his staunch belief that the Constitution commanded it. Nor is this conclusion so naive as it might first appear. From the time he first heard the law of the Constitution expounded by Cooley and Campbell, the doctrine of dual supremacy was incessantly dinned into his ears. That was the doctrine of the revered tribunal of 1895, of his mighty friend, Edward Douglas White, and the learned commentator, John Randolph Tucker. Therefore, the fact that it was congenial to him must not be allowed to obscure Sutherland's intense conviction that, in upholding the claims of the states, he was obeying the mandates of the Constitution.

On the central question of the supremacy clause versus the Tenth Amendment, Sutherland's position as developed on the Court was not entirely one-sided. In *Florida* v. *Mellon*,[72] for example, he faced a claim that the exemptions afforded by the federal inheritance tax, where a similar tax was levied by the state, constituted an invasion of the reserved powers of the states in that it forced them to adopt such a levy. The Justice met this argument with the following ringing affirmance of national supremacy: "The act is a law of the United States made in pursuance of the Constitution and, therefore, the supreme law of the land, the constitution or laws of the states to the contrary notwithstanding. Whenever the constitutional powers of the federal government and those of the states come into conflict the latter must yield."[73] These words have the appearance of being unequivocal. But there lurks in the qualifying adjective, "constitutional," enough reservations to take care of any case which carried an actual threat to the states.

In the dissents he filed in *Missouri* v. *Duncan*,[74] and

[72] 273 U.S. 12 (1927). [73] *ibid.* [74] 265 U.S. 17 (1924).

Lambert v. *Yellowly*,[75] a wholly different line of argument appears, and one which is, undoubtedly, much nearer to Sutherland's considered conviction. In the first case mentioned, the State had denied the capacity of a national bank to serve as an executor of an estate. The bank had appealed on the ground that an act of Congress demanded that it have this privilege whenever competing institutions did. For Mr. Justice Holmes this was enough, since, in his judgment, the authority of Congress was "independent" of any power reserved to the states.

Sutherland could not agree. His statement of the problem reveals his position: "The real question here, as I understand it, is not whether Congress may safeguard national banks against ordinary state legislation of a discriminative character; but whether Congress may intrude upon and prohibit the exercise of the *governmental* powers of a state to the extent that such exercise discriminates against such banks in favor of competing state corporations."[76]

It appears, then, that Sutherland's idea was that Congress could trespass upon the periphery of state power, but that it must avoid the region at the center. In that area, he declared the states to be "supreme and independent . . . exempt from the interference or control" of the general government.[77]

The second case, *Lambert* v. *Yellowly*, provides a more elaborate discussion. There the Court was considering just what legislation was allowed by the enforcement clause of the Eighteenth Amendment.[78] The statute under review had limited the amount of spirituous liquor which could be prescribed by physicians to "not more than a pint . . . for use by the same person within any period of ten days." The Court, speaking through Justice Brandeis, sustained the act as a legitimate means for securing the end an-

---

[75] 272 U.S. 581 (1926).

[76] *Missouri* v. *Duncan, supra* note 75, p. 25.　　　　[77] *ibid.*, p. 26.

[78] "The Congress and the several States shall have concurrent power to enforce this article by appropriate legislation." *U.S. Const.*, 18th Amend., sec. 2.

nounced by the amendment—that is, the prohibition of the manufacture and sale of liquor for "beverage purposes."

Sutherland was considerably troubled at this effort to substitute, by legislative fiat, the judgment of Congress for the informed discretion of a distinguished physician such as Dr. Lambert. He did not consider the problem of how much whiskey could be used to therapeutic advantage one which could be settled by the votes of a majority. But the main burden of his protest was that Congress had been delegated authority only over liquors to be used for beverage purposes. And although it had been empowered to enact appropriate legislation to implement its control, this did not warrant an interference with the power of the states to supervise physicians and regulate the practice of medicine.

It has been asserted many times, however, and occasionally by Sutherland, that a choice of *means* was available to Congress in carrying out its powers. Was not the limitation of the use of liquor for medicinal purposes a legitimate *means* for effecting control of beverage alcohol? Sutherland could not agree that it was. He explained:

By the legislation now under review, the authority of Congress is so exercised that the reserved power of the states to control the practice of medicine is directly invaded to the illegitimate end that the prescription and use of liquors for medicinal purposes is prohibited. . . . A grant of power for specified purposes does not include the power to prohibit for other and different purposes. Congressional legislation directly prohibiting the use of intoxicating liquor for concededly medical purposes does not consist with the *letter* and *spirit* of the Constitution and viewed as a means of carrying into effect the granted power is in fraud of that instrument and especially the Tenth Amendment.[79]

This appeal to the "letter and spirit" of the Constitution was a bold and clever stroke—bold in its invocation of the words of the nationalist hero, John Marshall, and its use of them to restrict, rather than expand, national power;

[79] *Lambert* v. *Yellowly, supra* note 76, pp. 603-604.

and clever in its resort to a standard so vague that it could not easily be controverted. For means to come within the letter and spirit of the Constitution, Sutherland explained, it was necessary for them to conform to its general design, which was to "give to the Federal Government control over national and international affairs, leaving to the several states the control of local affairs."[80]

An excellent example of the constitutional law produced by such a conception as Sutherland had of the Union is afforded by the case of *Macallen Company* v. *Massachusetts*,[81] decided in 1929. The case is concerned with the reciprocal immunity from taxation said to operate between the state and national governments. This immunity had its beginnings in the Taney ideal of nonclashing sovereignties, but it was 1870 before it received the judicial imprimatur. In that year, the Court held that the salary of a state judge was not subject to a federal income tax.[82] The decision purported to rest on Marshall's opinion in *McCulloch* v. *Maryland*,[83] relying particularly on the Chief Justice's aphorism that "the power to tax involves the power to destroy." This, it may be said, was somewhat illegitimate. Marshall's purpose was the assertion of national supremacy and he gave no countenance to a comparable authority in the states. Nevertheless, the immunity prospered, nourished, as it was, by the post-Civil War anxiety of the justices for the future of the states. It came to include within its prohibitions not only the direct and discriminatory interferences such as the taxation of the bank notes in the *McCulloch* case, but even levies on sales to government agencies [84] and patent royalties.[85]

[80] *ibid.*, p. 597.   [81] 279 U.S. 620 (1929).
[82] *Collector* v. *Day*, 11 Wall. 113 (1870).   [83] 4 Wheat. 316 (1819).
[84] *Panhandle Oil Co.* v. *Knox*, 277 U.S. 218 (1928); *Indian Motorcycle Co.* v. *United States*, 283 U.S. 570 (1931).
[85] *Long* v. *Rockwood*, 277 U.S. 142 (1928). On the development of the immunity doctrine, see Warner W. Gardner, "Tax Immune Bonds," 8 *Geo. Wash. L. Rev.* 1200 (1940). In recent years the immunity has been hewn to much more modest dimensions. See Thomas Reed Powell, "The

APPLICATION

Sutherland's initial reactions to the subtleties of the immunity theory were cautious enough. Thus, he joined a unanimous Court in denying its benefits to contractors on public projects,[86] and he was one of a protesting minority in the patent decision. But in the *Macallen* case, he enlarged the borders of the interdicted area. The case arose out of a Massachusetts levy which measured the franchise tax for corporations by their net income. In computing the net income, that from federal securities was included, although admittedly such securities could not be taxed directly. Sutherland pronounced this nothing but a clever legislative plot to nibble on forbidden fruit in spite of Stone's averment that he could discover no such "sinister purpose." That the legislature gave its trespass a *form* which had previously been considered legal could not excuse the fault. The following words of warning were spoken, not only for the instruction of state officials, but for the national taxing authorities as well:

> For one government—state or national—to lay a tax upon the instrumentalities or securities of the other is derogatory to the latter's dignity, subversive of its powers and repugnant to its paramount authority. These constitute compelling reasons why courts, in scrutinizing taxing acts like that involved, should be acute to distinguish between an exaction which in substance and reality is what it pretends to be, and a scheme to lay a tax upon a non-taxable subject by a deceptive use of words. The fact that a tax ostensibly laid upon a taxable subject is to be measured by the value of a non-taxable subject at once suggests the probability that it was the latter rather than the former that the law-maker sought to reach.[87]

More significant, in their relation to the federal system, are the cases arising under the commerce clause of the Constitution. The clause is at one and the same time a grant of power to the national government and a restric-

---

Waning of Intergovernmental Tax Immunities," 58 *Harv. L. Rev.* 633 (1945), and "The Remnant of Intergovernmental Tax Immunities," 58 *Harv. L. Rev.* 757 (1945).

[86] *Metcalf & Eddy* v. *Mitchell*, 269 U.S. 514 (1926).

[87] *Macallen* v. *Massachusetts, supra* note 82, pp. 628-629.

tion on the authority of the states. Both aspects of the clause were dealt with by Sutherland during the twenties. On its positive side, the cases arose under attempted applications of the Sherman Anti-trust Act. The first was *Industrial Association of San Francisco v. United States*,[88] which had its beginnings in a struggle between the building trades unions and the contractors of the San Francisco area in 1921. In an effort to weaken the unions, the contractors put in operation an elaborate system of controls, whereby the opportunity to purchase building materials was limited to those who would support an open shop policy. The Government sought to dissolve this conspiracy on the ground that it restrained trade in materials produced in other states, and that even as applied to California goods the result was to impede the flow of commerce.

In his opinion for a unanimous Court, Sutherland disposed of the first allegation by showing that the materials, although produced in other states, had come to rest in the hands of California retailers and had lost their interstate character. As to the second, the evidence had shown that, while permits were not required for the purchase of plumbing supplies, their shipment from other states had been seriously diminished because of the inability to secure complementary California materials. Sutherland's response to this argument was that it "ignores the all important fact that there was no interference with the freedom of the outside manufacturer to sell and ship or the local contractor to buy. The process went no further than to take away the latter's opportunity to use, and therefore his incentive to purchase. The effects upon, and interference with, interstate trade, if any, were purely incidental, indirect and remote."[89]

Sutherland was reminded of this passage by counsel for the defendant in the case of *Anderson v. Shipowner's Association*,[90] a 1926 decision. Anderson, a seaman, was asking for an injunction to prevent the shipowners from applying a scheme whereby they required every vessel to

[88] 268 U.S. 64 (1925).   [89] *ibid.*, p. 80.   [90] 272 U.S. 344 (1922).

hire only personnel authorized by the Association. Any such restraint on the exercise of so vital a right as that to earn a living quite naturally excited the hostility of the Justice, especially so since the victims were the seamen of whom he had so long been the ardent friend. But were the effects on interstate commerce here any less "indirect" and "remote" than in the *San Francisco* case, or that of *United Mine Workers* v. *Coronado Coal Company*,[91] where the Court had refused to apply the Act to the strike of a coal miners' local union? Sutherland's explanation of these two cases is interesting because of the message it bore for the future: "Neither the making of goods nor the mining of coal is commerce; and the fact that the things produced are afterwards shipped or used in interstate commerce does not make their production a part of it. Nor is building commerce; and the fact that materials to be used are shipped in from other states does not make building a part of such commerce."[92]

The difficult question in the case, however, was not the interstate character of the conspiracy, but rather whether the restraint of the use of labor was a restraint of trade. A variety of circumstances required that Sutherland be most circumspect in his answer. It will be recalled that much of organized labor's dissatisfaction with the *Adkins* case was founded in the treatment of labor as a commodity or an article of commerce. What rendered this so important to the unions was its relation to the Sherman and Clayton Acts. The latter had declared that "the labor of a human being is not a commodity or article of commerce."[93]

It was this that created the difficulty in the *Anderson* case, for if labor was not an "article of commerce," how could the anti-labor conspiracy of the shipowners be reached by the Sherman Act? Sutherland met the problem in a somewhat oblique fashion. He did not say that labor was or was not a commodity within the terms of the law.

[91] 259 U.S. 344 (1922).
[92] *Anderson* v. *Shipowner's Association, supra* note 91, p. 354.
[93] 38 Stat. 730, 731 (1914), 15 U.S.C. § 17 (1940).

Rather, he called the men who operated the ships "instrumentalities of commerce." By "unduly" interfering with the seamen's right to engage in this commerce, the shipowners were declared guilty of an unlawful conspiracy in restraint of trade. To all of which Sutherland added: "A restraint of interstate commerce can not be justified by the fact that the object of the participants in the combination was to benefit themselves in a way which might have been unobjectionable in the absence of such restraint."[94]

These words have a special relevance to the decision of the Court in *Bedford Cut Stone Company* v. *Journeymen Stone Cutters Association*,[95] decided some five months later. The national organization of the Union had ordered all members to refrain from handling stone on which non-union men had worked, a course of conduct which the company sought to halt by an injunction. The Court, by a vote of seven to two, approved the company's plea. Brandeis, in dissent, argued that the stone cutters had done none of the things which had been previously condemned. They were, he said, "innocent alike of trespass and of breach of contract. They did not picket. They refrained from violence, intimidation, fraud and threats. . . . They did not plan a boycott against any of the plaintiffs or against builders who used the plaintiff's product."[96] Their sole dereliction, Brandeis continued, was that they refused, in concert with each other, to work. The propriety of their conduct, he insinuatingly declared, could "hardly be doubted by one who believes in the organization of labor."[97]

Sutherland, while not overly friendly to organized labor, had other grounds for his doubts. The case for him was that of achieving what the law prohibited, to wit, the restraint of trade among the states. There was a "plain design," he said, "of suppressing or narrowing the interstate market."[98] The stone cutters' retort, of course, was

[94] *Anderson* v. *Shipowner's Association, supra* note 91, p. 363.
[95] 274 U.S. 37 (1927).   [96] *ibid.,* p. 59.   [97] *ibid.,* p. 58.
[98] *ibid.,* p. 47.

that their purpose was to win recognition of their union. But the reply came back that the union had restrained trade and this was not to be excused even if the general purpose was a lawful one.

This reasoning would seem to indicate that all strikes promoted on a multiple-state basis were illegal, for a "narrowing" of the interstate market would necessarily result from any abstention from work. Thus, it is easy to see why the case was commonly called a "slave decision."[99] Brandeis charged that the restraint placed on the workers by the majority opinion "reminds of involuntary servitude."[100] Sutherland, of course, had no such idea. He almost surely believed himself to be the bearer of freedom for the individual stone cutter or the individual local. Thus, he took pains to show that some of the locals had no grievance at all against their employers but were forced against their will by the national officers of the union to cooperate in the strike.[101] For a perfect stranger to come between an employer and his men was an interference with freedom far more serious than the prohibition of a nationwide strike—a strike in which the wishes of the individual, or even those of his local union, were swallowed up by a general interest.

The *Bedford* case is interesting, too, because of the conception of the scope of the commerce clause which it avows. Here the obvious question is: Was not the cutting of stone as entirely local as the mining of coal or the building of houses? On this point Sutherland conceded that "the product against which the strikes were directed . . . had come to rest in the respective localities to which it had been shipped, so that it had ceased to be a subject of interstate commerce."[102] But, he added hastily, the motive of the stone

---

[99] *Am. Lab. Leg. Rev.* xvii (1927), 139. The writer added sadly: "Henceforth it must be regarded as settled law that all strikes against the use of non-union material are unlawful, and that, in most cases, the anti-trust laws can be invoked against them."

[100] *Bedford Cut Stone Co.* v. *Journeymen Stone Cutters Ass'n, supra* note 96, p. 65.

[101] *ibid.*, pp. 43-45.   [102] *ibid.*, p. 46.

cutters was not a "local" one. Their conspiracy was to be "construed as an entirety; and when so regarded the local transactions became a part of the general plan,"[103] thereby rendering it subject to national control. In view of both earlier and later expressions, Sutherland's adoption of such a generous construction of the commerce power is somewhat surprising, for under it there would seem to be ample authority in the national government to govern the nation's industrial life. The explanation, perhaps, is that the coverage of the commerce clause expanded for Sutherland when "freedom" was the goal.

This view is supported by those cases in which Sutherland wrote opinions concerning the negative aspects of the commerce clause. As has been seen, he spoke often of the reserved rights of the states, but this should not beguile us into thinking that he allowed his jealousy of all power to recede into the background, even when the Fourteenth Amendment was not in issue. The object of the commerce clause for him was chiefly to secure the freedom of commerce from state interference. This is well illustrated by *Texas Transport & Terminal Company* v. *New Orleans*,[104] where he held a city license tax on steamship agents invalid as to those engaged exclusively in interstate trade. Similarly, a Missouri franchise tax on an interstate carrier measured by the proportion that its local assets bore to its total wealth was held unconstitutional.[105] In *Missouri* v. *Kansas Natural Gas Company*,[106] Sutherland explicitly acknowledged what was always probably the controlling factor for him in this type of problem. The case involved another Missouri statute, one which attempted to fix rates for the gas company. The company was a foreign corporation and sold only to wholesalers. In overthrowing the Act, Sutherland maintained that the limitations on a state's power over commerce were attributable directly to the Constitution and not to the will of Congress. In ex-

[103] *ibid.*, p. 47.   [104] 264 U.S. 150 (1924).
[105] *Monier* v. *Ozark Pipe Line Co.*, 266 U.S. 555 (1924).
[106] 265 U.S. 298 (1924).

APPLICATION

planation, he remarked: "The paramount interest is not local but national, admitting of and requiring uniformity of regulation. Such uniformity . . . may be necessary to preserve equality of opportunity and treatment among the various communities and States concerned."[107]

The important words here are "equality of opportunity." Pursued to its logical extreme, this concept would eliminate any state action whatsoever relative to interstate commerce since the only perfect equality would lie in every state following a policy of complete inaction. This fits in very nicely with the idea that the purpose of the commerce grant was to achieve the freedom of interstate trade. When the requirement is added that the freedom be equal, the barriers to state action at all become well nigh insurmountable.

4.

The third in Sutherland's trinity of constitutional ultimates was the separation of powers. Like the notions of limited government and dual federalism, this doctrine was, in the Justice's eyes, a foundation stone of the American governmental structure. But unlike them, it did not, in his hands necessarily result in an attrition of political authority. In this regard, the case of *Massachusetts* v. *Mellon*,[108] decided in 1923, is of the highest interest. Indeed, perhaps no other single decision in the Court's history has been fraught with such destructive implications for the idea of limited government, and, it must be added, that of dual federalism.[109] This is true because its result was to liberate the spending power of the national government from the threat of effective challenge. A government that can spend $71,000,000,000 in one year obviously is not confining its activities to the administration of justice and the national defense. Just as certainly it can not long occupy the same political level as a state operating on a budget of less than one per cent of that sum.

[107] *ibid.*, pp. 309-310.   [108] 262 U.S. 447 (1923).
[109] See Edward S. Corwin, *The Twilight of the Supreme Court*, New Haven, Yale University Press, 1934, pp. 149-179.

The case arose out of the Maternity Act of 1921 [110] which made grants to the states on stipulated conditions. Massachusetts sought to enjoin the payment of these grants by the Treasury on the ground that they involved a usurpation by Congress of powers reserved to the states. There was also a companion suit by a taxpayer which proceeded on the assumption that one could not be compelled to pay taxes for the support of unconstitutional undertakings. Sutherland disposed of the individual's plea by denying that his interest in the case was substantial enough to give him any standing in court to challenge the Act. It was said to be an interest "shared with millions of others . . . comparatively minute and indeterminable; and the effect upon future taxation, of any payment out of the funds, so remote, fluctuating, and uncertain, that no basis is afforded for an appeal to the preventive powers of a court of equity."[111]

The appeal of the state was another matter. No one could deny the vital interest of Massachusetts in preserving unimpaired her powers. Her suit, therefore, could not be dismissed for reasons similar to those applied to the taxpayer. Still, the Court refused to accede to the plea of the state. More than that, it confessed itself to be without the *competence* to do so. As Sutherland explained it, the Court was being asked "to adjudicate not rights of persons or property, not rights of dominion over physical domain . . . but abstract questions of political power, of sovereignty, of government."[112] This authority, he insisted, had not been confided to the judiciary:

The functions of government under our system are apportioned. To the legislative department has been committed the duty of making laws; to the executive the duty of executing them; and to the judiciary the duty of interpreting and applying them in cases properly brought before the courts. The general rule is that neither department may invade the province of the other and neither may control, direct or restrain the action of the

110 42 Stat. 224 (1921), 42 U.S.C. 161-174 (1940).
111 *Massachusetts* v. *Mellon, supra* note 109, p. 487.
112 *ibid.,* pp. 484-485.

other. . . . We have no power *per se* to review and annul acts of Congress on the ground that they are unconstitutional. That question may be considered only when the justification for some direct injury, suffered or threatened, presenting a justifiable issue, is made to rest upon such an act. . . . Here the parties plaintiff have no such case. Looking through forms of words to the substance of their complaint, it is merely that officials of the executive department of the government are executing and will execute an act of Congress asserted to be unconstitutional; and this we are asked to prevent. To do so would not be to decide a judicial controversy, but to assume a position of authority over the governmental acts of another and co-equal department, an authority which plainly we do not possess.[113]

Sutherland so often had a hand in nullifying legislation that the great restraint here indicated may be a source of surprise to some. Yet this is not the sole instance of his rejection of the notion that the judiciary operated from some lordly eminence. In *Kline* v. *Burke Construction Company*,[114] for example, he could not accept the theory that the Constitution itself guarantees a jurisdiction to the federal courts. In sweeping terms, he emphasized that their jurisdiction was derived from Congress. "That body," he said, "may give, withhold, or restrict such jurisdiction at its discretion, provided it be not extended beyond the boundaries fixed by the Constitution."[115] *Michaelson* v. *United States* [116] is another instance. There Sutherland spoke for the Court when it gave approval to the prescription by Congress of a jury trial in the case of criminal contempt—this in spite of the fact that administration of punishment for such an offense had always been deemed to be a judicial prerogative, and the result, therefore, would be to sanction a commingling of powers between the two departments.

Of course, this was something which could not be repeated on any large scale, as Sutherland's opinion in *Springer* v. *The Government of the Philippine Islands* [117] makes evident. The dispute in this case was over an act

[113] *ibid.*, p. 488.   [114] 260 U.S. 226 (1922).   [115] *ibid.*, p. 234.
[116] 266 U.S. 42 (1924).   [117] 277 U.S. 189 (1928).

of the Philippine legislature which made certain legislative officers members of the boards controlling government corporations, thereby depriving the Governor of the authority to appoint these members. The applicable law in the case was the Organic Act [118] for the government of the Islands. Sutherland conceived it as establishing the same general rule for the separation of powers as that prevailing in the American constitutions, state and federal. This rule, he argued, even where not expressly declared, was "basic and vital—not merely a matter of governmental mechanism."[119] The question, therefore, was what was the nature of the appointing power. Was it executive or legislative? Relying on the *Myers* case,[120] Sutherland declared it to be executive. Furthermore, the duties of the board, by a process of exclusion, were also said to be executive functions. Hence, even if there was an appointing power in the legislature, it was not permissible for it to authorize its own members to exercise executive authority.

5.

This completes, in its larger outlines, the portrayal of Sutherland's judicial activities in the period of the Taft chief justiceship. Taft's resignation on February 25, 1930, followed soon by the death of Sanford, effected a significant change in the personnel of the Court. This date, marking

[118] 32 Stat. 691 (1902), 39 Stat. 545 (1916).

[119] *Springer* v. *The Government of the Philippine Islands, supra* note 118, p. 201. Holmes' dissent reveals in a few lines the basic differences between him and Sutherland. Consider his opening paragraph (pp. 209-210): "The great ordinances of the constitution do not establish and divide fields of black and white. Even the more specific of them are found to terminate in a penumbra shading gradually from one extreme to the other. Property must not be taken without compensation, but with the help of a phrase (the police power) some property may be taken or destroyed for public use without paying for it, if you do not take too much. When we come to the fundamental distinctions it is still more obvious that they must be received with a certain latitude or our government could not go on."

[120] *Myers* v. *United States,* 272 U.S. 52 (1926). The division in the *Myers* case was the same as that in the *Springer* case. Holmes, Brandeis, and McReynolds dissented in each.

therefore as it does the close of one chapter of the Court's history and the beginning of another, has an equal relevance to Sutherland's judicial career. This is not to suggest that after 1930 his views underwent any radical alteration. The point is that, by that year, his major themes, with one notable exception, had had their initial statements. What was to follow, for all the turbulence and drama of the New Deal days, was but an intensive development of ideas already projected.

Judged by the frequency with which Sutherland's views prevailed in the twenties, the period was a resounding personal success for him. Not since the days of Fuller, Field, and Brewer had the Court so faithfully applied as a constitutional policy the idea of laissez faire. For this, Sutherland could have claimed the major credit. Through his opinions in the *Adkins, Tyson, Ribnik,* and other cases, he had hewn the power of government down to such dimensions that it could readily be controlled. Even the liberal wing of the Court seemed, on occasion, to yield assent.[121] The presumption of the legality of legislative action no longer obtained. Any exertion of governmental power had to be justified. And, apparently, there was but one sure justification—a prior sanction by the Court of an almost identical statute.

Such power as remained in legislative bodies now was bound by newly forged shackles. An exact equality was demanded—an equality which must prevail not only in the actual operation of a statute, but even in any set of circumstances, however improbable, which could be imagined. Furthermore, if an acknowledged power was so used that incidentally it accomplished a result which could not be achieved directly, then the power must yield. In addition to this, the Court had, under Taft, sharpened its ancient weapon of control when a frontal assault on power was impracticable. Dual federalism was still the law of the land and the Court was not to be deceived by any deceptive

---

[121] See *Murphy* v. *Sardell, supra* note 24, and *Williams* v. *Standard Oil Co., supra* note 50.

stratagems which sought to circumvent the requirements of the federal system. Finally, even at some sacrifice of the Court's prerogatives, legislators had been told that the separation of powers continued as the operative principle of the government of the United States.

In spite of its occasional violent disagreements, the Court under Taft maintained an admirable *esprit de corps*. The saving gentlemanly graces were always present. It was Sutherland's fortune to experience this warmth of feeling in a very special way. In 1927, he was almost forced to resign from the Court because of a severe intestinal disorder which kept him bedridden for several months. His place of confinement was the Johns Hopkins Hospital in Baltimore. There several of the justices visited him, bringing words of cheer and encouragement. By letter, the Chief Justice well summarized their feelings: "We all love you, George, and we would all regard it as the greatest loss to the country to have you become discouraged over your work, and we realize of what great importance it is to the country that you should be restored to your working capacity."[122]

Conscientious in the extreme and possessed of little surplus strength, Sutherland was forced, in these years, to limit his social activities to a minimum. The work of a justice he found to be "by far the hardest" he had ever undertaken.[123] His preoccupation with the work of the Court naturally restricted his activities in other fields. He did find time, however, to speak to the Utah Bar Association in 1924. His address was largely an account of the internal mechanics of the Court. The beginnings of the day's work were thus described by him: "At a quarter of twelve, or about that time every morning, the justices of the supreme court meet in the robing room at the Capitol. They shake hands with one another. That is a custom that has been in existence a great many years. It was originally

122 Taft to Sutherland, October 3, 1927.
123 20 *Rep. Utah State Bar Ass'n* 59 (1924).

instituted, perhaps, at a time when the justices do not agree as well as they do now."[124]

More interesting, perhaps, in the light of later developments was a spectacular reiteration by Sutherland of his faith in an inevitable progress. "I am always an optimist," he declared. "I think the world is getting better, and will continue to get better, and I do not fear for the final result."[125] These remarks were made to reassure his hearers after the Justice had confessed to the following apprehension:

I don't know whether I should be glad or sorry to see, if I could, the progress of another forty years. The Lord only knows what will happen, if we do as much in the next forty years as we have in the past! I sometimes am a little fearful—and I am saying this more or less seriously—at the progress of invention and discovery; the deadly gases, atomic energy, whatever that is—something hidden in matter, something that we actually perceive in the force of radium, but which is stored, as I understand, in all matter. And some day, perhaps within the next forty years, some learned scientist will discover how to release it and blow us all into eternity.[126]

In 1930, Sutherland had available the data for an equally startling prophecy in the field of political science. Already a bewildered nation had witnessed the beginnings of an economic catastrophe which in its ravages was to show no particular respect for the venerable doctrines of American constitutional law. The forces released were as destructive, in their way, as the atomic energy of which the Justice spoke. The difference was that a tried and proved means of control was at hand—or so it seemed to Sutherland and his colleagues. But was it? It is this question which suggests the theme of the succeeding chapter.

[124] *ibid.*   [125] *ibid.*   [126] *ibid.*

5

OVERTHROW, 1930-1937

WHEN Mr. Justice Holmes, nearing his ninety-first birthday, made his graceful "bow to the inevitable" in March 1932, and, in response to a nation-wide demand, Benjamin Nathan Cardozo was named as his successor, the "nine old men" of the Roosevelt era came together for the first time. Two years before, Charles Evans Hughes and Owen J. Roberts had succeeded to the seats left vacant by Taft and Sanford, but only after Hughes' qualifications had been vigorously challenged and President Hoover's first nominee for the Sanford seat, John J. Parker, had been rejected by the Senate. The fight on these two men had not been based on any want of ability or lack of judicial temperament. Rather, the somewhat novel objection was raised that their previous associations and sympathies were such as to produce decisions not consonant with the governmental philosophy of the protesting coalition of Democrats and insurgent Republicans. There could hardly have been a sharper reminder that the period of "normalcy" was over.[1]

For most people, of course, no such reminder was necessary. Beginning in October 1929, the stock market began a dizzy downward spiral that by 1933 had wiped out over eighty per cent of the paper values of industrial and

---

[1] For an account of the fight aroused by the appointments of Hughes and Parker, see Kenneth C. Cole, "The Role of the Senate in the Confirmation of Judicial Nominations," *Am. Pol. Sci. Rev.*, xxviii (1934), 875. The new Court soon settled into a fairly predictable pattern. As in the days of Taft, Sutherland, Van Devanter, McReynolds, and Butler were almost always to be found together. The liberal wing also retained its previous unity. The decisive votes, therefore, lay with Hughes and Roberts. In this situation, it is worthy of note that Roberts and Sutherland had adjoining offices while the Court was quartered in the Capitol. There may well have been some connection between this fact and the great influence Sutherland is said to have had on Roberts. See Edward S. Corwin, *Constitutional Revolution, Ltd.*, Claremont, Claremont Colleges, 1941, p. 55.

utility securities; bank failures mounted to an average of five a day; unemployment rose to an estimated 16,000,000; with large sections of the population living on a bare subsistence diet, staple food crops were left unharvested to rot in the fields. The "Hoover cart" made its appearance along with five cent cotton and forty cent wheat. Before such a hurricane of catastrophe, the national income shrank to less than half what it had been in 1929.

Even now it is too early to assess the changes wrought in American life by the ravages of this unparalleled economic disaster. It is certain, however, that it stimulated a fundamental revolution in American political thinking and practice. The rugged individualism of frontier days was forced to give ground before the cooperative notions inspired by the complexities of modern life. But the older idea never entirely surrendered, and in so far as it did, it did so only after the severest kind of a struggle. From this struggle the Supreme Court could hardly have escaped. Indeed, it is there that the lines dividing the opposing forces are seen most clearly.

Yet the repercussions of the depression were necessarily slow in making their way into the Supreme Court chamber. Further, when they did begin to penetrate that august remoteness, their origin could not have been easily divined. The reason for this lies in the fact that the issues presented bore the old familiar markings of other days. A discerning critic, however, might have been able, soon after Hughes took office, to deduce from the Court's business that things were not as they should be. He could have pointed to the persistent tampering by the taxing authorities with questionable sources of revenue; the unwillingness of utility commissions to allow sufficiently generous rate schedules; and the continued efforts by the states, notwithstanding the judicial edicts of the twenties, to subject the economic order to regulation.

The tax cases were the first harbingers for the justices of a radically new economic condition. They sharply reflected the shrinkage of governmental income and the mounting pressures calling for its expenditure. The reactions of the individual justices to this demand tell us much about them. Stone, for example, when considering appeals involving the reciprocal immunity doctrine—a doctrine which was based on the desire to preserve the states—emphasized that the states required sources of revenue to exist at all. He could, therefore, as a devoted believer in the federal system, plead for caution in any extension of the immunity.[2]

The increased need for revenue aroused in Sutherland, on the other hand, a heightened suspicion of legislative purposes. Thus, in *Educational Films Corporation* v. *Ward*,[3] decided in January 1931, he declared: "The duty of this court to examine taxing acts to see that the use of federal tax exempt subjects as a measure for taxes imposed in terms upon taxable subjects is not a cloak, under which the former in substance and effect are taxed, was never more imperative than now, when by reason of increased and increasing public expenditures, states and municipalities are driven to search in every direction for additional sources of revenue."

These were the opening lines of a protest against the Court's sanction of a franchise tax measured by net income from whatever source. The taxpayer here had resisted the inclusion in the measure of receipts from copyright royalties. Because of the tax's nondiscriminatory nature, Stone, for a majority, concluded that it did not offend. The *Macallen* case [4] was distinguished by saying that the legislature was there after forbidden fruit, but in the present case no such impurity of motive was discernible. Sutherland, for his part, did not argue this point. He chose rather the more general ground that the tax was invalid irrespective of intent. This conclusion rested on a precarious pyramid. A tax on a franchise measured by

[2] Samuel J. Konefsky, *Chief Justice Stone and the Supreme Court*, New York, The Macmillan Co., 1945, pp. 18-19.

[3] 282 U.S. 379, 394 (1931).

[4] *Macallen Company* v. *Massachusetts*, 279 U.S. 620 (1929).

income was really one on income; a tax on the income was really a tax on the copyright which produced it; and the levy on the copyright was in fact a levy on the United States Government!

A year after this decision, Sutherland was the author of the opinion in *First National Bank* v. *Maine*,[5] which presented another side of the problem of a state's jurisdiction to tax, the threat of multiple levies. The case arose out of an attempt by Maine to impose a death duty on the transfer of shares of stock in a Maine corporation, the decedent having been domiciled in Massachusetts. In earlier years, it would scarcely have been argued that the tax was beyond the state's authority. The transfer of shares necessarily occurred within Maine and was valid only because of Maine law. Certainly, therefore, there was a taxable event within the state, and this Sutherland conceded in general terms. But the Court's drive, launched in 1930, against what it considered to be the "grossly unfair" results of double taxation cast doubts on the validity of the levy. In a series of cases [6] the Court announced a new doctrine that inheritance taxes could be laid only by the domiciliary state upon bonds, notes, and credits owned by the decedent. This was achieved by attributing to these intangible assets a situs, which for purposes of convenience was said to follow the domicile of the creditor. Accordingly, only his state was conceded jurisdiction to tax. Following these cases, Sutherland concluded that they required an overthrow of the Maine levy.

The weakness of these decisions was well exposed by Justice Stone in a dissent which had the support of Holmes and Brandeis. The decisions, in his view, created a protection "which the Constitution has failed to provide" and he correctly perceived that the difficulty was of the Court's own making in ascribing a definite location to such a shadowy thing as a promise to pay a sum of money. Situs

[5] 284 U.S. 312 (1932).

[6] *Farmers Loan & Trust Co.* v. *Minnesota*, 280 U.S. 204 (1930); *Baldwin* v. *Missouri*, 281 U.S. 586 (1930); *Beidler* v. *South Carolina Tax Commission*, 282 U.S. 1 (1930).

was for him "not a dominating reality, but a convenient fiction which may be judicially employed or discarded, according to the result desired."[7]

It seems clear that in this case the "result desired" was the prime mover of the Sutherland opinion. He asserted that the failure to allow a situs to intangibles had "led to nothing but confusion and injustice by bringing about the anomalous and grossly unfair result that one kind of personal property cannot, for the purposes of imposing a transfer tax, be within the jurisdiction of more than one state at the same time, while another kind, quite as much within the protecting reach of the Fourteenth Amendment, may be, at the same moment, within the taxable jurisdiction of as many as four states. . . ."[8]

Here it is seen that Sutherland and those who agreed with him were striking at what they conceived to be "injustice" and unfairness. A similar motivation is evident in his dissent in *State Board of Tax Commissioners* v. *Jackson*.[9] In this case, the Court sustained an Indiana chain store tax which was graduated according to the number of stores operated "under the same general management, supervision, or ownership." The determining influence on the Court appears in these words of Mr. Justice Roberts: "In view of the numerous distinctions . . . between the business of a chain store and other types of store, we cannot pronounce the classification made by the statute to be arbitrary or unreasonable. That there are differences and advantages in favor of the chain store is shown by the number of such chains established and by their astonishing growth."[10]

Sutherland was willing to admit the differences of which his colleague wrote, but he insisted that these differences had no "just and reasonable relation" to the purpose of the statute—the raising of revenue. This was true because

[7] *First National Bank* v. *Maine, supra* note 5, p. 332.

[8] *ibid.*, p. 327. The *First National Bank* case was specifically overruled in *State Tax Commission* v. *Aldrich*, 316 U.S. 174 (1942).

[9] 283 U.S. 527 (1931).   [10] *ibid.*, p. 541.

the generalization—obviously a necessity in any taxing act—on which the legislature relied was not watertight. There were concerns, he argued, with only a single outlet which still were so large that they had all the advantages of a chain. This being true, it was manifestly unfair and a denial of equal protection to assess the chains at higher rates. Accordingly, he thought the whole statute must fall because in a few instances it worked unequally.

The reason why Sutherland demanded such perfection in legislators—indeed the explanation of his jealousy of power in every case—is adduced in a final paragraph. Once power is recognized, he argued, it knows no limits.

It may be that here the maximum of $25 for each store, while relatively high, is not, if considered by itself, excessive; but to sustain it will open the door of opportunity to the state to increase the amount to an oppressive extent. This court frequently has said, and it cannot be too often repeated in cases of this character, that the power to tax is the power to destroy; and this constitutes a reason why that power, however moderately exercised in given instances, should be jealously confined to the limits set by the Constitution.[11]

Sutherland's unwillingness to accept the legislature's generalization where a circumstance could be imagined in which it would be invalid appears in even bolder relief in his opinion for the Court in *Heiner* v. *Donnan*,[12] decided March 21, 1932. The statute in issue was a section of the Revenue Act which created a conclusive presumption that gifts made two years before death were made in contemplation of that event, with the result that property so disposed of was to be included in the assessment of inheritance taxes. Stone, speaking only for himself and Brandeis, found ample warrant for the legislation in its history. He pointed to the general use of this device to avoid the inheritance

11 *ibid.*, p. 552. This was not mere argument on Sutherland's part. In *Magnano Co.* v. *Hamilton*, 292 U.S. 40 (1934), he spoke for the Court in sustaining a Washington tax which had the effect of destroying the margarine business in that state. A tax, he said, may not be stricken down "simply because its enforcement may or will result in restricting or even destroying particular occupations or businesses." *Ibid.*, p. 44.

12 285 U.S. 312 (1932).

tax, and the ensuing loss of revenue, all of which did not impress Sutherland, as the following gives witness:

To sustain the validity of this irrebuttable presumption it is argued, with apparent conviction, that under the *prima facie* presumption originally in force there had been a loss of revenue. . . . This is very near to saying that the individual, innocent of evasion, may be stripped of his constitutional rights, in order to further a more thorough enforcement of the tax against the guilty, a new and startling doctrine, condemned by its mere statement. . . .[13]

Here, it seems, there are two rights in conflict—the right of society, on the one hand, to punish those who attempt to evade their lawful obligations to society itself; and, on the other, that of the individual to have his case, however unique, adjudged on its own peculiar facts. Sutherland, of course, was ready once more to declare that if a situation could be imagined in which the general statement relied on by the law was inapposite, the law would have to fall. He believed that a "young man abounding in health" could not be forced to yield, in the name of the common good, his rights to enjoy the fruits of his special circumstances. On this point Stone retorted that the presumption was not working in such a way as to require this result. He cited the fact that, of seventy-eight suits by the government, only one had involved a donor less than fifty years of age. This one exception in fact, however, or even one that could be imagined, was enough for Sutherland. The case for him was the possible though unlikely one of a youth "bereft of life by a stroke of lightning, within two years of making a gift . . . conclusively presumed to have acted under the inducement of the thought of death, equally with the old and ailing who already stands in the shadow of the inevitable end."[14]

The business of collecting taxes, then, although of the highest urgency, was not to be facilitated by unconstitutional shortcuts. Likewise, no plea of necessity could be allowed to win sanction for a weakening of the reciprocal

[13] *ibid.*, p. 328.   [14] *ibid.*, p. 327.

immunity operating between state and nation, or of double or discriminatory taxation. Necessity, therefore, so far as Sutherland was concerned, served only to create in him an acute apprehension that the crisis of the day was being used to mask a subtle assault on the Constitution. In this situation, he was convinced that the only course for the judiciary was to resist all beginnings of encroachment. They had always to remember that "every journey to a forbidden end begins with a first step." Once taken, it could never be retraced.

2.

The efforts of the states to find some solution for the increasingly grave problems brought by the depression began to come before the Court in 1932. The great question was, were the states to attempt to halt a social collapse with only those weapons left them by the *Adkins*,[15] *Tyson*,[16] and *Ribnik*[17] cases? Sutherland gave the answer for the Court in *New State Ice Company* v. *Liebmann*,[18] decided, when the country's economic demoralization was at its worst, on March 31, 1932. By the statute under review, Oklahoma required a certificate of public convenience and necessity of anyone engaging in the ice business. If it should be found that existing facilities in any community were sufficient to meet its needs, the license was not to be issued. The aim of the statute, of course, was to curb competition in the ice industry. Thus, the Court was presented with the question of whether a state's police power was broad enough to permit the deliberate encouragement of monopoly—a policy concededly at variance with the common law and the previously prevailing economic practice.

Brandeis, the lifelong foe of monopoly interestingly enough, concluded that the measure was not forbidden by the Fourteenth Amendment. He found in the facts con-

[15] *Adkins* v. *the Children's Hospital*, 261 U.S. 525 (1923).
[16] *Tyson* v. *Banton*, 273 U.S. 418 (1927).
[17] *Ribnik* v. *McBride*, 277 U.S. 350 (1928).
[18] 285 U.S. 262 (1932).

nected with the ice industry ample warrant for regulation. Although a believer in competition himself, he was willing to acknowledge that competition was no longer working and he refused to believe that the Constitution required it inexorably. "The people of the United States are now confronted with an emergency more serious than war," he warned. "The economic and social sciences are largely uncharted seas." For him, the only possible way to truth and a solution of the difficulties facing the country lay in the "process of trial and error." He accordingly admonished his colleagues that they were assuming a responsibility of the gravest kind when they undertook "to stay experimentation in things social and economic."[19]

Despite these trenchant words, Sutherland was willing to accept the responsibility involved in repudiating the statute. Indeed, in his view, he had no other alternative except to resign. To uphold the Constitution was an inescapable duty. The system of free competition was a part of the liberty guaranteed by the Fourteenth Amendment. And while willing to concede again that "all businesses are subject to some measure of public regulation," still he could find nothing in the ice industry to justify its withdrawal from the general rule. Furthermore, liberty of contract, the right to enter a calling, is a liberty with "which the state is not entitled to dispense in the interest of experiments." Just as there is an absolute prohibition of interference with the freedom of the press, just so "the opportunity to apply one's labor and skill in an ordinary occupation with proper regard for all reasonable regulations is no less entitled to protection."[20]

In *Stephenson* v. *Binford*,[21] decided later in the same year, Sutherland did indeed make a gesture toward recognizing in the states a police power with which the manifold problems of the day could be met. The Texas statute under review was much like that which he had earlier condemned in *Frost Trucking Co.* v. *Railroad Commis-*

[19] *ibid.*, pp. 306-311.   [20] *ibid.*, p. 280.   [21] 287 U.S. 251 (1932).

sion.[22] All carriers for hire on public roads were required to have either a certificate of public convenience and necessity or a permit; rates were to be fixed by a commission; and it was specifically declared that the object of the act was to ensure that the public highways should serve "the best interest of the general public." Anxious to find a distinction between this and the earlier case, Sutherland noted that here private carriers were to receive "permits" while in the *Frost* case a "certificate" similar to that required of the common carrier was demanded. This, plus the more positive evidence that regulation of highways was the end in view, was enough to sustain an exercise of power which five years before had been denounced as unconstitutional. Sutherland, in his eagerness to uphold the act, refused to heed even a suggestion that the rate provisions unduly interfered with freedom of contract. Admitting that there was an interference, it was not such "as the Fourteenth Amendment forbids. While freedom of contract is the general rule, it is nevertheless not absolute but subject to a great variety of legitimate restraints, *among which are such as are required for the safety and welfare of the state and its inhabitants.*"[23]

If one gives the italicized words their logical meaning, it is hard to escape the conclusion that Sutherland thought the regulation of the ice business, or employment agencies, or ticket brokers, or women's wages, unconstitutional only because the welfare of the state did not demand such regulations. After all, was the "safety and welfare" of the people—as determined by the Supreme Court, of course—the measure of constitutionality? One could readily have responded in the affirmative if this were the sole defense of the statute. But Sutherland produced another and one much more in harmony with the views he had formerly expressed. He explained: "When the exercise of that freedom [of contract] conflicts with the power and duty of the state to safeguard its property and preserve it for those

[22] 271 U.S. 583 (1926).
[23] *Stephenson* v. *Binford, supra* note 21, p. 274. The italics are mine.

uses for which it was primarily designed, such freedom may be regulated and limited to the extent which reasonably may be necessary to carry the power and duty into effect."[24]

So, just as in *Euclid* v. *Ambler*,[25] the state may act to *protect* property, and where the property is its own, it has even the *duty* to do so. Looked at from this standpoint the case supplies no warrant for thinking that Sutherland had come to regard general considerations of public welfare as sufficient justification for impairment of contractual liberty. Thus he could hold, about this same time, that neither the bankruptcy nor commerce powers of the federal government were equal to upsetting a "private agreement" which gave extravagant benefits to the reorganizers of a bankrupt railroad.[26] And in *Coombes* v. *Getz*,[27] the protection of the contract clause was held to extend not only to contracts but to statutory liabilities masquerading as such.

Of the cases reviewed so far in this chapter, none was decided later than 1932, and only *Stephenson* v. *Binford* after the presidential election of that year. It was 1934 before Sutherland was to speak again on the issue of contract versus the police power. In the meantime, the country had witnessed the unparalleled scenes of economic disaster and confusion which culminated in the bank holiday of March 1933. In the face of such calamities, the abdication of Respectability was complete. It was even suggested by one of the Money Changers fleeing from the Temple that the Constitution be suspended and dictatorial power handed over to the new President.[28] True, the situation had improved somewhat when the Court convened for its October term, but the atmosphere of crisis had not been dispelled. Huey P. Long was demanding that wealth be shared and Dr. Townsend found it an easy matter to convince the older people that $200 a month after reach-

24 *ibid.*   25 272 U.S. 365 (1926).

26 *United States* v. *Chicago, Milwaukee, St. Paul and Pacific Railway Company*, 282 U.S. 311 (1931).

27 285 U.S. 434 (1932).

28 William Kay Wallace in the *New York Times*, March 26, 1933.

ing the age of sixty-five would be useful not only to them but a blessing to the country at large. The fulminations of these two and others harmonized with the tramp of the unemployed to produce a turbulent symphony of protest and alarm, and one not inaudible in the chambers of the Supreme Court as the great case of *Home Building & Loan Association* v. *Blaisdell* [29] was argued.

Blaisdell, like thousands of his countrymen, had borrowed money which he was now unable to repay. At the time of the loan, he had mortgaged his home, and, in the usual course of events, his forfeiture would have required its surrender to the mortgagee, in this case the Home Building & Loan Association. But events were far from usual. The legislature of Minnesota, where Blaisdell lived, had, after citing the "general and extreme stagnation," the "almost complete lack of credit," and "the inherent and fundamental purpose of our government . . . to safeguard the public and promote the general welfare of the people," provided for a temporary stay of a creditor's right to the foreclosure of his mortgage. While the debtor remained in possession he was to pay a reasonable rental value which was to be applied, after fixed charges such as interest and taxes had been deducted, to his deficiency. Acting under this statute, a Minnesota court had added two extra years to the period during which Blaisdell would be allowed to redeem his mortgage and had further provided that he should remain in possession, subject, however, to the payment of a monthly rental.

What was the Supreme Court to do in answer to the Loan Association's plea that the stay authorized by the legislature was unconstitutional? Undeniably, conditions of acute distress prevailed in Minnesota. The State's Attorney General reminded the Court of tax delinquencies reaching 78 per cent, of ten cent butter and twenty-nine cent wheat.[30] On the other hand, the Constitution spoke in

[29] 290 U.S. 398 (1934). The argument took place on November 7 and 8, 1933.

[30] See *ibid.*, pp. 423-424 for a summary of the Attorney General's statement as to economic conditions.

unequivocal words: "No state shall . . . pass any . . . law impairing the obligation of contract."[31]

Throughout its history this provision had uniformly been held to bar similar statutes.[32] Nevertheless, the Court's response, spoken by the Chief Justice and agreed to by the barest majority, was to affirm the validity of the proceedings.

In its disposal of the embarrassing array of precedent, the method of the opinion is somewhat oblique. What its author does is to appeal to a line of cases which had sanctioned the exercise of police power in regard to health, welfare, and morals of the people, irrespective of its effect on contracts.[33] By a transfer of the reasoning of those cases to the case at hand, where the contract itself was the sole immediate object of the legislation, the Chief Justice claimed to find prior authority for the result achieved. He conceded that there was no warrant for an absolute repudiation but thought a "temporary restraint" permissible if made necessary by a great public calamity. This power, he was careful to say, was not created by the emergency; rather, the emergency furnished the occasion for its use. The question, then, as presented by the Chief Justice, was whether or not the economic emergency of the preceding years was the sort which justified extraordinary action.

The heart of the Chief Justice's argument is revealed in the conceptions which he summoned to his aid in giving the answer. The words of Marshall were recalled: "We must never forget that it is a constitution we are expounding"—"a constitution intended to endure for ages to come, and, consequently, to be adapted to the various crises of

[31] *U.S. Const.* Art. I, § 10.

[32] See especially *Bronson* v. *Kinzie*, 1 How. 311 (1843), where a statute providing a stay of a year was overthrown. The only difference was that no provision was made to secure to the mortgagee the rental value of the property.

[33] As, e.g., in *Stone* v. *Mississippi*, 101 U.S. 814 (1880), where it was held that a state could prohibit lotteries even when it had previously granted a charter to a corporation organized to conduct them.

human affairs."[34] There was a reminder, too, of the words
of Mr. Justice Holmes in *Missouri* v. *Holland*:[35]

... when we are dealing with words that are also a constituent
act, like the Constitution of the United States, we must realize
that they have called into life a being the development of which
could not have been foreseen completely by the most gifted of its
begetters. ... The case before us must be considered in the light
of our whole experience and not merely in that of what was said
a hundred years ago.

These citations well serve the purpose for which the
Chief Justice included them—to demonstrate that the
Court, in determining what the contract clause prohibited,
was not bound by the notions of the framers. Along the
same line, Hughes declared: "If by the statement that
what the Constitution meant at the time of its adoption it
means today, it is intended to say that the great clauses
of the Constitution must be confined to the interpretation
which the framers, with the conditions and outlook of their
time, would have placed upon them, the statement carries
its own refutation."[36]

While rejecting the controlling authority of opinion of
1787, the Court brought forward as the true guide to
construction the "growing appreciation of public needs
and of the necessity of finding ground for a rational compromise between individual rights and public welfare";[37]
emphasis, too, was to be placed on the need of "reasonable
means to safeguard the economic structure upon which the
good of all depends."[38] When judged by these standards,
the goal of the statute under review was declared to be
"legitimate" and its provisions "appropriate" to the
emergency.

Sutherland's troubled reaction to these propositions is
contained in one of his most notable opinions. His argument
reveals not only his own basic convictions but those of the

---

[34] *McCulloch* v. *Maryland*, 4 Wheat. 316, 407, 415 (1819).
[35] 252 U.S. 416, 433 (1920).
[36] *Home Building & Loan Ass'n* v. *Blaisdell*, *supra* note 29, pp. 442-
443.
[37] *ibid.*, p. 442.   [38] *ibid.*

Chief Justice as well. The crucial issue between Hughes and Sutherland is rooted in a fundamental disagreement as to the nature of the Constitution itself. Is it any more than an organization of power for certain declared ends? Or is it a grant of power which at the same time prescribes the only means available for its exercise? How does an emergency affect the institution of judicial review? Are the functions of courts varied by periods of crisis? What is the proper role of government? Is its duty to preserve the social fabric so overwhelming that constitutional limitations are to be laid aside?

On each of these problems Sutherland rejected emphatically what Hughes had had to say. From the very first his opinion is fraught with a recognition that vital principles were at stake:

Few questions of greater moment [Sutherland began] than that just decided have been submitted for judicial inquiry during this generation. He simply closes his eyes to the necessary implications of the decision who fails to see in it the potentiality of future gradual but ever-advancing encroachments upon the sanctity of private and public contracts. The effect of the Minnesota legislation, though serious enough in itself, is of trivial significance compared with the far more serious and dangerous inroads upon the limitations of the Constitution which are almost certain to ensue as a consequence naturally following any step beyond the boundaries fixed by that instrument. And those of us who are thus apprehensive of the effect of this decision would, in a matter so important, be neglectful of our duty should we fail to spread upon the permanent records of the Court the reasons which move us to the opposite view.[39]

In advancing his idea of the nature of a constitution, Sutherland relied mainly on the writings of his preceptors at the Michigan Law School, Judges Campbell and Cooley. Quoting the latter, he argued that constitutions were framed "with the varying moods of public opinion" in mind and thus "with a view to putting the fundamentals of government beyond their control." The Constitution was therefore not "a mere collection of political maxims to be

[39] *ibid.*, p. 448.

adhered to or disregarded according to the prevailing sentiment," but a *law* enacted by the people in their sovereign capacity. As such, in the words of Judge Campbell, it could not be changed by "events," nor was it "competent for any department in the government to change . . . or declare it changed, simply because it appears to be ill adapted to a new state of things." Indeed, this changeless quality in the Constitution was indispensable. Without it, there was a mere promise of the sovereign to conform. This promise became a constitution only when it could not be set aside except in the agreed manner and when there was a guarantee of individual rights. According to Cooley, and doubtless Sutherland was in agreement, a government was not constitutional unless it protected these rights, whatever the demands of necessity or of the general welfare.[40]

Sutherland's disagreement with the Chief Justice on the nature of the judicial function was just as emphatic. Hughes had asserted that the generality of the contract clause required "a process of construction . . . to fill in the details." The anguished dissenter retorted that it was not a judge's business to *interpret*; he had only to *apply* the Constitution. That instrument carried its own interpretation since it spoke "in such plain English words that it would seem that the ingenuity of man could not evade them."[41] Therefore a judge must "declare the law as written, leaving it to the people themselves to make such

---

[40] In this part of his dissent Sutherland places great emphasis on *Ex parte Milligan*, 4 Wall. 2 (1866), where it was held that not even the Civil War furnished an occasion for the disregard of any of the provisions of the Constitution. Sutherland, however, did not always demand such constitutional absolutism. See e.g., *United States* v. *Macintosh*, 283 U.S. 605, 622 (1931), where Sutherland quotes with approval John Quincy Adams' famous definition of the war power—one quite incompatible with the idea of constitutional limitations.

[41] *Home Building & Loan Ass'n* v. *Blaisdell, supra* note 29, p. 449. Professor Corwin has noted the kinship between the idea that the "scriptures speak unmistakably" and a similar notion applied to the Constitution. See Edward S. Corwin, *The Twilight of the Supreme Court*, New Haven, Yale University Press, 1934, pp. 107-108. Such a theory was a commonplace, of course, in the Utah of Sutherland's youth.

changes as new circumstances may require."[42] Not only could it not be changed by events; it could not be changed by judges so long as they acted judicially, for that was but to recite the law as it had been given by the people, who alone were sovereign in the American political system.

And certainly the Constitution could not be changed by an emergency. "No doctrine, involving more pernicious consequences was ever invented by the wit of man than that any of its provisions can be suspended during any of the great exigencies of government. Such a doctrine leads directly to anarchy or despotism."[43] Again, "if the provisions of the Constitution be not upheld when they pinch as well as when they comfort, they may as well be abandoned."[44] This attitude fairly raises the question of whether or not Sutherland was willing to see the country go to rack and ruin in order that it could continue to indulge in the doubtful luxury of a literal reading of the Constitution. Certainly the knowledge that the great charter had been preserved would have been of little solace to a Blaisdell, stripped of his worldly possessions and reduced to the condition of a wolf forced to pillage and rob for his sustenance.

To any such criticism, however, Sutherland made a ready answer and one fundamentally divergent from the Hughes view of "an increased use of the organization of society in order to protect the very bases of individual opportunity." Such was not the task of government. "Indiscretion or imprudence was not to be relieved by legislation, but restrained by the conviction that a full compliance with contracts would be exacted."[45] The Blaisdells

---

[42] *Home Building & Loan Ass'n* v. *Blaisdell, supra* note 29, p. 452, quoting from Cooley, *Constitutional Limitations*, 8th ed., p. 124.

[43] *ibid.,* p. 450, quoting from *Ex parte Milligan,* 4 Wall. 2, 121 (1866).

[44] *ibid.,* p. 483.

[45] *ibid.,* p. 454. According to Herbert Spencer, there was really mercy in this course—the "mercy of severity." Consider the following:

"Pervading all nature we may see at work a stern discipline, which is a little cruel that it may be very kind. That state of universal warfare maintained throughout the lower creation, to the great perplexity of many worthy people, is at bottom the most merciful provision which

were suffering from their failure to adapt themselves to the social world in which they lived. In Sutherland's view, the intervention of government must therefore necessarily meet with failure. After all, the present exigency was

nothing new. From the beginning of our existence as a nation, periods of depression, of industrial failure, of financial distress, of unpaid and unpayable indebtedness, have alternated with years of plenty. The vital lesson that expenditure beyond income begets poverty, that public or private extravagance, financed by promises to pay, either must end in complete or partial repudiation or the promises be fulfilled by self-denial and painful effort, though constantly taught by bitter experience, seems never to have been learned. . . .[46]

Thus regarded, the illness of society could not be cured by "legislative devices to shift the misfortune of the debtor." Indeed, in Sutherland's view, the malady was not a social one at all. Rather, its ravages infected only individuals who could be rendered whole "only by industry and frugality, not by relaxation of law or by a sacrifice of the rights of others." Salvation, then, lay in the reconstruction of the individual in the only manner by which this was possible—his own slow and painful efforts and goaded always by the threat of suffering for his failures. In any event, the words of the Court in *Edwards*

---

the circumstances admit of. It is much better that the ruminant animal, when deprived by age of the vigor which made its existence a pleasure, should be killed by some beast of prey, than that it should linger out a life made painful by infirmities, and eventually die of starvation. By the destruction of all such, not only is existence ended before it becomes burdensome, but room is made for a younger generation capable of the fullest enjoyment; and, moreover, out of the very act of substitution happiness is derived for a tribe of predatory creatures. Note further, that their carnivorous enemies not only remove from herbivorous herds individuals past their prime, but also weed out the sickly, the malformed, and the least fleet or powerful. By the aid of which purifying process, as well as by the fighting, so universal in the pairing season, all vitiation of the race through the multiplication of its inferior samples is prevented; and the maintenance of a constitution completely adapted to surrounding conditions, and therefore most productive of happiness, is assured." *Social Statics*, New York, D. Appleton & Co., 1883, pp. 352-353.

[46] *Home Building & Loan Ass'n* v. *Blaisdell, supra* note 29, pp. 471-472.

v. *Kearzey*[47] were as pertinent as ever. "Policy and humanity," it had said, "are dangerous guides in the discussion of a legal proposition. He who follows them far is apt to bring back the means of error and delusion."[48]

This insistence that "natural forces" should be allowed to wrench from the weak and the helpless a bitter atonement for their errors has connotations bordering on the brutal. That there was a limit however is shown by the case of *Local Loan Company* v. *Hunt*,[49] decided just three months after the *Blaisdell* case. There Hunt had given the company a lien on his wages as security for a loan. Later, he was adjudged a bankrupt. Nevertheless, the company continued to attempt to enforce its lien in a state court. The Supreme Court, however, speaking through Sutherland, refused to permit this. The difference between the *Blaisdell* case and the one at hand was slight. In the latter, the individual had mortgaged himself, so to speak, while in the Minnesota case, he had mortgaged his property. The distinction, however, was vital for Sutherland. He observed that "the power on an individual to earn a living was a personal liberty," to which property rights would have to yield.[50] Without it, the self-denying Spartan

---

[47] 96 U.S. 595, 604 (1877).

[48] Some further words were spoken on the *Blaisdell* case in *Worthen Co.* v. *Thomas*, 292 U.S. 426 (1934) where the Court overthrew a statute in which the relief granted to creditors was neither temporary nor conditional. Sutherland apparently regarded this as a vindication of his opinion in the *Blaisdell* case. In a special concurrence, he said that there was no difference between the two cases. Although four months had elapsed, he took occasion to denounce once again the error of the majority in the earlier case. The "fixed and secure boundaries of the fundamental law" had been abandoned. He continued: "We reject as unsound and dangerous doctrine, threatening the stability of the deliberately framed and wise provisions of the Constitution, the notion that violations of those provisions may be measured by the length of time they are to continue or the extent of the infraction, and that only those of long duration or of large importance are to be held bad. . . . We do not possess the benevolent power to compare and contrast infringements of the Constitution and condemn them when they are long-lived or great or unqualified, and condone them when they are temporary or small or conditioned."

[49] 292 U.S. 234 (1934).　　　　　　　　　　　　[50] *ibid.*, p. 245.

qualities would be unequal to their task and pauperism the result. In other words, governmental intervention, through the familiar instrument of a bankruptcy proceeding, is permissible to the extent that it seeks to enable the individual to exercise his right of contest and struggle. Beyond that, he is to be left on his own to stand or fall in accordance with his own capacities.

Their victory in the *Blaisdell* case was not the sole triumph of the states in 1934 in their assault on the restraints previously thought to be imposed on them by the Constitution. Less than two months later, the power to impose price regulation and a limit on competition was recognized in *Nebbia* v. *New York*.[51] Language was used which indicated that the legislature's judgment on the appropriateness of such measures was to be final.[52] There was, of course, the inevitable protest by the inseparable four, authored this time by McReynolds. More important, the formulator of the new doctrine was none other than Mr. Justice Roberts, the Court's swing man. Plainly, he was no longer yielding to the magic words of old— "contract," "equal protection," "due process." In this situation the conservatives resorted to a change of tactic. The privileges and immunities clause [53] was at hand, untarnished from recent use. Perhaps it would appeal to the errant Roberts, and even the Chief Justice, where the more familiar words had not. The experiment was delayed for something over a year until the case of *Colgate* v. *Harvey*,[54] but when tried, proved to be a sweeping success. Only Stone, Brandeis, and Cardozo refused to endorse the opinion prepared by Sutherland for the Court.

[51] 291 U.S. 502 (1934).

[52] "So far as the requirement of due process is concerned, and in the absence of other constitutional restriction, a state is free to adopt whatever economic policy may reasonably be deemed to promote public welfare, and to enforce that policy by legislation adapted to its purpose. The courts are without authority either to declare such policy, or, when it is declared by the legislature, to override it." *Ibid.*, p. 537.

[53] ". . . No State shall make or enforce any law which shall abridge the privileges or immunities of citizens of the United States. . . ." *U.S. Const. Amend.* xiv, § 1.

[54] 296 U.S. 404 (1935).

The case arose out of a Vermont income tax which drew a distinction between income gained from loans made in the state and loans made outside, the latter being assessed at a higher rate. Sutherland first attacked this classification as being a denial of equal protection. He refused to see in the statute any other purpose than that of raising revenue, and to this object the discrimination was said to bear "no substantial or fair relation." His entire discussion of this point is based on the same assumption which underlies so many of his opinions—that the social context producing the statute is irrelevant. Thus a revenue measure was considered by him capable of having but a single function. It had no relation to the social structure or the general welfare but was purely and simply to produce necessary funds. In any event, this was to be believed in the absence of a specific declaration by the legislature to the contrary.

Here, Stone entered a biting caveat. He thought "a decent respect to an independent branch of the government" compelled acceptance of the presumption that the legislature was acting with a view to the "broader advantages." And to prove that a state was not barred from seeking to advance the special interests of its citizens, he cited the fact that the national government had favored the citizens of some states to the detriment of those in others by use of a protective tariff.

It was not enough, however, for Stone to contravert the equal protection argument. For at this point Sutherland confounded him by dusting off the privileges and immunities clause of the Fourteenth Amendment and sending it forth to serve the cause of liberty and laissez faire. This clause had, of course, never before been employed by the Court to strike down a state legislative effort—this in spite of argument in forty-four cases that its use was appropriate.[55] "Feeble indeed," Stone exclaimed at this resurrection of the "almost forgotten" words. But Suther-

[55] *ibid.*, pp. 445-446. The most notable example, of course, was the opinion in the Slaughter House Cases, 16 Wall. 36 (1873).

land was not impressed. In his view a provision could not be dismissed which "extended and completed the shield of national protection."

Even if it be assumed, however, that there are privileges and immunities inhering in United States citizenship which a state is not at liberty to transgress, the problem remained as to whether the Vermont act amounted to such a transgression. In other words, does one derive a right by virtue of his United States citizenship to invest money in an out-of-state enterprise? Sutherland summarily announced that he did.

As citizens of the United States we are members of a single great community consisting of all the states united and not of distinct communities consisting of the states severally. No citizen of the United States is an alien in any state of the Union; and the very status of national citizenship connotes equality of rights and privileges, so far as they flow from such citizenship.[56]

The equality which Sutherland had in mind was the equal freedom from all state interference and this was such a glittering goal that it overrode his devotion to the principle of dual federalism. That rights vital to the states were involved was made clear by Stone, who thought the opinion created "an inexhaustible source of immunities incalculable in their . . . harm to local government."[57] But here, as with the commerce clause, the equality of governmental inaction was a value superior, in Sutherland's view, to the claims of the states. Now this concept had been lodged in yet another provision of the Constitution and any successful attack on it would face the necessity of reducing an additional redoubt. *Blaisdell* and *Nebbia* to the contrary, the struggle to restrain state power was not yet lost.

3.

Colgate v. *Harvey* was decided December 16, 1935. By that date, the center of interest was no longer state legislative power. Rather, the Court's challenge to Franklin

[56] *Colgate* v. *Harvey, supra* note 54, p. 426.   [57] *ibid.*, p. 447.

Roosevelt and the New Deal was the absorbing topic of the day. Twelve months before the nine justices had been officially informed for the first time of the strange happenings in the other two departments.[58] Sutherland, of course, was not dependent on a lawyer or his brief for knowledge of what was going on in the political branches. He doubtless retained sufficient interest in affairs to follow them in a general way. What he saw of the new movement could not have been reassuring. To begin with, his old enemies, the surviving Progressives, were lined up almost solidly in the Roosevelt camp. Had they not been present, however, there was more than enough in the new movement to arouse disturbing memories and the new President, with his assertion of aggressive leadership, inevitably recalled that earlier Democratic "autocrat," Woodrow Wilson.

A pliant Congress was ready to do the President's bidding. The feverish legislative activity of the first hundred days of the Roosevelt administration is even now within the recollection of most adult Americans. Democrats and Republicans alike responded to presidential demands "with an alacrity suggesting spontaneous combustion." Bills that formerly would have required weeks, and even months, for their passage received the Congressional imprimatur in a few hours. Dissent was scarcely in evidence until James M. Beck, on May 25, 1933, raised his voice in the House of Representatives to utter a lonely protest. The bill under consideration was the National Industrial Recovery Act. Beck solemnly warned his colleagues that "the shadows of a lasting night" were falling upon the constitutional edifice. And the disaster was not lessened in any degree by "the irresistible charm" of FDR. Dictatorship was in the offing. The President was no longer the executive known to the Constitution. Plainly, that instrument had passed into the limbo. Worst of all, not even the Supreme Court provided a ray of light in the darkening gloom. The trouble all started with the opinion in the Lottery case.[59]

[58] *Panama Refining Co.* v. *Ryan*, 293 U.S. 388 (1935).

[59] *Champion* v. *Ames*, 188 U.S. 321 (1903). Beck had himself represented the Government in this case, but with obvious doubts.

That ruling, Beck said, "while sound in theory, was one of the most fateful and mischievous decisions in its effect upon the expansion of federal power that the Supreme Court ever rendered, because it has been wrongfully interpreted to give to Congress this tremendously coercive and tyrannous power over commerce."[60]

The legislators, however, were in no mood to heed such direful warnings and the bill promptly passed. Feeling assured, no doubt, that his friend on the Supreme Court would prove to be a more sympathetic audience, Beck sent a copy of his address to Sutherland. The Justice, in acknowledging receipt, expressed his "deep interest" and characterized Beck's effort as a very "forceful and clear statement" and as one which made "a strong appeal to thoughtful men." But from the vantage point of the bench, he was not ready to admit the passing of the Constitution. "I have an abiding faith," he wrote, "in the vitality of the Constitution, and I think it will endure beyond the present crisis and other crises which our people will from time to time face in the future."[61]

The confidence here reflected was not shaken by the *Blaisdell* and *Nebbia* cases. The Justice's optimism can be accounted for only by ascribing it to his knowledge that the Court must have its innings. The first of these finally came toward the end of 1934 and was attended by a result distinctly reassuring. An all but unanimous Court held that Congress had exceeded its power in attempting to delegate authority, unchecked by statutory guides, to the President to prohibit the transportation of "hot oil" in interstate commerce.[62]

Scarcely a month later the famous "gold clause" cases[63] were decided. A Congressional Joint Resolution,[64] supplementary to the dollar devaluation program, had decreed that contracts which called for payment in gold or in

---

[60] 77 *Cong. Rec.* 4215 (1933).   [61] Sutherland to Beck, June 5, 1933.
[62] *Panama Refining Co.* v. *Ryan, supra* note 58. Cardozo was the lone dissenter.
[63] *Norman* v. *Baltimore & Ohio Railroad*, 294 U.S. 240 (1935); *Perry* v. *United States*, 294 U.S. 330 (1935).
[64] 48 Stat. 113 (1933), 31 U.S.C., §§ 462, 463, 821 (1940).

currency of equivalent value were to be "discharged, upon payment, dollar for dollar, in any coin or currency which at the time of payment is legal tender for public and private debts." As Professor Corwin has observed: "No such drastic legislation from the point of view of property rights had ever before been enacted by the Congress of the United States."[65]

Just what the resolution was designed to accomplish is well shown by the facts of the two cases before the Court. In one a holder of a bond of the Baltimore and Ohio Railroad, on which $22 was due, was suing for $38, the equivalent in the new currency. There was no denying that this was what he had specifically contracted for. In the other suit, a bond of the United States, it, too, containing a similar promise, was the basis of the action. The Court's answer, delivered by the Chief Justice, to the two bondholders, while not exactly the same in each case, achieved a similar result. On the private loan, it was held that, since Congress had authority to regulate the value of currency, the insertion of gold clauses into contracts was an unconstitutional attempt to obstruct the legislative power. The holder of the government bond, on the other hand, was solemnly assured that the government could not abrogate its promise and that therefore his cause of action was a valid one. But, the Court hastened to add, the litigant had suffered no damages by the government's breach of a contract which could not be breached. Hence that gentleman, much perplexed no doubt, was unceremoniously dismissed as a seeker after unjust enrichment![66]

Mr. Justice McReynolds spoke for the dissenting four, expanding considerably the vehemence of his opinion on the occasion of its oral delivery. "This is Nero at his worst," he mourned.[67] Even the written opinion has been characterized as "one of the most vehement ever delivered

---

[65] Edward S. Corwin, *Constitutional Revolution, Ltd.*, Claremont, Claremont Colleges, 1941, p. 42.

[66] I am indebted to Professor Corwin for calling Mr. Perry's plight to my attention. See *ibid.*, p. 45.

[67] *ibid.*, p. 46.

from any bench."[68] One does not have to rely on Sutherland's formally noted concurrence to know that he shared
his colleague's revulsion. In the papers left by the Justice,
there is a memorandum[69] obviously prepared for use in
conference when the cases were to be discussed. In this
paper Sutherland pointed out that the extent of Congressional power over the currency previously recognized was
the power to say what should be legal tender. The due
process of law clause was said to forbid the destruction
of the contractual obligations under review, to say nothing
of the fact that there was no delegated power under which
such an object could be achieved. The memorandum next
proceeded to attack the government's argument that the
gold clause constituted an obstruction to the authority of
Congress to fix the value of money. Obviously, this authority was

not obstructed by the payment of the 15-grain dollars to equal the
stipulated amount of the 25-grain dollars. The result might be
to greatly interfere with the business of the country. It might
conceivably result in business chaos, of which the Attorney General spoke. That would not interfere in the slightest degree with
the power of Congress to measure the value of the dollar by any
quantity of gold it saw fit. The contemplation of such a result
might induce Congress to a greater degree of care in exercising
its power, but it does not interfere with the power itself.

There was, it seems, an unanswerable reasonableness in
this argument which could be overcome only by apprehension of the chaos which Sutherland seemed willing for the
country to experience in order that it and its representatives might learn a needed lesson. There is comparable
persuasiveness, too, in some succeeding words on the Government's obligation, although they obviously reflect the
Justice's intense emotional upset. Stigmatizing as "utterly
dishonest" the view that the Government creditor's damages must be measured by the dollars alone permitted to
circulate, he incredulously inquired: "Can the government,

[68] *ibid.*

[69] A complete copy of the memorandum may be found in Appendix B.

which is forbidden to vary the terms of its contract, accomplish the same result by a legislative manipulation which prevents the terms being carried into effect?

Sutherland's answer was an indignant "No." Interestingly, it has all the appearances of being the original of the McReynolds dissent. The only difference is that the memorandum is even more violent than the official protest! This part of it is worth reproducing in full:

I think the best way to deal with the case at hand is to cite the history—to point out the fact that a bond issue was made by the present administration calling for gold-dollar payments a short time before the legislation under attack was passed; that, with callous indifference to its solemn engagement, it undertook to destroy its effect . . . that it gathered the gold into its treasury, thereby impounding the very thing it had promised to pay; that it had cynically and in disregard of all moral principle boasted that the result of its gold manipulation has been to bring to it a profit of between two and three billions of dollars—a profit made possible in part at least by the dishonorable attempt to annul promises made to its own citizens who mistakenly trusted to its honor. An individual as a contractor has as much authority to avoid his obligations as the government. Suppose an individual, lacking the power to annul or lessen the amount of his monetary obligation, should attempt to secrete or manipulate his assets so as to put them beyond the reach of his creditors. The Court would denounce that as a fraud, and sweep it aside as ineffective; and a boast on the part of a dishonest debtor that he had reaped a great profit by the fraud would not be received with a high degree of patience.[70]

The principal perpetrator of this "dishonorable attempt" by a "dishonest debtor," "fraud," "disregard of all moral principles," and "callous indifference" was, of course, Franklin Roosevelt. During the somber winter, when the Court was holding such acts to be within the fundamental law, Sutherland must have had his moments of doubt as to the ultimate triumph of which he had earlier been so positive. But the month of May brought regeneration. In short order the Court declared invalid the Railroad

[70] cf. Justice McReynolds dissenting in the Gold Clause Cases, 294 U.S. 361, 380-381 (1935).

Retirement Act, the Frazier-Lemke Act, and the National Industrial Recovery Act, employing language which rendered the entire New Deal program constitutionally suspect.[71] Chief Justice Hughes, in the latter case, gave this welcome declaration: "The persons employed in slaughtering and selling in local trade are not employed in interstate commerce. . . . The recuperative efforts of the Federal Government must be made in a manner consistent with the authority granted by the Constitution."

But this was not all. On the same May 27th which saw the end of the Frazier-Lemke Act and the NIRA, the Court also made known its holding in *Rathbun* v. *United States*,[72] with Sutherland the author of the unanimously supported opinion. The issue involved was the extent of the President's power of removal. Since the earliest days of the Constitution, this question had been hotly argued,[73] and the energy of FDR's leadership, securing as it seemed, a new preeminence for the chief executive, endowed it with special significance in 1935.

The case had its beginnings in 1933 when the President had removed from office William E. Humphrey, a member of the Federal Trade Commission. The Act, which established the Commission, after providing for seven-year terms, stipulated that the President was authorized to remove a member only for "inefficiency, neglect of duty, or malfeasance in office." FDR did not purport to act for any of these reasons, but simply because, as he stated it, his and the Commissioner's minds did not "go along together."

Humphrey's resistance to the attempt of the President to oust him was hardly justified by the one previous judicial utterance on the subject. In 1926, Chief Justice Taft, with Sutherland's approval, had denied in sweeping terms the right of Congress to restrain the President in

[71] *Railroad Retirement Board* v. *Alton Railroad Co.*, 295 U.S. 330 (1935); *Louisville Bank* v. *Radford*, 295 U.S. 555 (1935); *Schechter Poultry Corp.* v. *United States*, 295 U.S. 495 (1935).
[72] 295 U.S. 602 (1935).
[73] See Edward S. Corwin, *The President's Removal Power Under the Constitution*, New York, National Municipal League, 1927.

any manner in discharging executive employees.[74] And this in spite of an acknowledged legislative power to establish the office and fix its terms. In other words, where the two powers conflicted, that of the Congress must yield.

In reaching this conclusion Taft relied largely on the so-called "decision of 1789." In that year the first Congress, in setting up the departments of the new government, refused to make their principal officers expressly removable by the President. Yet, the relevant acts did refer to the time when "the said principal officer shall be removed from office by the President of the United States."[75] Did this mean that Congress was there granting to the President a power of removal, or did it constitute a recognition by Congress that the President already had the power by virtue of the Constitution?

Taft eagerly embraced the second interpretation. But he went further to argue that the opening clause of Article II[76] carried with it a substantive grant and that therefore the President was endowed with all executive authority known to the Constitution. In other words, any officer of the Government outside the legislative and judicial departments was a creature of the President's, exercising his authority, and therefore ultimately responsible to him. Moreover, it was argued that the President could not discharge his duty to "take care that the laws be faithfully executed" without complete control. Besides this, the Chief Justice, himself a former President, urged that the same practical considerations of harmonious administration which governed in the case of cabinet officers extended to all employees of the executive branch.

In addition to Sutherland there were on the Court when the *Rathbun* case was decided three other justices who had concurred in the earlier Taft opinion.[77] In these cir-

---

[74] *Myers* v. *United States*, 272 U.S. 52 (1926).

[75] See Corwin, *The President's Removal Power Under the Constitution*, pp. 8-23.

[76] "The executive Power shall be vested in a President . . ." *U.S. Const.* Art. II, 1.

[77] Van Devanter, Butler, and Stone. Brandeis and McReynolds had dissented.

cumstances, it is a notable tribute to Sutherland's dialectical skill that he should have been selected to conduct the
retreat which a unanimous Court now found necessary.
This difficult task Sutherland performed with a minimum
of embarrassment to himself and his colleagues. He began
with a resort to a familiar judicial technique—the steriliza-
tion of an inconvenient precedent.

> The office of a postmaster is so essentially unlike the office now
> involved that the decision in the Myers case cannot be accepted as
> controlling our decision here. A postmaster is an executive officer
> restricted to the performance of executive functions. He is charged
> with no duty at all related to either the legislative or judicial
> power. . . . The necessary reach of the decision goes far enough
> to include all purely executive officers. It goes no further—much
> less does it include an officer who occupies no place in the execu-
> tive department and who exercises no part of the executive power
> vested by the Constitution in the President.[78]

So much for Myers and the office of postmaster. The
Commissioner occupied an entirely different position. He
was required by Congress to use *his* discretion in the implementation of legislative and judicial policies and the
authority of Congress to make this demand could not "well
be doubted." Accordingly, Congress could protect its
creature, "for it is quite evident that one who holds his
office only during the pleasure of another, cannot be de-
pended upon to maintain an attitude of independence
against the latter's will."[79]

It will be recalled that Sutherland had always been a
believer in a rigid separation of powers. How then could
he say that the Commissioner occupied no place in the
executive department? And after this is dismissed as an
unconsidered dictum,[80] might it not be asked if the *Rathbun*

[78] *Rathbun* v. *United States, supra* note 72, pp. 627-628.

[79] *ibid.*, p. 629.

[80] Professor Corwin in his *The President, Office and Powers*, New York,
New York University Press, 1940, p. 357, quotes the following anecdote
by Professor Cushman: "In 1937 Mr. Justice Sutherland was on the
bench during the oral argument in the *Shipping Board* cases. One who
was present in Court at this time reported the following interesting
colloquy which took place. Mr. James W. Ryan, counsel for the shipping

decision does not allow an intermeddling by Congress in the matter of administration which would be inadmissible within the confines of a pure theory? There is some temptation to answer affirmatively. Yet the Constitution, in so far as it commands a separation, obviously assumes that the legislature shall be the dominant branch in matters of policy. Thus, the "necessary and proper" clause gives Congress the authority to enact laws needed to execute not only its powers but "all other Powers vested by this Constitution in the Government of the United States, or in any Department or Officer thereof." And surely the President is not left defenseless. His prerogative in certain matters is guaranteed by the Constitution itself. Moreover, there is his participation in the legislative process through the veto, and in the extra-constitutional role of

---

company, was urging upon the Court the argument, earlier summarized, that the United States Shipping Board could not constitutionally be put by executive order or by act of Congress 'in' the executive branch. The Shipping Board, he argued, was not an 'executive agency' and could not be an 'executive agency' because it was not *in* the executive branch of the Government.

"Justice Sutherland, who had been sitting back in his chair and asking occasional questions during the course of the argument, leaned forward quickly when he heard this.

" 'Did you say that the Shipping Board was not *in* the executive branch of the Government?' he said—as though he did not believe he had heard correctly. Several other Justices smiled condescendingly at counsel as though he were making a farfetched proposition.

" 'Yes, your Honor,' Mr. Ryan replied.

" 'What makes you think that? Where do you find any legal basis for such a conclusion?' the Justice wished to know.

" 'Why in your Honor's opinion in the *Humphrey* case, this Court held that the Federal Trade Commission and similar regulatory agencies were not in the executive branch of the Government. The Shipping Board fell within the same general category as the Federal Trade Commission and the Interstate Commerce Commission.' Mr. Ryan then proceeded to read certain portions of that opinion.

" 'What branch of the Government do you think the Shipping Board was in, if it was not in the executive branch?' the Justice wanted to know.

" 'In the legislative branch, your Honor.'

"Justice Sutherland shook his head, as though he disagreed, and seemed to be thinking the question over as the discussion went on to other points." 24 *Corn. L. Q.* 13-53 and 163-197, at pp. 52-53 (1938).

party leader. Considered in this light, the efforts of Sutherland in the *Rathbun* case must be applauded as in full conformity with the framers' ideas of the relationships of the three departments.[81]

The rout suffered by the Administration on May 27 was received in the conservative community as an unmistakable signal that the darkness of the Roosevelt night would not endure forever.[82] The stock market advanced and with it the hopes of the Republicans for the 1936 elections.[83] Was it not now provable that the New Deal was unconstitutional and therefore un-American? Those who looked to the Supreme Court for the final answers to such questions had a ready reply.

Others were ready, too, but with a different set of answers. William Green for the American Federation of Labor let it be known that the workers of America did not intend to relinquish the benefits they had recently won.[84] The left-wing weeklies were more direct; the nine guardians of the covenant had made a mistake which, in some unprescribed manner, must needs be corrected. Even in the daily press, doubts that the justices alone were equipped to interpret the Constitution made their appearance.

Most important of all, however, were the reactions of

[81] Despite the great question of political organization involved, the immediate practical effects of the opinion received more attention. For example, Mr. Justice Jackson, then a Government lawyer, declared: "In *Humphrey's* case the Court 'disapproved' its own statement on which the President had relied. The Court switched its doctrine and rebuked the President by holding the removal of Humphrey to be illegal. Within the Administration there was a profound feeling that the opinion of the Court was written with a design to give the impression that the President had flouted the Constitution, rather than that the Court had simply changed its mind within the past ten years. The decision could easily have forestalled this by recognizing the President's reliance on an opinion of Chief Justice Taft. But the decision contained no such gracious acknowledgment." Robert H. Jackson, *The Struggle for Judicial Supremacy*, New York, Alfred A. Knopf, 1941, pp. 108-109.

[82] The lower federal courts certainly took this view. Some 1600 injunctions were soon issued against the enforcement of New Deal legislation. See *ibid.*, p. 115.

[83] *New York Times*, May 28, 1935; *ibid.*, June 3, 1935.

[84] *ibid.*, May 30, 1935.

the culprits. On May 31, Franklin Roosevelt received the press at the White House. His demeanor was strangely grave. The Court, he said, had interpreted the Constitution as if "the horse and buggy days" still prevailed. The President went on to point out that the direst results had attended previous efforts of the Court to rule. All in all, it was evident that he did not propose to yield.[85] This was made abundantly clear a few weeks later by his letter to Congressman Hill in which he urged the passage of the Guffey Coal Bill, however reasonable the doubts as to its constitutionality.[86] Congress, for its part, responded by also refusing to accept as final the Court's reading of the Constitution. Before the end of the session in August, it passed the Guffey Bill, the Wagner Labor Relations Act, the Social Security Act, and a new pension measure for the railroad workers.

The justices, so long accustomed to the unconditional acceptance of their rulings, might well have been occasioned considerable pain by this exhibition of disrespect. Still, the result for Sutherland and his conservative colleagues was but to strengthen their resolution. So long as the flames of arbitrary and usurped authority licked at the Temple of the Constitution, it was their duty to make full use of the one sure extinguisher, judicial review. With the liberal three, on the other hand, it is possible that the defiance registered by Congress and President suggested that a force was abroad in the land which nine men would be unable to check—and this even though they wore robes and were denominated Justices of the Supreme Court.

This interpretation is countenanced by the opinions rendered the following January, when the Agricultural Adjustment Act was declared unconstitutional.[87] Speaking for the majority, Mr. Justice Roberts thought it wise to explain that in overthrowing the acts of Congress, the Court did not assume, as was often charged, "a power to overrule or control the action of the people's representa-

---

[85] *ibid.*, June 1, 1935.   [86] *ibid.*, July 7, 1935.
[87] *United States* v. *Butler*, 297 U.S. 1 (1936).

tives. This is a misconception," he said. The judicial branch had but one duty, he further explained—"to lay the article of the Constitution which is invoked beside the statute which is challenged and to decide whether the latter squares with the former."[88] After a resort to this procedure, he found that the questioned tax was illegal because it interfered with the power reserved by the states to regulate agriculture. Of course, it was true that Congress had power to tax for the general welfare, and this was in addition to the other powers granted, but, even so, the phrase did not embody a limitless grant. Most assuredly, it did not extend to such purely local matters as the growing of crops. The opinion fairly seemed to imply that the differences between Court and Congress would disappear if only the legislators would understand, once and for all, that there is no authority in the Constitution for converting the United States "into a central government exercising uncontrolled police power."[89] Should Congress persist in its errors, the Court had no alternative but to follow the supreme law.

Stone, with the concurrence of Brandeis and Cardozo, entered a dissent which is remarkable in many ways and in none more so than the manner in which he reproached his colleagues for the action taken. If ruin was on the way, or if the states were about to lose their independence, the Court, acting alone, could not avert the catastrophe— certainly not by a "tortured construction of the Constitution—justified by recourse to extreme examples. . . ."[90] There was far more danger, said Stone, in avoiding the "frank recognition that language, even of a constitution, may mean what it says: that the power to tax and spend includes the power to relieve a nationwide economic maladjustment."[91] As a preface to these remarks, Stone uttered a reminder that "while unconstitutional exercise of power by the executive and legislative branches of the government is subject to judicial restraint, the only check upon

[88] *ibid.*, p. 62.   [89] *ibid.*, p. 77.   [90] *ibid.*, p. 87.   [91] *ibid.*, p. 88.

our own exercise of power is our own sense of self-restraint."[92] George Sutherland, listening in silence, would not forget these words.

The uses to which the Stone opinion could be put were not lost on the critics of the Court. To prove their charge that the Court was in error they could bring as chief witnesses the three dissenters, men who were not mere politicians depending for their position on the sufferance of the crowd but judges, learned and respectable. This fact made it imperative for the conservatives to meet head-on the challenge hurled so forcefully by Stone. In this situation, they naturally turned to Sutherland, who, through the years, had always been their most effective spokesman.

The first installment of their reply came in *Jones* v. *Securities Exchange Commission*,[93] decided April 6, 1936. This case, while not involving any broad review of legislative power, was well adapted to the delineation of perhaps the most fundamental difference among the justices—the clash between liberty and authority. Jones had registered with the SEC a statement covering a proposed issue of trust certificates. On investigation, the Commission came to the conclusion that the truth of some assertions made by Jones was doubtful. Accordingly, it ordered a hearing and, by subpoena, commanded Jones to produce certain books and papers. Jones' reaction to this was to attempt to withdraw his original statement, thus depriving the Commission of jurisdiction. However, the Commission denied that he could stifle the inquiry by any such maneuver and sought the aid of the District Court in forcing Jones to appear before the examiner.

The Supreme Court, with the customary division, held that Jones could thus fustrate the investigation by what Cardozo characterized in his dissent, as "precipitate retreat on the eve of exposure." The opposing opinions present an interesting contrast in approach. Sutherland, for the majority, is thinking of the right of the individual to be free from "a general, roving, offensive, inquisitorial, compulsory investigation." Cardozo, on the other hand, has in mind "the host of impoverished investors." With this difference in emphasis, the conclusion seemed inevitable to Sutherland that "an abandonment of the application was of no concern to anyone but the registrant. The possibility of any other interest in the matter," he continued, "is so shadowy, indefinite, and equivocal that it must be put out of consideration as altogether unreal."[94]

Here, it seems, is the heart of Sutherland's quarrel with government. His immersion in the individualistic ideas of previous centuries had made the community for him a shadowy, ephemeral thing with no real existence at all. Accordingly, he was bound to say:

> The action of the Commission finds no support in right principle or in law. It is wholly unreasonable and arbitrary. It violates the cardinal principle upon which the constitutional safeguards of personal liberty rests—that this shall be a government of laws—because to the precise extent that the mere will of an official or an official body is permitted to take the place of an allowable official discretion or to supplant the standing law as a rule of human conduct, the government ceases to be one of laws and becomes an autocracy.[95]

In the face of such a threat, Sutherland characteristically warned, courts "must never cease to be vigilant to detect and turn aside the danger at its beginning."[96] Nor should "the fear that some malefactor may go unwhipped of justice" stay the judges in the performance of their duty. "The philosophy that constitutional limitations . . . may be brushed aside upon the plea that good, perchance, may follow, finds no countenance in the American system of government."[97] After all, it was in the name of ending "unlawful inquisitorial investigations" that the Star Chamber had been abolished.[98]

If denunciations of autocracy and the tyranny of the

[94] *ibid.*, p. 23. [95] *ibid.*, pp. 23-24. [96] *ibid.*, p. 24. [97] *ibid.*, p. 27.
[98] *ibid.*, p. 28. Sutherland's reference to the Star Chamber provoked Cardozo to prophesy: "Historians may find hyperbole in the sanguinary simile." Sutherland's opinion in this case is more violent even than that in the *Blaisdell* case. In thought and phraseology, it closely parallels his speech to the American Bar Association in 1917.

Stuarts had any relevance in the America of 1936, they could apply only to Franklin Roosevelt and the New Deal. Even as they were uttered the Court had under consideration the case of *Carter* v. *Carter Coal Company*.[99] On its face the issue presented was quite different from that considered in the *Jones* decision. Carter was asking if the commerce clause authorized a scheme of national regulation of the coal industry. There were, however, certain obvious parallels. There was the threat of governmental power seeking to pre-empt individual prerogative by invoking such a "shadowy" and "unreal" concept as public interest. There was the resort to the "roving, offensive, inquisitorial commission." Therefore, it would seem that Sutherland could have had little disposition to view the Guffey Act with favor.

It would be misleading, however, to suggest that the opinions in the *Carter* case represent mere shadow boxing. They concern a problem quite able of its own weight to challenge the exertions of all serious thinkers on the American constitutional system. It is the problem of federalism, of centralization versus decentralization, of the commerce clause versus states' rights. These questions had been before the Court in the *Schechter* case but they were somewhat obscured by others. Furthermore, the business of marketing poultry was hardly of vital national interest. The *Carter* case, however, involved one of the nation's most basic industries. Thus the occasion was at hand where the issues could be more clearly drawn. John Dickinson in his argument for the Government well summarized the situation:

Much may turn upon the decision of this Court and upon the opinion of this Court. The issues, in a certain sense, are momentous, far more momentous than the provisions of this particular Act. The issue of federal power is here at stake—the issue of whether there lurk within the interstices of the Constitution crevices through which effective governmental ability to deal with great public questions may unconsciously have sifted away.[100]

99 298 U.S. 238 (1936).   100 *ibid.*, p. 268.

The Guffey Coal Act declared the production, distribution, and use of bituminous coal to be affected with a "national public interest," and its purpose to be the promotion of the interstate commerce of this commodity. There was further a legislative finding that the production and distribution of coal directly affected interstate commerce. Accordingly, the National Bituminous Coal Commission was created. Under its authority, the mine owners of the country were to agree to a bituminous coal code. This code was to establish regulations of wages and hours, and minimum prices, throughout the industry. To secure the compliance of all operators a sales tax was levied on all coal mined, the proceeds of which were to be refunded in case of acceptance of the code by the operator.

Before reviewing Sutherland's opinion declaring such a scheme beyond the power of Congress, it would be helpful to consider briefly the prior interpretation of the commerce clause. In general, the precedents reveal two sharply differing lines of thought. What may be described as the nationalist view was first expounded by John Marshall in the case of *Gibbons* v. *Ogden*.[101] Marshall began with a minimal definition of commerce as traffic, or buying and selling. But he hastened to add that it was "something more." This something more was said to be "intercourse," thereby bringing transportation within the clause even when unconnected with traffic. The power of Congress to "regulate" was said to be that of prescribing "the rule by which commerce is to be governed." And Congress had this authority "as absolutely as it would . . . in a single government." It was complete in itself, knowing no limitations other than those written into the Constitution.

This view of the commerce clause, with the weight of the great Chief Justice's tremendous reputation behind it, has had an enduring vitality. Under it both traffic and transportation were subject to the national authority. What of production? In 1936 the nationalist could look especially to two cases for a satisfying answer—*Swift &*

[101] 9 Wheat. 1 (1824).

Company v. *United States*,[102] decided in 1905, and *Stafford* v. *Wallace*,[103] decided in 1922. Holmes in one and Taft in the other both emphatically affirmed that production was within the reach of Congress when such activity was but a part of the "stream" of the nation's commerce. Commerce was said to be a practical conception and no "nice and technical" inquiry into the non-interstate character of some of its "necessary incidents and facilities" was to be permitted to frustrate the purpose of the framers to create a system of "national protection and control."[104]

This represents only a part of the story, however; only a lesser part, perhaps. Marshall, himself, had thought it necessary to concede that the grant to Congress did not "comprehend that commerce which is completely internal," and thirteen years after *Gibbons* v. *Ogden* it was asserted from the bench that the power must necessarily be measured by that reserved to the states.[105] This idea was brought to its highest development by the Court of 1895 which Sutherland admired so much. In the famous *Sugar Trust* case[106] decided that year, the justices held that the Sherman Anti-trust Act could not be invoked against those who had monopolized the refined sugar of the country for the purpose of *sale*. Thus, commerce in its original sense—that of buying and selling—was no longer under the control of Congress. Nor could any mere "indirect" effect, the Court held, produced by sales or production justify national action. Only transportation was undeniably within the clause. Even as to this, the power of Congress was not absolute. *Hammer* v. *Dagenhart*,[107] decided in 1918, authoritatively stated that the power of regulation did not carry with it a general authority to prohibit. And conceding that it did, if it were so used as to interfere in an area reserved to state jurisdiction, this result would render the exercise illegal.

---

102 196 U.S. 375 (1905).   103 258 U.S. 495 (1922).   104 *ibid.*, p. 519.
105 *New York* v. *Miln*, 11 Pet. 102, 139 (1837).
106 *United States* v. *E. C. Knight Co.*, 156 U.S. 1 (1895).
107 247 U.S. 251 (1918).

Thus, in 1936, the Court could find authority for a conclusion either overthrowing or sustaining the Guffey Act. Sutherland, in the years before, had generally followed the restrictive interpretation, although in the *Bedford* case,[108] it will be remembered, he had specifically asserted that acts, otherwise local, were amenable to the commerce power when part of a general plan of national scope. His senatorial speeches well show that he regarded commerce to be principally transportation[109] and he had denied from the bench that control of production could be accomplished merely because transportation followed.[110] Moreover, in 1932, he had declared that the power of Congress over foreign and interstate commerce, although given in identical terms, was not the same.[111] And, finally, he had many times accepted the continued independence and vitality of the states as a mandate of the Constitution by which all of its particular provisions were to be evaluated.

Convinced as he was of the rectitude of these propositions, it was inevitable that Sutherland should have found the Guffey Act to be invalid. Even so, his opinion gives evidence of being founded on a fresh consideration of the problem. He began by attributing to Congress the notion that there was some general federal power in existence apart from the specific grants of the Constitution, seemingly feeling that this was the basic constitutional heresy of the day. That this is a fair representation of the Congressional view may well be questioned. While Congress has no general power to legislate, still conditions of national import supply perfectly valid occasions for the use of such power as it does have. And this may be said to

[108] *Bedford Cut Stone Co.* v. *Journeymen Stone Cutters Ass'n*, 274 U.S. 37 (1927).

[109] See especially 51 *Cong. Rec.* 12807-12808 (1914).

[110] *Anderson* v. *Shipowners Ass'n*, 272 U.S. 359 (1926).

[111] *Atlantic Cleaners & Dyers* v. *United States*, 286 U.S. 427 (1932). For a history of how this idea came to be inserted into judicial interpretation of the Constitution, see Edward S. Corwin, *The Commerce Clause versus States Rights*, Oxford University Press, 1936, pp. 23-52.

have been the limit of the Congressional claim. Further, Congress had specifically linked its authority over the chaotic conditions in the coal industry to the commerce clause but Sutherland dismissed this as pure "assumption" and "opinion" which could not be controlling on the courts.

The nub of this dispute is not the existence of an authority to legislate for the general welfare. That there is no such authority must be conceded. But even so, must not the general welfare be considered to provide a light for Congress—and the Court—in the exercise of their functions? Sutherland's answer to this query is perhaps better stated in the *Jones* case than anywhere else. Such conceptions as "general welfare" or "public interest" have no light to shed! They are themselves but invisible phantoms lurking in the darkness of the shadow.

The great mass of legislative power, Sutherland went on to explain, was found in the states, indestructible and supreme in their sphere. The Constitution demanded their preservation. Hence it could not be construed in such a way "as to reduce them to mere geographical subdivisions of the national domain."[112] If this seemed extreme in the circumstances, it was necessary only to recall "that every journey to a forbidden end begins with the first step."[113] And those ends not recognized by the Constitution must be regarded as forbidden for that instrument "is in every real sense a law—the lawmakers being the people themselves, in whom under our system all political power and sovereignty primarily resides."[114] Further, "the Constitution speaks for itself in terms so plain that to misunderstand their import is not rationally possible."[115] It was not necessary to add that the judges, far from thwarting the popular will, were its defenders against a treacherous revolt. They would do their duty where others had failed.

Did Congress, by virtue of the commerce clause, have the authority to prescribe a comprehensive scheme of

[112] *Carter* v. *Carter Coal Co., supra* note 99, p. 296.
[113] *ibid.*, p. 295.   [114] *ibid.*, p. 296.   [115] *ibid.*

regulation for the coal industry? Sutherland's emphatic negative answer is couched in the boldest terms. He appealed to the great nationalist hero, John Marshall. Commerce, Sutherland conceded, did indeed include not only transportation, but the purchase and sale, and exchange of commodities between the citizens of the different states as Marshall had said. But Marshall had never ruled that production was within the ambit of the clause. Nor had he left any doubt that the discretion of Congress in the exercise of its powers applied only to *means*, not *ends*. "To an end not within the terms of the Constitution," Sutherland emphasized, "all ways are closed."[116]

The argument does not end here, however. It can be conceded that mining is a local operation; still, it obviously affects interstate sales and regulation of the one may be absolutely essential to a regulation of the other. To this argument, Sutherland responded that the "extent of the effect" produced was not relevant.

If the production by one man of a single ton of coal intended for interstate sale and shipment, and actually so sold and shipped, affects interstate commerce indirectly, the effect does not become direct by multiplying the tonnage or increasing the number of men employed, or adding to the expense of the business, or by all combined.[117]

This is to say that wages and hours, because of their local character, can never affect commerce any way but "indirectly." Hence, there can not be, whatever the extent of this effect, the direct relationship which authorized the intervention of Congress. This involved Sutherland in a singular contradiction when he came to consider the price-fixing provisions of the Act, which, since they applied only to sales and not to production, were not forbidden—at least by the commerce clause. Here he was faced with the declaration of Congress that these provisions were to be regarded as separable in the event other sections were voided. Price-fixing, however, was to Sutherland quite as

116 *ibid.*, p. 291.   117 *ibid.*, p. 308.

objectionable as interferences with the reserved rights of
the states—a fact to which the *Adkins* case and others bear
eloquent witness. Yet, this interference with the natural
desires of the mine owners could not be frontally assailed
since Roberts, whose support it was necessary to retain for
a majority, had only recently declared that the question of
price regulation was one for the legislature.[118] In this
dilemma, Sutherland sought his way out by asserting that,
since prices and wages were so closely related, Congress
could not make the two sections separable however much it
tried! This being the case, the price provisions had to fall
with the rest of the Act, making unnecessary a struggle
over the question of their validity standing alone.

Unlike the *Schechter* decision, the *Carter* case involved
an industry vital to the very existence of interstate commerce and this was known long before John L. Lewis
rendered it observable to even the dullest intelligence. It
therefore presented the country with the most decisive
possible denial that the Constitution contained within its
grants any authority for meeting the most serious of the
problems facing the nation in 1936. The opinion, both in
the expressions it employed and in the result it achieved,
struck the idea of American nationalism a blow such as it
has seldom, if ever, received. In this connection, Sutherland's explanation of the constitutional crisis to an English friend is highly suggestive. Only a day or two after
the argument in the *Carter* case closed, he wrote his friend:

I note what you say about our action in declaring certain laws
unconstitutional. The difficulty is that you do not give sufficient
consideration to the difference between our government and that
of Great Britain. The United States is made up of forty-eight
different states, each of them possessing, so far as its own affairs
are concerned, supreme authority. *The United States itself is a
creature of the Constitution,* and has only the powers which the
Constitution either expressly or by necessary implication grants.
The written Constitution is itself a law, and declares in precise
words that it is the *supreme* law. The fact that it is made by the

118 *Nebbia* v. *New York, supra* note 51, p. 537.

people of all the states instead of by some legislative body does not make it any the less a law. When a case is brought before our court, it is the most normal judicial function to determine what the law is; and if an act of legislation (either a state law or an act of Congress) conflicts with a rule laid down in the Constitution, the court must say so or be guilty of failing to perform the duty which it has solemnly taken an oath to discharge.

Of course, Parliament is supreme in Great Britain; but you haven't there a galaxy of independent states whose rights in many respects have never been surrendered. *A parallel situation would be to say that Parliament had supreme power to pass all sorts of legislation absolutely binding upon the various dominions, whether they dealt with their local concerns or not.* However, the story is a long one, and I must not weary you with it.[119]

4.

Two weeks after the *Carter* case, on June 1, the Court, following Sutherland's opinion in the *Adkins* case, held invalid a New York minimum wage law for women.[120] Even Hamilton Fish protested at this, making the practical observation that the decision would cost the Republicans one million votes in the November elections.[121] With the approach of the quadrennial referendum, what the two parties proposed to do, if anything, about the constitutional crisis was the vital question of the day. The Republicans made clear that they would support no tampering with the Court, asserting that regulations of wages and working conditions by the states was still, somehow, constitutionally possible.[122] For their part the Democrats pledged themselves, in spite of the Court's pronouncements, to continue the New Deal on all fronts. Should it prove necessary, they proposed to have the people "clarify" the meaning of the Constitution for the justices by means of

[119] Sutherland to Dr. S. Hughes, March 16, 1936. *Cf.* Sutherland's opinions in *United States* v. *Curtiss-Wright Export Corp.*, 299 U.S. 304 (1936) and *United States* v. *Belmont*, 301 U.S. 324 (1937), for view to the contrary when the foreign relations power was in issue. The italics are mine.

[120] *Morehead* v. *New York ex rel Tipaldo*, 298 U.S. 587 (1936).

[121] *New York Times*, June 3, 1936.   [122] *ibid.*, June 12, 1936.

an amendment.[123] But amendment or no amendment, it was plain that neither they nor their leader considered the last word to have been spoken.

Something resembling the final verdict did come on November 3rd. If the overwhelming Roosevelt triumph signified anything, it meant that the American people did not intend that government should resume its former role merely of arbiter and policeman. But was it likely that this message would penetrate the marble walls of the Supreme Court building? All that had gone before hardly warranted an affirmative answer. Constitutional questions, Sutherland had said in the *Adkins* case, could not be resolved by a counting of heads.

But even Sutherland did not relish the job of standing athwart the popular will. Writing Senator Bailey of North Carolina in the middle of January 1937, he remarked:

There is a more or less prevalent opinion abroad in the land that some judges are ruthless from pure depravity, and are indifferent to what others think about their decisions. There may be such, although I doubt it. At any rate, I am not one of them. I think almost every man prefers approval rather than disapproval of what he does. And there is nothing wrong in the sentiment provided what he does is not influenced by his desire for approval or his fear of disapproval.[124]

On February 5, the President at last revealed his hand. On that date he asked Congress for authority to enlarge the Court if none of the justices over seventy were willing to accommodate by resigning. His original justification of this plan was that the heavy and important work of the Court was generally too exhausting after the age of seventy had been reached. Sutherland at this time was just short of his seventy-fifth birthday. Not being strong physically, he was ready to resign and would have done so but for the Roosevelt attack.[125] His resolution to continue so

---

[123] *ibid.*, June 26, 1936.

[124] Sutherland to Josiah W. Bailey, January 13, 1937.

[125] "It was so good of you to write me about my retirement. I should have gone nearly a year ago had it not been for the fight on the Court,

long as the Court was under fire must have been strengthened by the numerous appeals received from all over the country urging that course. Among them was a testimonial from sixty-one citizens of Poughkeepsie, New York, who wrote to "express our appreciation and admiration of you and your coadjutors, and of your just and fair decisions and to beg you on no account to resign from the bench now at the height of your power and usefulness."[126]

As the battle developed, Sutherland never publicly abandoned the customary reticence of the judiciary on political questions. But, privately, he encouraged as best he could the opponents and received from them reports of the latest decisions of strategy.[127] The most eloquent denunciations of the plan were those of Sutherland's friend, Senator Bailey. On February 13, the Senator delivered a radio speech defending the Court against every charge. It had not usurped legislative power, nor had it rendered any ruling not in accord with the Constitution. The function of the Court, Bailey said,

is truth and righteousness. . . . It has no earthly power. . . . The Supreme Court has neither purse nor sword. It can not defend itself even against criticism. Its decrees prevail only by reason of the spiritual appeal of justice to the human heart—It has guarded the rights of the people, it has preserved the rights of the states, it has maintained the rights and powers of the Union—and all without purse, without patronage, without propaganda, without force; but not without power—not without the power in it and in ourselves which makes for righteousness.[128]

Much impressed by Bailey's remarks, Sutherland wrote the Senator a letter of gratitude: "I am unable to refrain from breaking the silence which is supposed to enshroud

---

which I am glad to say is now a thing of the past, and which I think will never be revived." Sutherland to a Mr. Preston (initials unknown), January 18, 1938.

[126] Martha I. Young (and others) to Sutherland, March (date not given) 1937.

[127] Besides Bailey, Sutherland corresponded over the Court question with Senator Tom Connally of Texas.

[128] 81 *Cong. Rec.* (Appendix) 209 (1937).

the judiciary to tell you how deeply your words have moved me. I am quite sincere in saying that in my judgment there never has been a better speech."[129]

Meanwhile the business of the Court moved on. Once more the question of the validity of a minimum wage for women was to be considered. When the decision[130] came on March 29, it was revealed that the conservatives had lost Mr. Justice Roberts, and with him their majority. Out of respect to his recent concurrence in the *Morehead* case, that decision was distinguished and Sutherland's opinion in the *Adkins* case made the object of attack. While recognizing "the earnestness and the vigor which characterized" that opinion, the Court nevertheless declared it could no longer be followed.

The issue of wage-fixing was, of course, a vital one to Sutherland and its authorization by the Court could not be witnessed in silence. Yet his protest at the overruling of one of his greatest efforts was on more general grounds. The burning question of the day was the role of the judiciary in the American constitutional system. The opponents of the Court had subjected it to a severe indictment. The most serious charge was that the Court itself had been guilty of acting unconstitutionally. It had converted itself, so it was claimed, into a superlegislature which had usurped Congressional prerogative and arrogated to itself the right to rule. The clincher to the argument was sought in the general disagreement, on or off the Court, as to the correctness of its rulings. If, it was urged, a statute could be declared void only if it was clearly so beyond all reasonable doubt, then the sizable and respectable array of opinion which considered valid the questioned enactments was proof positive that a reasonable doubt did exist as to their invalidity.

It is as a defense, then, of his entire judicial career that Sutherland's opinion in the *West Coast Hotel* case is to be read. As such, it is perhaps the clearest statement of

[129] Sutherland to Bailey, February 22, 1937.
[130] *West Coast Hotel Co.* v. *Parrish*, 300 U.S. 379 (1937).

judicial prerogative produced by the great struggle of the Roosevelt era. Basically, it is grounded on a conception of the Constitution as a grant of power from the people. Aside from this grant there was no authority at all to govern. Moreover, the people had not surrendered a general power to govern but only authority to act in certain specified instances. And even this authority had not been given in one combined mass but in nicely separated lots. Thus the people had "created three separate, distinct, independent and coequal departments of government." Sutherland continued: "It seems unnecessary to repeat that the powers of these departments are different and are to be exercised independently. . . . Each of the departments is an agent of its creator; and one department is not and cannot be the agent of another. Each is answerable to its creator for what it does, and not to another agent."[131]

With power thus distributed in isolated packages, it was not likely to be dangerous to the liberties of the individual so long as it was prevented from coming together and uniting in a single, unified onslaught. Here is where judges were to come into the picture. "Some agency," Sutherland said, "of necessity, must have the power to say the final word as to the validity of a statute assailed as unconstitutional."[132] The identity of this agency had not been left in doubt. "The Constitution makes it clear that the power has been intrusted to this Court when the question arises in a controversy within its jurisdiction."[133] The Court, then, was an agent of the people, charged with the duty of overseeing the other two branches to make certain that they heeded the popular mandate.

This much, however, was only part of the argument. Juvenal's eternally pertinent query—*quis custodiet ipsos custodes?*—posed a problem which had to be considered. It was this problem which had evoked Stone's searing language in the AAA case. "The only check upon our own exercise of power," he had declared, "is our own sense of

---

[131] *ibid.*, p. 405.   [132] *ibid.*, p. 401.   [133] *ibid.*

self-restraint."[134] Sutherland now rejoined that such a notion was "both ill considered and mischievous."[135] Why? Because "self-restraint belongs in the domain of will and not of judgment."[136] It was all strangely reminiscent of the classic pronouncement of John Marshall in *Osborn* v. *U.S. Bank*.[137] "Judicial power as contradistinguished from the power of the laws, has no existence. Courts are the mere instruments of the law, and can will nothing. . . . Judicial power is never exercised for the purpose of giving effect to the will of the judge."

A judge, then, was only a conduit by which the law—in the case of the Constitution, the *people's law*—was transmitted and applied to particular cases. Hence, so long as he remained faithful to the judicial oath, he was in theory and in fact utterly incapable of violating the Constitution! That could take place only when he fell so low as to project his *will*—or his own personal feelings—into the case. And the fact that this took the form of self-restraint could not save it from being labeled an usurpation of power. Thus, if the Court had become a superlegislature, it was not the work of Sutherland and his colleagues on the Right, but of the erstwhile dissenters themselves.

The judicial function, the Justice insisted, "does not include the power of amendment under the guise of interpretation." He continued: "If the Constitution, intelligently and reasonably construed in the light of these principles, stands in the way of desirable legislation, the blame must rest upon that instrument and not upon the court for enforcing it according to its terms. The remedy in that situation—and the only true remedy is to amend the Constitution."[138]

The twelfth day of April, however, revealed that the Chief Justice and four of his colleagues had sought another solution of the dilemma, whether true or not. A new reading

---

[134] *United States* v. *Butler*, 297 U.S. 1, 79 (1936).

[135] *West Coast Hotel Co.* v. *Parrish, supra* note 130, p. 402.

[136] *ibid.*   [137] 9 *Wheat.* 738, 866 (1824).

[138] *West Coast Hotel Co.* v. *Parrish, supra* note 130, p. 404.

of the Constitution was in evidence as the Court, on that day, sustained the National Labor Relations Act.[139] Congress, the Court now held, could not be denied the power to control intrastate activities "if they have such a close and substantial relation to interstate commerce that their control is essential or appropriate to protect that commerce."[140] Further, the opinion of the Chief Justice carried with it the first recognition by the Court that liberty was capable of destruction by agencies other than government and that political power could promote, by positive measures, its wider diffusion and enjoyment.[141]

McReynolds voiced the inevitable dissent of the unconvinced and unrepentant four to these propositions. Sutherland's role on this historic day was to make the conservative attack on the application of the provisions of the Labor Act to the Associated Press. The Labor Board had ordered that body to reinstate an editorial employee discharged for union activity. The AP claimed that, thus construed, the Act was a violation of the First Amendment, a plea Sutherland was quick to uphold.

His opinion quickly reached the crucial issue—one not so evident in 1937 as a decade later, but known to Edmund Burke as long ago as 1790. "Liberty, when men act in bodies, is Power," the great Traditionalist had declared.[142] This was clear to Sutherland, too, as the following words well indicate:

For many years there has been contention between labor and capital. Labor has become highly organized in a wide effort to secure and preserve its rights. The daily news with respect to labor disputes is now of vast proportions; and clearly a considerable part of petitioner's editorial service must be devoted to that subject. Such news is not only of great public interest, but an unbiased version of it is of the utmost public concern. To give a group of employers on the one hand, or a labor organization on the other,

---

[139] *National Labor Relations Board* v. *Jones & Laughlin Steel Corp.*, 301 U.S. 1 (1937).
[140] *ibid.*, p. 37.
[141] *ibid.*, pp. 33-34.
[142] *Reflections on the Revolution in France* (Everyman's Ed.), p. 9.

power of control over such a service is obviously to endanger the fairness and accuracy of the service.[143]

Aside from the issue immediately to be decided, Sutherland's opinion is of exceptional interest as a recognition on his part that judges acting alone were unable to stem the march of authoritarianism. A quarter of a century before he had declared that persistent majorities must have their way or else anarchy would be the result.[144] Even though in dissent at the moment and unconvinced as ever, his remarks show that he no longer thought of the Court as being able to save the people from themselves. Accordingly, it is to them that his appeal is specifically addressed. There is a moving reminder that

freedom is not a mere intellectual abstraction; and it is not merely a word to adorn an oration upon occasions of patriotic rejoicing. It is an intensely practical reality, capable of concrete enjoyment in a multitude of ways day by day.[145]

The authoritarian flood had breached the dam erected by the Constitution. Yet, in itself, this was a relatively small matter. The serious thing was "the sinister menace to the security of the dam, which those living in the valley will do well to heed."[146] Judges, acting as the sluice gate operators, could do their part but the master controls were in other hands, those of the American people. To them, then, went this final fervent plea for vigilance:

Do the people of this land—in the providence of God, favored, as they sometimes boast, above all others in the plenitude of their liberties—desire to preserve those so carefully protected by the First Amendment: liberty of religious worship, freedom of speech and of the press, and the right as free men peaceably to assemble and petition their government for a redress of griev-

[143] *Associated Press* v. *National Labor Relations Board*, 301 U.S. 103, 138 (1937).

[144] There was an important qualification, however. Majorities must be "acting within the scope of their legitimate functions." *The Law and the People*, Sen. Doc. No. 328, 63d Cong., 2d Sess. 7 (1913).

[145] *Associated Press* v. *National Labor Relations Board*, *supra* note 143, p. 137.

[146] *ibid.*, p. 136.

ances? If so, let them withstand all *beginnings* of encroachment. For the saddest epitaph which can be carved in memory of a ravished liberty is that it was lost because its possessors failed to stretch forth a saving hand while yet there was time.[147]

[147] *ibid.*, p. 141. While Sutherland was never convinced that the new reading of the Constitution was admissible, his expressions in later cases were markedly temperate in tone. Thus, in *Carmichael et al.* v. *Southern Coal & Coke Co.*, 301 U.S. 495 (1937), and *Steward Machine Co.* v. *Davis*, 301 U.S. 548 (1937), he agreed that states might tax employers for unemployment relief and that the Social Security Act was within the powers of Congress. His protest was directed solely to the administrative features of each statute under review. In his private correspondence, the Justice displayed no excited alarm but he was certain that some day the trend must be reversed. On April 21, 1937, for example, he wrote to his friend, Dean Bates of the Michigan Law School: "The world is passing through an uncomfortable experience; and in many respects will have to retrace its steps with painful effort. The tendency of many governments is in the direction of destroying individual initiative, self-reliance, and other cardinal virtues which I was always taught were necessary to develop a real democracy. The notion that the individual is not to have the full reward of what he does well, and is not to bear the responsibility for what he does badly, apparently, is becoming part of our present philosophy of government."

6

PERSONAL LIBERTY
AND NATIONAL SURVIVAL

GEORGE SUTHERLAND contributed so much to the
political structure which was shattered by the constitutional revolution of 1937 that history must inevitably
identify him with a lost cause. His last years on the Court,
however, were not always dimmed by the clouds of defeat.
Indeed, few American judges have ever enjoyed such a
spectacular success as he achieved in the cases dealing with
the foreign relations power. His influence in this field
today overshadows that of all other justices and it is not
likely that it will ever be diminished. Likewise, Sutherland
had a leading role in another major development which
has a continuing significance—the enlargement, both in
meaning and application, of the Bill of Rights. This
chapter will deal with his contribution in these two fields.
The coupling of the two is by no means arbitrary, for
certainly one of the great problems of the present era is
how the liberty of the individual can be maintained when
a nation is acutely conscious of the pangs of insecurity.

Thus far the emphasis in this discussion has been given
to Sutherland's concern for the freedom of the individual
from the "meddlesome interference" of the state in economic matters. It is hardly necessary to add that he was
possessed of an equal concern for the preservation and
enhancement of those intimate personal liberties mentioned
with particularity in the Bill of Rights. Sutherland, of
course, was unwilling to admit that the liberty of contract
and the freedom to dispose of and control one's property
were any less personal or any less vital to the individual
than, for example, freedom from arbitrary arrest.[1] Despite

[1] "The assertion, which is so often and so loosely made, that the courts
in their decisions respecting the Constitution exalt the rights of property

his opposition, however, the distinction was made. The result has been what Sutherland would doubtless have considered a paradox. As the power of the state has grown with respect to the control and direction of the economy, at the same time, the Supreme Court has encircled the individual with new protections in the enjoyment of his civil rights. Richer meanings have been given to old freedoms and the Bill of Rights has largely been made applicable to state action.[2]

In this general extension of the blessings of liberty Sutherland had an important part. The problem of liberty for him was procedural as well as substantive. The forms of Anglo-Saxon jurisprudence seemed to him to have proved their worth. Furthermore, the Constitution specifically commanded certain of them—trial by jury, for example. Thus, when one Colts was indicted for driving an automobile in the District of Columbia so recklessly "as to endanger property and individuals," Sutherland quite readily affirmed the defendant's contention that the offense was not a petty one which lent itself to summary adjudication but was of such a serious nature as to require the agreement of twelve men before conviction.[3]

---

above the rights of man makes a strong appeal to the emotions, but it is untrue in fact and misleading in what it implies. There is nothing more obstructive to the process of reaching just conclusions than catch phrases of this character in which plausible sophistry is made to do the duty of passionless logic. There is no such thing as rights of property apart from the rights of man. The vice and the fallacy of the phrase consist in the suggestion which it makes to the average mind that property as a distinct entity may have rights antagonistic to the rights of man. The language of the fifth amendment is, 'No *person* shall be *deprived* of life, liberty, or *property* without due process of law.' The thing protected by the Constitution is not the right of property but the right of a person to property, and this right to property is of the same character as the right to life and liberty." George Sutherland, "The Courts and The Constitution," Sen. Doc. No. 970, 62d Cong., 3d Sess. 15 (1912).

[2] On the history of this development, see Charles Warren, "The New Liberty Under the Fourteenth Amendment," 39 *Harv. L. Rev.* 431 (1926); John Raeburn Green, "Liberty Under the Fourteenth Amendment," 27 *Wash. U. L. Q.* 497 (1942).

[3] *District of Columbia* v. *Colts*, 282 U.S. 63 (1930).

A more questionable example of Sutherland's devotion to the jury system and one which demonstrates just how inflexible constitutional guaranties were for him is furnished by the case of *Dimick* v. *Schiedt*.[4] In issue was the Seventh Amendment, which provides that "in suits at common law, where the value in controversy shall exceed twenty dollars, the right of trial by jury shall be preserved." Schiedt had obtained a judgment for $500 in a lower federal court. The trial judge regarded this award by the jury as so inadequate that he was ready to accede to Schiedt's motion for a new trial. However, when Dimick agreed to pay $1500, the judge declined to grant the motion. Schiedt's consent to this arrangement was neither asked nor given, and he persisted in his effort to secure authorization for a new proceeding, arguing that the judge could not take away from him his right to have a fair-minded jury assess his damages.

The trial judge obviously had in mind the salutary objective of avoiding the needless expense and delay of further litigation. He had also to bolster him the familiar practice which allowed a judge by the threat of a new trial to obtain a *plaintiff's* consent to a *reduction* in an award deemed to be excessive. The acquiescence of the defendant in such a case is immaterial. These considerations, however, were not convincing to Sutherland. Procedural liberal though he was, he strongly argued that the Constitution required a jury verdict when required by the common law as it existed at the time of the adoption of the Amendment—not that law as it exists today. Thus, when a part of the common law is incorporated by reference in the Constitution, it immediately loses all capacity for growth and flexibility. Once this was determined, the result was easy. The procedure of the trial judge being unknown in 1791, it could not be admitted one hundred and forty years later.

Stone, in dissent, asserted that his adversary had resorted for the materials of his decision to "the legal scrap heap of a century and a half ago."[5] He called attention to

---

[4] 293 U.S. 474 (1935).　　　　　　[5] *ibid.*, p. 495.

one of Sutherland's earlier opinions [6] which had urged that the common law be adapted to modern life " in accordance with present day standards of wisdom and justice rather than in accordance with some outworn and antiquated rule of the past." Sutherland's response, of course, was that the common law is one thing and the Constitution another. So far as the rules of the common law were incorporated in the Constitution, they took on the changeless characteristics of the Constitution itself.

In *Patton* v. *United States*[7] Sutherland had further opportunity to state his views on the jury question. The question then before the Court arose out of a defendant's agreement to continue his trial with eleven jurors, one having been disqualified by illness midway in the proceedings. After a conviction by the reduced number of jurors, the defendant argued on appeal that the Constitution established the jury "as a part of the frame of government" and it was not possible, therefore, for it to be dispensed with in the trial of a case, even with the consent of the accused. Before disposing of this problem, Sutherland had first to announce that the "constitutional jury means twelve men as though that number had been specifically named."[8] To the objection that the change from twelve to eleven was so slight as to be trivial, he rejoined characteristically: "To uphold the voluntary reduction of a jury from twelve to eleven upon the ground that the reduction—though it destroys the jury of the Constitution—is only a slight reduction, is not to interpret that instrument but to disregard it. It is not our province to measure the extent to which the Constitution has been contravened and ignore the violation, if in our opinion, it is not, relatively, as bad as it might have been."[9]

The argument that trial by full jury could not be waived nevertheless failed because it was said to be a

---

[6] *Funk* v. *United States*, 290 U.S. 371, 382 (1933). In this case, Sutherland wrote an extremely liberal opinion asserting the competence of a wife to testify in behalf of her husband in a criminal case. The common law rule was otherwise.

[7] 281 U.S. 276 (1930).   [8] *ibid.*, p. 292.   [9] *ibid.*

privilege, not an indispensable governmental institution. Accordingly, just as a trial could be dispensed with altogether by a plea of guilty, so the jury's functions could be assumed by eleven men or by the judge himself when the defendant gave an "express and intelligent consent," but only then. There must always be, Sutherland warned, "a caution increasing in degree as the offenses dealt with increase in gravity."[10]

Other cases demonstrate Sutherland's great concern for the preservation of personal liberty. His approach was always one of emphasis on the unequal nature of the struggle waged by government and the individual. With all the resources of society at its command, government was under an overwhelming obligation to proceed with the utmost fairness and justice whoever the accused might be. Thus, when a Government attorney took liberties with the truth in his summation to the jury, Sutherland ordered a new trial:

The United States Attorney is the representative not of an ordinary party to a controversy but of a sovereignty whose obligation to govern impartially is as compelling as its obligation to govern at all; and whose interest therefore in a criminal prosecution is not that it shall win a case, but that justice shall be done. . . . He may prosecute with earnestness and vigor—indeed, he should do so. But while he may strike hard blows, he is not at liberty to strike foul ones. It is as much his duty to refrain from improper methods calculated to produce a wrongful conviction as it is to use every legitimate means to bring about a just one.[11]

The safety of the individual lay, then, in the perfect and even application of the *law*. The peril latent in such an attitude is illustrated by a case[12] in which Sutherland seems definitely to have failed as a guardian of liberty. It concerned the Georgia conviction of a Negro Communist

[10] *ibid.*, p. 313. Besides making possible the waiver of jury trial in the federal courts, the Patton case has also been used to sustain the validity of waiver of indictment by a grand jury. See *United States* v. *Gill,* 55 Fed. (2d) 399 (1931) and note (1948), 21 *So. Calif. L. Rev.* 193. See also Rule 7 of the Federal Rules of Criminal Procedure.

[11] *Berger* v. *United States,* 295 U.S. 78, 88 (1935).

[12] *Herndon* v. *Georgia,* 295 U.S. 441 (1935).

agitator whose offense was an "attempt to incite insurrection." At the trial, the court had given in its instructions to the jury an unexceptionable exposition of the "clear and present danger" doctrine; but in the Georgia appellate tribunal's review, a new standard was introduced—one that sanctioned the conviction of the defendant if his remarks were intended to achieve an insurrection "at any time." At this, the defendant's counsel made the objection that the statute as thus interpreted was unconstitutional. Sutherland's reply for the Supreme Court to this argument was distressingly technical. The objection came, he said, too late to be heard because the defendant had been amply warned by decisions of the Georgia Supreme Court in *other* cases that it would not follow the "clear and present danger" standard.

This Mr. Justice Cardozo hotly denied. The cases which Sutherland thought should have been so plain in their meaning to the defendant proved to be not crystal clear even to the judges. In any event, they were not agreed as to just what the defendant might have deduced from them. The main point of Cardozo's dissent was the unreasonableness in requiring a defendant to protest a ruling that had not been made. He challenged as "novel doctrine" the proposition that "a defendant who has had the benefit of all he asks, and indeed of a good deal more, must place a statement on the record that if some other court at some other time shall read the statute differently, there will be a denial of liberties that at the moment of the protest are unchallenged and intact."[13]

2.

Sutherland's insistence on the traditional procedures of the law was accompanied by an equal emphasis on pre-

[13] *ibid.*, p. 448. Herndon finally won his release by a habeas corpus proceeding. See *Herndon* v. *Lowry*, 301 U.S. 242 (1937). Sutherland joined in Van Devanter's dissent. Similarly, it should be noted that he dissented from the Court's holding in *Near* v. *Minnesota*, 283 U.S. 697 (1931), where a criminal libel statute was overthrown as an unconstitutional interference with freedom of speech.

serving constitutional guaranties in fact as well as in form. In the first of the celebrated *Scottsboro* cases,[14] the Court was faced with just such a problem, and it was Sutherland who wrote the opinion setting aside the Alabama proceedings on the grounds that the right to counsel had been recognized in such a manner as really not to provide the defendant with a fair trial. Although well known, the facts will bear repetition.

Powell was one of nine Negro boys charged with raping two white girls. On the day of the alleged offense the Negroes were on a freight train moving through Alabama. On the same train were a number of white boys and the two white girls. A fight between the Negroes and the white boys took place with the result that the latter were thrown off the train. It was alleged that the attacks on the girls occurred immediately afterwards. Meanwhile, the white youths had sought the aid of a sheriff's posse. As a result, the train was met at Scottsboro and the Negroes seized.

Sutherland's opinion makes very real the tension which prevailed in the following days. The whole trial was conducted at the point of a soldier's bayonet. The Justice's description of the affair follows:

> It is perfectly apparent that the proceedings from beginning to end, took place in an atmosphere of tense, hostile, and excited public sentiment. During the entire time, the defendants were closely confined or were under military guard. The record does not disclose their ages, except that one of them was nineteen; but the record clearly indicates that most, if not all, of them were youthful, and they are constantly referred to as "the boys." They were ignorant and illiterate.[15]

The plea of the defendants was that they had been denied due process of law in that they had not been accorded the assistance of counsel of their own choice. Sutherland's first task, then, was to dispose of the objection that due process could not include the right of counsel. The argument ran that, since in respect to the federal government, the Sixth Amendment specifically included such a

14 *Powell* v. *Alabama*, 287 U.S. 45 (1932).   15 *ibid.*, pp. 51-52.

guarantee, it was not part of the due process of the Fifth Amendment, there being no superfluous language in the Constitution. And if not a part of the Fifth Amendment, it could not be encompassed by the same words in the Fourteenth. The Justice conceded the force of this reasoning but replied that "it must yield to more compelling considerations," such, for instance, as the violation of those "fundamental principles of liberty and justice which lie at the base of all our civil and political institutions."[16] By requiring of the state courts that their procedures satisfy the federal judiciary in certain essentials, Sutherland greatly facilitated the development of the new liberty which gives the nation a bill of rights against state action. *Powell* v. *Alabama* will always remain one of its principal bulwarks.[17]

The basis for federal jurisdiction having been established, Sutherland next addressed himself to the question of whether or not the assistance of counsel had been denied Powell. The record showed that at the arraignment, the court, assuming without inquiry that the defendants were unable or not inclined to produce a lawyer of their own selection, had appointed "all the members of the bar" to represent them. It was not until the morning of the trial six days later that one of the local lawyers was made definitely responsible for the defense. This arrangement Sutherland dismissed "as little more than an expansive gesture."[18] He thus condemned the whole affair: "The defendants, young, ignorant, illiterate, surrounded by hostile sentiment, haled back and forth under guard of soldiers,

---

[16] *ibid.*, p. 67 quoting from *Herbert* v. *Louisiana*, 272 U.S. 312, 316 (1926).

[17] In the light of the later cases of *Palko* v. *Connecticut*, 302 U.S. 319 (1937) and *Betts* v. *Brady*, 316 U.S. 455 (1942), it can not be said that by the Powell decision, the absolute guarantee of counsel in the Sixth Amendment was absorbed into the Fourteenth. Counsel was necessary because in the circumstances prevailing, a fair hearing would have otherwise been impossible. But this is not inevitably so. See *Betts* v. *Brady, supra.* See also *Carter* v. *Illinois*, 329 U.S. 173 (1947), and *Foster* v. *Illinois*, 332 U.S. 134 (1947).

[18] *Powell* v. *Alabama, supra* note 14, p. 56.

charged with an atrocious crime regarded with especial horror in the community where they were to be tried, were thus put in peril of their lives within a few moments after counsel for the first time charged with any degree of responsibility began to represent them."[19] The Justice demanded that counsel be made available while there was yet time for inquiry and reflection as to the best possible defense. Any other course was "not to proceed promptly in the calm spirit of regulated justice but to go forward with the haste of the mob."[20]

Sutherland was the Court's spokesman in yet another step in the broadening of the liberty protected by the Fourteenth Amendment. The occasion was the case of *Grosjean* v. *American Press Company*,[21] where the Court overthrew a Huey Long license tax on Louisiana newspapers of over 20,000 circulation. The tax was measured by the receipts from advertising. Liberally interpreting the *Powell* case, Sutherland asserted:

> We concluded that certain fundamental rights, safeguarded by the first eight amendments against federal action, were also safeguarded against state action by the due process of law clause of the Fourteenth Amendment, and among them the fundamental right of the accused to the aid of counsel in a criminal prosecution.
>
> That freedom of speech and of the press are rights of the same fundamental character, safeguarded by the due process of law clause of the Fourteenth Amendment against abridgment by state legislation, has likewise been settled by a series of decisions of this court. . . .[22]

The question, therefore, was whether the Louisiana tax amounted to an abridgment of the freedom of the press. In answer, Sutherland concluded that the purpose of the First Amendment was to bar the adoption of "any form of previous restraint upon printed publications, or their

---

19 *ibid.*, pp. 57-58.   20 *ibid.*, p. 59.   21 297 U.S. 233 (1936).

22 *ibid.*, pp. 243-244. The decisions Sutherland referred to are *Gitlow* v. *New York*, 268 U.S. 652 (1925) and *Near* v. *Minnesota*, 283 U.S. 697 (1931). He also included, inferentially, *Stromberg* v. *California*, 283 U.S. 359 (1931).

circulation. . . ."[23] This was not to suggest that newspapers were immune from taxation. The tax was bad, said Sutherland, because "in the light of its history and of its present setting, it is seen to be a deliberate and calculated device in the guise of a tax to limit the circulation of information to which the public is entitled in virtue of the constitutional guarantees. The free press stands as one of the great interpreters between the government and the people. To allow it to be fettered is to fetter ourselves."[24] The vital interest at stake, Sutherland asserted, was the "natural right" of a people to be informed about "the doings or misdoings" of their rulers. Whatever other good might be achieved from a free press, its greatest utility was the protection it offered to the individual in his never ending struggle with organized society.

3.

In his approach to the problem of liberty—indeed, in his approach to all constitutional questions—Sutherland gave abundant evidence that he considered the limits of the Constitution to be absolute and inflexible. On several notable occasions, however, when constitutional rights were arrayed against the supreme duty of the nation to survive, he unhesitatingly chose national survival as the absolute to which even the most cherished constitutional principles must yield. Ironically, it was by this adventure in constitutional relativism that Sutherland achieved perhaps the most enduring success of his career. Obviously, only the most intense conviction that American nationalism was a supreme good could have persuaded him, inflexible constitutionalist that he was, to forsake his usual absolutist views. The roots of his consuming attachment to this country are not difficult to find. There was his own spectacular reenactment of the traditional American success story. Doubtless, his experience fostered the notion that here at last was a country in which the individual with ability and

[23] *Grosjean* v. *American Press Company, supra* note 21, p. 249.
[24] *ibid.*, p. 250.

industry could not be prevented from having his just deserts. More than that, there was the solution afforded by the Constitution of the seemingly insoluble political riddle, the problem of authority. Only in America had there been attained that "happy equipoise where liberty and authority exactly counterbalance."[25]

Many times, both before and after his appointment to the bench, Sutherland gave strong expression of his ardent patriotism. On the occasion of the Independence Day celebration in Provo in 1888, he aroused the enthusiasm of his hearers with an appeal that rang the traditional changes—the wisdom of the Fathers and Scott's lines from *Marmion*.[26] Years later, he stoutly opposed an honor for Robert E. Lee on the ground that the great Virginian had devoted his talents to the destruction of American unity.[27] In the first World War, he was one of the earliest advocates of a strong assertion of American rights, and it was particularly pleasing to him that the Americanism of those who, like himself, were of English birth, was never compromised by a hyphen.[28] The clearest expression of his devotion to the ideal of American unity is to be found in an address which he delivered at the University of Michigan in 1920, entitled "The Supreme Allegiance." It was a warning against adherence to the League of Nations so long as the unequivocal guarantee of Article X remained in the Covenant. In the course of his remarks, he declared:

To my mind, one of the most dangerous [of current theories] is that which challenges and belittles the spirit of nationalism and which seeks to substitute for the warmth and intimacy of loyalty and love of country, that vague and vacuous communion of the tribes known as "internationalism." . . . The nation is something

[25] George Sutherland, "Superfluous Government," an address delivered before the Cleveland Chamber of Commerce, December 8, 1914, and printed in pamphlet form, p. 13.

[26] *Utah Inquirer* (Provo), July 6, 1888.

[27] Undated memorandum in the Sutherland papers.

[28] *The London Times*, July 22, 1924, in which a short address by Sutherland to a joint meeting of American and English lawyers is reported.

more than so many millions of people occuying a geographical subdivision of the earth's surface, speaking the same language and subject to the same laws. These are its visible and tangible constituents, but what gives it organic life and meaning is the spirit of unity which dwells within. . . .

. . . *The institutions under which we live are of such transcendent worth that their protection is the imperious and paramount duty of all whose rights are made safe by the marvelous counterpoise of liberty and law which they afford. They are ours and ours alone; an example which others may emulate but a possession never to be thrown into the grist of some common political universalism.*[29]

These sentiments supply a background which renders understandable Sutherland's otherwise puzzling choice of company in *Meyer* v. *Nebraska*.[30] The statute there overthrown prohibited the teaching of any language except English in the Nebraska schools, public or private. A majority of seven concurred in an opinion by McReynolds asserting that the right to teach a foreign language was a property right which the Fourteenth Amendment protected. Holmes dissented, but his protesting partner this time was not Brandeis, but the perfervid patriot from Utah. Sutherland, of course, could usually be relied on to denounce such interferences with the liberty of the individual and his property. But, he must have reasoned, these were values which could flourish only in a strong and unified America, and to this end, the right to teach foreign languages had to yield.

Much the same notion is apparent in Sutherland's opinion for the majority in the celebrated *Macintosh*

[29] George Sutherland, "The Supreme Allegiance," an address delivered at the University of Michigan, February 24, 1920, and printed in pamphlet form, pp. 10-12. The italics are mine.

[30] 262 U.S. 390 (1923). While the *Gitlow* case was the first in which the Court explicitly brought freedom of speech within the Fourteenth Amendment, the *Meyer* case actually furnished the "bridge" over which the justices escaped from their former decisions denying any such result. In the course of his opinion, McReynolds made a rather lengthy catalogue of the "liberties" included in the Amendment. Among these, he said, was the liberty "to enjoy those privileges long recognized by the common law as essential to the orderly pursuit of happiness by free men." (p. 399)

case,[31] decided May 25, 1931. Macintosh, of Canadian birth and citizenship, had been for some years a professor in the Yale Divinity School when he sought to be naturalized. Among other things, the law required the prospective citizen to declare on oath that he would "support and defend the Constitution of the United States against all enemies." This Macintosh was willing to do, but with the reservation that he would bear arms only in such wars as he considered to be morally justified.

The case thus presented to the Supreme Court the question whether a promise to "support and defend the Constitution" was compatible with the Professor's intention to oppose a war he believed to be unjust. The Chief Justice, speaking for a minority of four, sought to show that the majority was adding to the statute a provision which had not been specifically included. The consideration that Congress had always shown conscientious objectors was cited to prove the existence of a Congressional policy which the Court should follow unless it was clearly indicated that a deviation was intended.

Sutherland's opinion for the majority proceeds on the broad ground that the Constitution recognized virtually no limitation on the war power and that therefore Macintosh could not be devoted to its principles when he attempted to reserve the right of private judgment. The war power was one, said Sutherland, which "tolerates no qualifications or limitations unless found in the Constitution or in applicable principles of international law. In the words of John Quincy Adams, 'this power is tremendous; it is strictly Constitutional; but it breaks down every barrier so anxiously erected for the protection of liberty, property and of life.' "[32]

The rights of conscience, therefore, could not be allowed to challenge the commands of the nation in seasons of danger. "We are a Christian people," Sutherland continued, "according to one another the equal right of religious freedom, and acknowledging with reverence the duty

[31] *United States* v. *Macintosh*, 283 U.S. 605 (1931).   [32] *ibid.*, p. 622.

of obedience to the will of God."[33] But this proposition could not be allowed to obscure another which the justice deemed even more fundamental: *"We are a nation with a duty to survive*; a nation whose Constitution contemplates war as well as peace; whose government must go forward on the assumption . . . that unqualified allegiance to the nation and submission and obedience to the laws of the land, as well those made for war as those made for peace, are not inconsistent with the will of God."[34]

4.

From the Macintosh dissent, there emerges the dominant idea in all Sutherland's thinking on the relationship of the United States to the outside world. National survival is a supreme duty to which not only scruples of conscience, but even the great organizational principles of the Constitution must yield. This is the central idea of Sutherland's remarkable opinion in *United States* v. *Curtiss-Wright Export Corporation*,[35] decided December 18, 1936. There he succeeded in winning the approval of his brethren for the notion that the power of the government in the field of foreign relations does not depend for its existence on the Constitution. Rather, it is an inherent power arising by virtue of the United States' membership in the family of nations. Therefore its exercise is not subject to the usual constitutional restraints.

The case had its beginnings in the indictment of the defendant company for selling arms to Bolivia in violation of a Congressional Joint Resolution[36] and the provisions of a Presidential proclamation. The Resolution declared it to be unlawful to sell any arms or munitions of war to countries involved in the Chaco dispute *if the President should find that such prohibition might "contribute to the re-establishment of peace" and then make such finding known*. The President duly issued the required proclamation on the same day that the Resolution was passed, May

33 *ibid.*, p. 625.   34 *ibid.* The italics are mine.
35 299 U.S. 304 (1936).   36 48 Stat. 811 (1934).

29, 1934. The Company, after its indictment early in 1936, strenuously denied that the President's proclamation was a law the violation of which could be punished in judicial proceedings. Counsel pointed out that the prohibition of the sale of arms was left to the unfettered discretion of the Chief Executive and that the result was that his will was thereby substituted for that of Congress, the only body legitimately empowered to make law.

At this point, it is interesting to recall the definition of autocracy given by Sutherland only a few months before in the *Jones* case.[37] It was, he had written, the substitution of "the mere will of an official . . . [for] the standing law as a rule of human conduct." In the present case, however, this was not the issue for him; rather the question was the place of the United States in the family of nations. The Resolution was designed, he said, "to affect a situation entirely external to the United States"[38] and, therefore, was to be judged on different grounds than if it had related solely to internal affairs. His development of this difference follows:

> The two classes of powers are different, both in respect of their origin and their nature. The broad statement that the federal government can exercise no powers except those specifically enumerated in the Constitution, and such implied powers as are necessary and proper to carry into effect the enumerated powers, is categorically true only in respect of our internal affairs. In that field the primary purpose of the Constitution was to carve from the general mass of legislative powers *then possessed by the states* such portions as it was thought desirable to vest in the federal government, leaving those not included in the enumeration still in the states. That this doctrine applies only to powers which the states had, is self-evident. And since the states severally never possessed international powers, such powers could not have been carved from the mass of state powers but obviously were transmitted to the United States from some other source. . . .

> As a result of the separation from Great Britain by the colonies, acting as a unit, the powers of external sovereignty passed from

[37] *Jones* v. *Securities and Exchange Commission*, 298 U.S. 1, 23 (1936).
[38] *United States* v. *Curtiss-Wright Export Corporation*, *supra* note 35, p. 315.

the Crown not to the colonies severally, but to the colonies in their collective and corporate capacity as the United States of America. . . . Rulers come and go; governments end and forms of government change; but sovereignty survives. A political society can not endure without a supreme will somewhere. Sovereignty is never held in suspense. When, therefore, the external sovereignty of Great Britain in respect of the colonies ceased, it immediately passed to the Union.[39]

The conclusion to be drawn from all this was a theory of the foreign relations power which rendered it independent of constitutional limitations. "The powers to declare and wage war, to conclude peace, to make treaties, to maintain diplomatic relations with other sovereignties, if they had never been mentioned in the Constitution," Sutherland explained, "would have vested in the federal government as necessary concomitants of nationality. . . . As a member of the family of nations, the right and power of the United States . . . are equal to the right and power of the other members of the international family. Otherwise, the United States is not completely sovereign."[40]

This much of Sutherland's opinion was devoted to the justification of a well-nigh limitless power for the federal government in the field of foreign relations—a power, it may be repeated, existing independently of the Constitution. Its exercise therefore could not be circumscribed by the usual constitutional restraints. This is not to say, however, that in the distribution of this authority the Constitution was dismissed as irrelevant. Indeed, that instrument is invoked as conferring on the President an authority to act in external matters irrespective of legislative action. Thus Sutherland warned:

It is important to bear in mind that here we are dealing not alone with an authority vested in the President by an exertion of legislative power, but with such an authority plus the very delicate, plenary and exclusive power of the President as the sole organ of the federal government in the field of international relations—a power which does not require as a basis for its

[39] *ibid.*, pp. 316-317.   [40] *ibid.*, p. 318.

exercise an act of Congress, but which, of course, like every other governmental power, must be exercised in subordination to the applicable provisions of the Constitution.[41]

A second result of the *Curtiss-Wright* case, then, is that it emphatically confirms the vast authority of the Presidential office in the international sphere. After establishing an inherent power in the federal government, the opinion makes plain that the greater part of this power is the President's to do with what he will or can. The extent to which this is true vividly appears in *United States* v. *Belmont*,[42] decided a few months later in May 1937. The case was an outgrowth of the executive agreement which accompanied the recognition of the Soviet government in November 1933. The terms of this agreement provided that all claims against American nationals held by the Soviet were to be assigned to the United States for collection. One such claim was the confiscated account of a Russian corporation in the Belmont bank in New York. The bank, however, refused to turn the funds over to the United States on the grounds that the policy of the State of New York was against the recognition of property rights acquired by expropriation and, in the lower federal court, this policy was deemed to be controlling.

The Supreme Court reversed, with Sutherland the author of the opinion. The heart of his reasoning appears in the following paragraph:

Plainly, the external powers of the United States are to be exercised without regard to state laws or policies. The supremacy of a treaty in this respect has been recognized from the beginning—and while this rule in respect of treaties is established by the express language of cl. 2, Art. vi, of the Constitution, the same rule would result in the case of all international compacts and agreements from the very fact that complete power over international affairs is in the national government and is not and can not be subject to any curtailment or interference on the part of the several states. In respect of all international negotiations and compacts, and in respect to our foreign relations generally,

41 *ibid.*, pp. 319-320.   42 301 U.S. 324.

state lines disappear. As to such purposes the state of New York does not exist. . . .[43]

This is strong language, and the fears it has aroused in those anxious for the preservation of state autonomy and the survival of ancient forms in lawmaking are understandable. Reduced to its simplest terms, it means that the President's will in certain matters can replace state law. This result, however, can be evaluated only against the background of the actual facts in the *Belmont* case. The recognition of the Soviet regime was for years one of the most controversial issues in American politics. When the appropriate branch of the Government finally decided to take positive action, it would have been something worse than ridiculous if the State of New York had been allowed to obstruct such a policy. It is to Sutherland's everlasting credit that he was able to comprehend this. It was not easy for him to have a clear view of the situation. He believed in the rights of the states as firmly as anyone. He could have had little sympathy with Franklin Roosevelt and still less for the Soviet policy of expropriation.[44] But the common sense of high statesmanship enabled him to see that the real issue was none of these but rather the capacity of the United States to speak in a single, intelligible voice to the nations of the world.

The benefits of the *Belmont* case so readily apparent in

[43] *ibid.*, p. 331. *Cf.* "That there should ever have been any doubt as to the complete supremacy of the national power in all matters of foreign relation is an anomaly that, under the new and enlarged world responsibilities we are assuming, is no longer tolerable. The eyes of foreign governments see only the Nation. State boundaries are as meaningless to them as county boundaries in Great Britain are to us. In *Chisholm* v. *Georgia*, Mr. Justice Wilson said 'As to the purposes of the Union, therefore, Georgia is not a sovereign state'; to which may be added: and for the purposes of external sovereignty the *state* of Georgia does not exist." George Sutherland, *The Constitution and World Affairs*, New York, Columbia University Press, 1919, pp. 163-164.

[44] Sutherland dismissed this problem by declaring that the policy of the Constitution against expropriation applied only to nationals of the United States. But what if one of our nationals is the victim of expropriation? Would an executive agreement acquiescing be binding on the Courts? *Cf. United States* v. *Pink*, 315 U.S. 203 (1942).

public international law spill over into the sphere of private law as well. The case supplies a principle which might well go far in eliminating many troublesome international conflict of laws problems. Its reasoning sustains if, indeed, it does not command, a national common law to take the place of the bewildering maze of state decisions in international conflicts of laws cases.[45]

5.

Sutherland's success in winning the Court to his view of the foreign relations power was a personal triumph of proportions seldom encountered in judicial biography. It was a triumph, too—and this Sutherland would have willingly conceded—for Judge James V. Campbell, his teacher at the Michigan Law School nearly sixty years before. In his lectures on the general subject of "The Jurisprudence of the United States," Campbell hammered home to his students what one of them labeled as "his one-sided view of the separation of the colonies from Great Britain."[46] What this "one-sided view" was appears in the following quotations from student notebooks recording the Judge's remarks:

In 1774 the Colonies were joined in anticipation of a war with Great Britain which broke out in 1775 and resulted in their independence. . . . The Congress of 1774 answers to nothing today except our convention and was nothing more or less than a popular assembly.

In 1775 they acted as a government and took necessary steps to carry on war and their power was at once recognized, and this Congress took the responsibility of declaring the independence of

45 The effects of the *Belmont* case on private international law have been approvingly noted by Prof. Elliot E. Cheatham in his article, "Stone on Conflict of Laws," 46 *Col. L. Rev.* 719, 731 (1946).

46 Manuscript notebook of Alexander Hamilton, Jr. containing lecture notes taken at the University of Michigan Law School (1880), p. 96. This notebook and those cited in subsequent notes are in the library of the University of Michigan. No notebook is available covering the period when Sutherland attended the University but it is reasonable to assume that he heard from Campbell substantially what earlier students had. This surmise is corroborated by the list of Campbell's lecture topics given in Chapter 1.

the thirteen colonies without even consulting their constituents. At the suggestion of Congress the colonies organized their state governments.[47]

The first Congress represented the colonies and the people; but not the governments of the colonies *viz.* The colonies in the first Congress were not represented as they are now. They did many things in the first Congress that would not be allowed to Congress now. It is impossible in case of war not to interfere with the relations of other governments. Therefore there must be some tribunal or committee which should represent the American people in war, as in 1776, in reference to foreign nations; to hold the people together under one head. Congress was therefore a revolutionary power, and took all the duties of government upon it.[48]

No state either before or after the revolution has ever been regarded as a nation. Before the revolution the colonies expected Parliament to regulate national affairs. The government of the United States in fact preceded the present state governments.[49]

On the situation as it exists under the Constitution, Campbell laid great stress on the continued applicability of the law of nations. He told his students:

The implications of knowledge of laws in the Constitution are from 1st the law of nations . . . rules applying to all governments of whatever kind without which no government can exist. . . . In our own government we must possess every power that has been found to be absolutely necessary to all other nations. A nation may be regarded in two lights: first as to its duties to other nations and second as to its duties to its inhabitants; and these two relations must harmonize in order to have prosperity in the nation.

The law of nations does not deal with internal duties but external, and there must somewhere be a power to regulate the external as well as the internal relations of a nation.[50]

Finally Campbell had a word on the duty of the courts. Judges, he said, "cannot question the power that makes a treaty. It is only their duty to enforce. It is wholly political and not in the least judicial."[51]

[47] Manuscript notebook of Marshall Davis Ewell (1866), p. 8.
[48] Hamilton notebook (1880), p. 156.
[49] Manuscript notebook of De Forest Paine (1872), p. 259.
[50] Ewell notebook (1866), pp. 6-7.
[51] Paine notebook (1872), p. 280.

The foregoing material convincingly supports the thesis that it was Campbell who planted in Sutherland's brain the ideas which bore fruit in the *Curtiss-Wright* case. In his *Constitutional Power and World Affairs*,[52] Sutherland called attention to Campbell's opinion in *Van Husen* v. *Knouse*[53] which argues that a power essential to government and which is prohibited to the states, must necessarily be found in the general government. The reference is accompanied by a warm tribute to Campbell whom Sutherland called one of the "most scholarly and independently learned jurists the country has ever known." Of course, Campbell's interpretation of Revolutionary history was not original with him. Justice Story took much the same view in his *Commentaries*,[54] and Abraham Lincoln,[55] George Bancroft,[56] and Von Holst[57] gave it popular currency. Yet, it was Campbell's advocacy that proved decisive. His feat in winning Sutherland to a complete acceptance of his views is one of the clearest and most dramatic examples in our history of the power of a teacher.

Sutherland did not wait until he had the opportunity to speak judicially to set forth his views on the foreign relations power. As early as 1910, he had developed his thesis in an article published in the *North American Review*.[58] The first World War and its aftermath stimulated him to develop it still further in his lectures at Columbia in 1918.

[52] George Sutherland, *Constitutional Power and World Affairs*, p. 58.

[53] 13 Mich. 313 (1864). Professor Corwin has pointed out that the thesis of the *Van Husen* case could, with as much logic, be used as a basis for the exercise by the national government of power in internal affairs. See Edward S. Corwin, *The Twilight of the Supreme Court*, New Haven, Yale University Press, 1934, pp. 220-221.

[54] Joseph Story, *Commentaries on the Constitution of the United States*, Boston, Little Brown & Co., 5th ed., 1873, pp. 144-167. Secs. 198-218.

[55] In his famous message to Congress on July 4, 1861. See Richardson, *Messages and Papers of the Presidents* (1897), p. 3228.

[56] See generally his *History of the United States of America*, vols. 4 and 5.

[57] H. Von Holst, *The Constitutional and Political History of the United States*, Chicago, Callaghan and Company, 1889, pp. 1-64.

[58] George Sutherland, "Internal and External Powers of the National Government," *North American Review*, cxci (March 1910), 373.

With acute perception, he forecast that "we shall feel the weight of our extra-territorial responsibilities in many unaccustomed ways." He concluded:

In this broadened field of endeavor, we must cease to think in terms of states and states' rights and think only in terms of nationality. We must cease to measure the authority of the general government only by what the Constitution affirmatively grants, and consider it also in the light of what the Constitution permits from failure to deny. There is no danger that we shall thereby destroy the reserved rights of the states, or overrun the domain of local government—against these unfortunate consequences we must always be on our guard—but we shall avoid the unspeakably absurd confusion of having an agency to speak for us upon all matters of legitimate international concern with a vocabulary so limited that upon some of them—and, in the light of our expanded world relations, not inconceivably the most vital of them—it cannot speak at all.[59]

6.

While the Sutherland theory of the foreign relations power has been generally praised, it has also evoked the most stringent criticism.[60] Professor C. Perry Patterson, for example, has charged that it is a "revolutionary" doctrine and one "subversive of our constitutional system."[61] "Executive totalitarianism" and the obliteration of the dual nature of the Union are pictured as inevitable results.[62] The burden of Professor Patterson's argument is that the states once actually were sovereign and independent. His proof consists of various recitals to this effect by the states themselves, the severe restrictions imposed by the states on delegates to the Continental Congress, the language of Article II of the Articles of

[59] *Constitutional Power and World Affairs*, p. 172.
[60] See particularly C. Perry Patterson, "In re The United States v. Curtiss-Wright Corporation," 22 *Tex. L. Rev.* 286, 445 (1944) and David M. Levitan, "The Foreign Relations Power: An Analysis of Mr. Justice Sutherland's Theory," 55 *Yale L. J.* 467 (1946). The Levitan article makes considerable use of Van Tyne, "Sovereignty in the American Revolution: An Historical Study," *Am. Hist. Rev.* XII, 529 (1907).
[61] Patterson, *supra*, p. 286.
[62] *ibid.*, p. 462.

Confederation,[63] and the behavior of the states themselves. There is, it must be conceded, an element of strength in this criticism. But, it must be added, even during the period of the Articles—indeed, from the time of the first Continental Congress—the advocates of state sovereignty were constantly confronted with the opposing theory. James Wilson stated it succinctly in August 1776: "As to those matters which are referred to Congress, we are not so many states, we are one large state. We lay aside our individuality whenever we come here."[64]

The speculation, however, on one side or the other of this thorny problem can hardly be as decisive of the issue as the behavior of the parties. As Gerhart Niemeyer has suggested, "Sovereignty is not only a conception; it is likewise a real fact—."[65] In this light, the important question would seem to be whether the states from 1776 to 1787 actually comported themselves as members of the international community. That there was some such activity is certain; and Section 10 of Article I of the Constitution,[66] as Professor Corwin has observed, "quite clearly recognized the states as retaining a certain rudimentary capacity in this field."[67] Yet even under the Articles the consent of Congress was required for a state to negotiate with a foreign power,[68] and that the most significant portion of our foreign relations was carried on by agents of Congress is a fact too well known to be controverted. Indeed, Rufus King declared in the Convention:

[63] "Each State retains its sovereignty, freedom, and independence, and every power, jurisdiction and right, which is not by this confederation expressly delegated to the United States, in Congress assembled."

[64] Quoted in Merrill Jensen, *The Articles of Confederation*, Madison, University of Wisconsin Press, 1940, p. 168.

[65] In John B. Whitton (ed.), *The Second Chance*, Princeton, Princeton University Press, 1944, p. 56.

[66] "No State shall enter into any Treaty, Alliance, or Confederation. . . .

"No State shall, without the consent of Congress, . . . enter into any Agreement or Compact with another State, or with a foreign Power."

[67] Edward S. Corwin, *The President, Office and Powers*, New York, New York University Press, 1941, p. 203.

[68] Articles of Confederation, Art. VI.

The states were not "sovereigns" in the sense contended for by some. They did not possess the peculiar features of sovereignty,—they could not make war, nor peace, nor alliances, nor treaties. Considering them as political beings, they were dumb, for they could not speak of any foreign sovereign whatever. They were deaf, for they could not hear any propositions from such sovereign. They had not even the organs or faculties of defence or offence, for they could not of themselves raise troops, or equip vessels, for war.[69]

To Professor Patterson's charge that the Sutherland doctrine is violative of our political theory the reply must again be that it contains an admixture of the truth. Inherent power is not compatible with the constitutional or delegated variety. But is this more than to say that war is the eternal enemy of democracy? Can one doubt after our recent experience that the government of the United States has at its disposal any and all means necessary for its preservation, whether granted by the Constitution or not? And does the disguise of these powers in constitutional garments, however ill-fitting and bulging at the seams, serve the cause of democracy? It seems more likely to obscure the terrible truth that until the problem of war is mitigated, our democracy will continue to be threatened.

Happily, the uses to which the Sutherland theory can be put are not exclusively those of war and international strife. At a time when the peoples of the world are painfully searching for some power extensive enough to impose a semblance of order on the international community, it is a heartening thing to know that the Constitution of the United States does not prohibit this country from making its full contribution. The process by which we have been forced into two world wars and led to join in a worldwide effort for the maintenance of peace and security is not likely to diminish its intensity. Nor is it in any way certain that the concept of world organization has reached its final institutional form. It is, of course, possible that whatever shape world institutions take, the hopes placed in

[69] 5 Elliot's Debates 212.

them will prove to be illusory. But that these hopes may be indulged in at all is because the United States, as a member of the international community, is as free and sovereign as its fellows. For this freedom, the nation will ever owe a debt of gratitude to George Sutherland.

7

AN IDEA IN RETROSPECT

THE defeat, in the summer of 1937, of the President's Court plan brought to George Sutherland a warm glow of contentment. To him, it seemed that the integrity of the Supreme Court as an institution of American government had been vindicated—not only for the present, but for all the foreseeable future.[1] So convinced, he was then willing to contemplate retirement. On January 6, 1938, he notified the President of his intention to leave the bench twelve days later. The customary letter from his colleagues on the occasion was highly appreciative. It read:

My dear Justice Sutherland:

Upon your retirement from regular active service on the bench, we wish to give you renewed assurance of our warm affection and of our high appreciation of the distinguished ability and unremitting devotion which have characterized your long participation in the work of the Court. Not only have you brought to our deliberations learning and dialectical skill, a wide knowledge of affairs enriched by varied and eminent public service, and a habit of thoroughness and precision, but you have matched tenacity of purpose with an unvarying kindliness and have mellowed our deliberations with unfailing humor. We keenly regret the loss of this companionship which will ever remain a delightful memory. We trust that in your retirement from the constant labor of active service you will find fresh vigor and the abiding satisfaction which comes from the consciousness of arduous duties performed with complete fidelity.[2]

The Justice gracefully responded:

My dear Brethren:

I have read your letter, and make my reply to it with mingled emotions of gratitude for the more than generous things you say,

[1] Sutherland to a Mr. Preston (initials unknown), January 18, 1938. See above Chapter 5, note 125.
[2] 303 U.S. vi (1938).

and sorrow that these amenities end the completeness of that close and affectionate comradeship which reaches back so many years. It is very hard for me to step out of this circle, where I have taken comfort for so long. I leave the Court with keen regret. I have loved the work in which we have been engaged together; and only a definite conviction that the time has come reconciles me to the unwelcome thought of laying it down. The memory of our association will remain; but this, although very dear, will not compensate me for the loss of the reality. May health and happiness attend you all throughout the coming years.[3]

Sutherland responded, also, to each of the many letters that came from friends all over the country. His feelings are perhaps best portrayed by the following excerpt: "I leave the Court with extreme regret. The work has been congenial, and it was very hard to put it aside; but circumstances were such that it seemed, if not absolutely necessary, at least wise and proper that I should do so."[4]

There were, in addition, the plaudits of the press. The comment of the *New York Herald Tribune* was representative: "The country loses a singularly able mind and a character as staunch as it is above reproach. . . . The presence of his admirably logical mind and his complete loyalty to the truth as he saw it were always of the highest value."[5]

After leaving the Court, Sutherland continued to live in Washington and, under the provisions of the new Retirement Act, returned once to the Bench to sit with the Second Circuit Court of Appeals in hearing the case of the convicted judge, Martin T. Manton.[6] His last years were enriched by the company of his wife, daughter, and a grandson in whose beginnings at the bar the Justice took a great pride.[7] In 1941 came an honor he particularly valued. Brigham Young University awarded him an honor-

[3] U.S. vii (1938).

[4] Sutherland to a Mr. Preston, January 18, 1938.

[5] *New York Herald Tribune*, January 7, 1938.

[6] For Sutherland's opinion upholding Manton's conviction, see *United States* v. *Manton*, 107 F. 2d 834 (1939).

[7] The Justice's wife survived him, dying in 1944. His daughter is Mrs. Walter Bloedorn of Washington, D.C. His grandson is Mr. George Sutherland Elmore of the District of Columbia Bar.

ary degree, the fifth in its history. For the occasion Sutherland prepared an address which was read to a large gathering in Provo.[8] It was in the nature of a valedictory, containing mellow recollections of days long gone and the sage advice of a man who had reached his goal. His goal, he suggested, had been not merely to be a good lawyer, or a good legislator, or a good judge. These were as nothing compared to the ambition of being "a good man." He died quietly in Stockbridge, Massachusetts, just at the beginning of a summer holiday, on July 18, 1942.[9]

2.

In formulating an estimate of Sutherland, it is essential to dismiss at once the easy generalization that he was the prisoner of a blind conservatism which rendered him altogether incapable of beholding the new with any degree of sympathy. This is clearly an over-simplification. In rebuttal, one has only to recall Sutherland's insistence on procedural reform, or his advocacy of the Postal Savings Bank Bill, or his struggle to secure a Workmen's Compensation Act. Or one might consider his opinion in *Funk* v. *United States*,[10] which is as liberal in its approach to the law of evidence as any ever written. He there wrote:

The fundamental basis upon which all rules of evidence must rest—if they are to rest upon reason—is their adaptation to the successful development of the truth. And since experience is of all teachers the most dependable, and since experience also is a continuous process, it follows that a rule of evidence at one time thought necessary to the ascertainment of truth should yield to the experience of a succeeding generation whenever that experience has clearly demonstrated the fallacy or unwisdom of the old rule. . . .

To concede this capacity for growth and change in the common law by drawing "its inspiration from every fountain of justice," and at the same time to say that the courts of this country are forever bound to perpetuate such of its rules as, by every reason-

---

[8] "The Spirit of Brigham Young University," reprinted in the University publication, *The Messenger*, vol. 18, no. 10.
[9] *New York Times*, July 19, 1942.   [10] 290 U.S. 371 (1933).

able test, are found to be neither wise nor just, because we have once adopted them as suited to our situation and institutions at a particular time, is to deny to the common law in the place of its adoption a "flexibility and capacity for growth and adaptation" which was "the peculiar boast and excellence" of the system in the place of its origin.[11]

These are not the words of one devoted to the past for its own sake. They show that Sutherland was capable of progressive, realistic thinking. How, then, did it happen that he should have been such a resolute defender of the old order? The words of Justice Holmes in *Gitlow* v. *New York* [12] suggest an answer. "Every idea is an incitement," Holmes wrote. "It offers itself for belief and if believed it is acted on." Sutherland was obsessed with a particular idea—an idea of government. In his case, it was indeed an incitement. He believed in it and acted on it. And the intensity of his belief needs no other witness than the consistency of his actions.

The idea of government which was the moving influence in Sutherland's life was based on his conviction that the individual is, in a sense, the only political reality. On the individual, therefore, Sutherland fixed his gaze and never let it wander. Whatever enhanced individual freedom was good; whatever restricted it was bad. Nor was there any mystery of how this freedom might be achieved. It was simply a matter of reducing governmental restraint to an absolute minimum. Men did not need the aid of government. They were entirely self-sufficient or must inevitably become so if only government would leave them free to exercise their talents.

Moreover, Sutherland and those of similar mind, were prepared to argue that their emphasis on individual freedom did not entail a sacrifice of the common good. The nature of man was such that if given free scope it would in the long run produce the ideal commonwealth. Men would become adapted to their environment and with perfect adaptation, there would come perfect bliss. It was in this

[11] *ibid.*, pp. 381, 383.   [12] 268 U.S. 652, 673 (1925).

spirit that Sutherland, in the *Adkins* case,[13] wrote: "To sustain the individual freedom of action contemplated by the Constitution is not to strike down the common good but to exalt it, for surely the good of society as a whole cannot be better served than by the preservation of the liberties of its constituent members."

Such a theory suggests the question of why government is necessary at all. Sutherland might have responded that it is necessary only for protection against foreign aggression and to keep a measure of order as men follow conflicting desires and impulses. He considered war an ever-present possibility which rendered it certain that people lacking adequate means of defense could never maintain their freedom. A freedom that ended in slavery or annihilation was valueless. Safety could be found only in organized government. The whole power of the state was to be available to meet any foreign attack and thereby guarantee on the domestic front the tranquillity essential to the enjoyment of freedom. But this power, great as it was, was to be used only against outsiders. It was not recognized as legitimate when employed internally.

Besides the power to repel attack, Sutherland conceded to government an authority to act when two or more individuals were pursuing mutually contradictory ends. It was the quality of the action which he was willing to permit in this situation which distinguishes him from his opponents. He did not believe that it was the duty of government to intervene in the name of the common good and say which of the contestants should prevail. The perfect answer to this question was not to be found in legislatures or majorities, but in the mysterious forces of nature. If men would only wait, the answer would appear. All that government should do was to preserve social order and see to it that the rules of the contest were fairly enforced.

The reader might wonder just what Sutherland's conception of government has to do with his contribution to

[13] *Adkins* v. *Children's Hospital*, 261 U.S. 525, 561 (1923).

American constitutional law. Was he not a member of a court which decided cases and controversies between contending parties and decided them in accordance with the standing law rather than any particular theory of government? It is well known that this is the traditional description of the Court and its function. Yet, it is clear today, and perhaps it has always been so, that the Supreme Court has been and is something more than a court of law. It has been and is an agency of government.[14] Throughout its history, it has determined questions which far transcend the interests of the litigants and which are by every conceivable test, concerned with matters of policy. For example, the important thing about the *Dred Scott* case,[15] so far as the whole people of the United States were concerned, was not that the unfortunate Negro should resume his status as one of Mr. Sandford's chattels. The result of the case more important than all others was that the slavery question was removed from the purview of the usual political processes, and thereby rendered incapable of solution except by war.

Other examples of the Court's involvement in policy, some as dramatic and some less. so, can be cited in almost any volume of the Reports. But it would be to no purpose. The point is that every judge who ever sat on the Supreme Court of the United States, with possibly a single exception,[16] has been, with varying degrees of awareness, the advocate of a political theory. Each of them has employed his own particular conception of the ideal polity as a lens with which to bring the Constitution into some sort of focus. This has been true of men as different as Marshall, Taney, Miller, Field, White, and Brandeis. And it was true of Sutherland.

Sutherland's theory of government is important, then, because it prompted his theory of the Constitution. He

---

[14] For an excellent exposition of this idea, see Charles P. Curtis, *Lions under the Throne*, Boston, Houghton Mifflin Company, 1947.

[15] *Scott* v. *Sandford*, 19 How. 393 (1857).

[16] I refer, of course, to Holmes.

conceived the Constitution as miraculously providing for his ideal state. To begin with, it was *law*. But it was no ordinary law. It was the people's law and as such, the only authentic expression of their political will. It had one, and only one, true meaning—that with which it was endowed at the time of its adoption, and this supplied a constant standard with which exact compliance was always required.

The great miracle of the Constitution was accomplished, Sutherland believed, by the manner in which it dealt with authority. There was no such thing as a general power to govern. Rather, authority was cut up into small bits. And lest two of these bits should merge and thereby become dangerous, each power was assigned a special compartment from which it was not to be allowed to escape. In achieving and maintaining such a distribution, the principles of federalism and the separation of powers were the chief reliance. Power was so widely diffused among the states and the three departments that it nowhere existed in sufficient strength to threaten the liberties of free men.

Just as it was Sutherland's idea of government which prompted his idea of the Constitution, it was, in turn, the latter which produced his conception of judicial power. The plan of government envisioned by the Constitution was not self-operative. Overseers were needed to supervise the delicate adjustment, to reinforce the barriers so jealously erected, and to compel authority to remain in the compartment to which it had been assigned. To Sutherland it was plain that the people had entrusted this duty to the judiciary. One thinks immediately, of course, of *Massachusetts* v. *Mellon*,[17] where the Justice expressly disclaimed any such role for the courts. But one should think, too, of a whole roster of other cases where Sutherland unhesitatingly accepted such a responsibility. It is, perhaps, well to recall again his words in the *West Coast Hotel* case:[18]

[17] 262 U.S. 447 (1923).
[18] *West Coast Hotel Co.* v. *Parrish*, 300 U.S. 379, 401 (1937).

Under our form of government, where the written constitution, by its own terms, is the supreme law, some agency of necessity must have the power to say the final word as to the validity of a statute assailed as unconstitutional. *The Constitution makes it clear that the power has been intrusted to this court* when the question arises in a controversy within its jurisdiction; and so long as the power remains there, its exercise can not be avoided without betrayal of the trust.

The words following those italicized represent an important qualification. But after they are given the fullest possible effect, the courts remain, under Sutherland's conception of judicial power, the most potent agency of government. To the judiciary was committed the supreme task of marking the bounds beyond which the other branches of the government could not pass. In discharging this function, the courts proceeded in a manner entirely different from other bodies and it was this that justified their preeminence. They alone were not corrupted by *will*. The exertion of will was unavoidable, and even appropriate, in the case of the legislature. But a judge was rendered incapable of its use on taking his oath. He surrendered his own will to become the mouthpiece of the law.

Today, less than ten years after his death, there has been a complete, and probably final, repudiation of much of Sutherland's thought. Few would contend for his extravagant notion of judicial prerogative. Nor can anyone, with the experience of the past twenty years in mind, believe that constitutional power is so anemic as Sutherland imagined. Governmental authority is no longer confronted by a judicial obstacle course. Sutherland's idea of individual liberty persists, but it is everywhere on the defensive and its staunchest defenders have realized that his prescription of absolute laissez faire can no longer be of service to them.

Even granting all this, Sutherland's achievement remains a sizable one. In cases where he did not become enmeshed in his hostility to government, his opinions continue to have a vital influence. Few judges have contributed so much to the delineation of the powers of the judicial and executive departments. Sutherland is today influential in both the fair and efficient administration of justice. And in the field of foreign affairs, he seems destined to enjoy a lasting preeminence.

Sutherland is important for the further reason that his career brightly illuminates the problem of the theorist as judge. He stands apart from his conservative colleagues primarily because he was a man of ideas. His superiority was that of a man with a theory, of the architect as compared to the carpenter. Paradoxically, Sutherland's concern with theory was the source of his greatest weakness as a judge. So addicted was he to speculative thinking that he came to depend on it too much. There were vast areas in the world of fact with which he was almost wholly unfamiliar. In a day when knowledge of sociology and economics was required of statesmen as never before, Sutherland knew little of either. Thus he could not know that when he talked of Willie Lyons' freedom of contract, he was speaking of something that did not exist.

In this connection, it is worthy of remark that it was Sutherland who was the target of Holmes' famous aphorism that "a page of history is worth a volume of logic."[19] All too often, Sutherland's logic was a logic merely of words and not of realities. In the *Jones* case,[20] for example, he eloquently pleaded the cause of freedom and the necessity for a government of laws and not of men. But the whole opinion rings a little hollow when one remembers the simple facts of the case. The SEC was not threatening Jones with the thumb and the screw but seeking merely to discover whether or not he had fraudulently attempted to deceive the public—surely a legitimate inquiry. Or one might consider the utterly unrealistic concept of equality which moved Sutherland to denounce the tax on mortgages of over $5,000 in *Louisville Gas & Electric Co.* v. *Cole-*

[19] See ante p. 104.
[20] *Jones* v. *Securities and Exchange Commission*, 298 U.S. 1 (1936).

man.[21] His opinion, while condemning inequality in law, could have had no other effect but to accentuate it in fact. Indeed, there is ground for saying that the whole Sutherland theory of government was for him, as well as for multitudes of others, nothing more than a theory. He not only tolerated governmental intervention of the "right" kind; he demanded it. It was one thing for government to enjoin a strike; it was another for it to limit the charges of an employment agency. It was one thing for government to erect a barrier against imports; it was quite another for it to prescribe a minimum wage.

It must also be conceded that Sutherland, whatever his knowledge of political theory, suffered from the familiar difficulty of not knowing enough. He was a devoted student of the philosophical intricacies of nineteenth century individualism but had little interest in other systems. His exclusive preoccupation with but a segment of man's ideological experience rendered him intellectually parochial. He was so immersed in the Spencerian philosophy that he had no power to criticize it judiciously, no measuring stick with which to approach it selectively, no vantage point from which to see how much of Spencer was merely the expression of an age. In short, he had not the capacity for transcending his own experience.

But it will not do to quarrel with Sutherland because he was not an Olympian. His theoretical deficiencies come to mind only because his singular excellence stimulates questioning. This questioning cannot obscure his very real ability as a political philosopher or the fact that this ability elevated him to a distinguished place in the history of constitutional interpretation. An excellent illustration of the advantages he derived from his superior theoretical insights is furnished by the case of *Euclid* v. *Ambler,*[22] where Sutherland wrote the opinion upholding a zoning statute in the Cleveland suburb. Had he been a creature of impulse, he might well have joined Butler, McReynolds,

[21] 277 U.S. 32 (1927).   [22] 272 U.S. 365 (1926).

and Van Devanter in rejecting the statute. It was a novelty and its approval by the Court undoubtedly involved a recognition of a vast growth in political power. But Sutherland had the perspicacity to see that the statute was consistent with his theory in two essential details. First of all, the condition that produced it was a direct result of overpopulation which was, in turn, the real reason for government. In the second place, his analysis showed him that the effect of the statute would be beneficial to property, for it would protect the individual in the enjoyment of his own possessions. Here again one of the basic functions of government, from his viewpoint, was brought into play. The result was the fine opinion on which so much of our municipal law of today is based.

Other cases demonstrate the advantages which came to Sutherland because of the symmetry of his theoretical foundations. The *Adkins* opinion[23] is a good example. One has only to compare it with its precursor, Peckham's effort in *Lochner* v. *New York*,[24] to realize how effective a statement it is. Whereas Peckham's opinion requires the illumination of perhaps the most notable Holmes dissent, Sutherland's remarks in the *Adkins* case carry their own message. Peckham talks of unreasonableness and arbitrary power without ever revealing, except in the haziest kind of way, the basis for his conclusions. Sutherland, on the other hand, made comprehensible the philosophy of government and of society on which he outlawed the minimum wage. Divided and isolated as people were, it was not a subject which could be encompassed by the general terms of a statute. Equally clear was his demonstration that, from his viewpoint, the employer was being unjustly deprived of his property by being required to surrender something for which he received no equivalent. Moreover, Sutherland presented an alternative to the philosophy of the minimum wage. Granted his premises he could reasonably argue that he was not the foe of progress but its

[23] *Adkins* v. *Children's Hospital, supra* note 13.
[24] 198 U.S. 45 (1904).

proponent. And he could do this with force and persuasion because he, too, had definite ideas as to how to achieve the good of society and the ability to express these ideas with precision and clarity.

Finally, Sutherland is of enduring significance because he so insistently recalls to us the problem of the individual in a world of ever increasing complexity. The claims of the individual are no longer taken for granted. The pressing necessity for cohesion in society and the more and more frequent resort to the power of government to obtain this cohesion have too often engendered a state of mind in which the individual is considered only secondarily, if at all. But it may perhaps be symptomatic of a shift in emphasis that so convinced a socialist as Bertrand Russell should recently ask the same question that Sutherland asked years ago.[25] How can the creative impulses of the individual be stimulated in a controlled and equalitarian society? It is not necessary to subscribe to Sutherland's rejection of either controls or equality to appreciate his supreme concern for the individual. We can be grateful that he keeps before us the truth succinctly expressed by John Stuart Mill:

The worth of a State, in the long run, is the worth of the individuals composing it, . . . a State which dwarfs its men, in order that they may be more docile instruments in its hands even for beneficial purposes—will find that with small men no great thing can really be accomplished. . . .[26]

Sutherland's devotion to this idea made of him, in an era of fundamental change, the voice of much of the American experience. If we may believe that a judge's "authority and his immunity depend upon the assumption that he speaks with the mouth of others,"[27] Sutherland is a man to be reckoned with. As the last great spokesman for the tradition of individualism, he holds a strategic place

[25] See Bertrand Russell, *Authority and the Individual*, New York, Simon and Schuster, 1949.

[26] *On Liberty*, New York, Oxford University Press, 1942, p. 144.

[27] Learned Hand, "Mr. Justice Cardozo," 39 *Col. L. R.* 9 (1939).

in the history of the Supreme Court. He was, as Holmes said of Marshall, great because he was *there*.[28] Another who was there, the late Chief Justice Stone, has left this prophecy concerning the contribution of George Sutherland:

The time will come when it will be recognized, perhaps more clearly than it is at present, how fortunate it has been for the true progress of the law that, at a time when the trend was in the opposite direction, there sat upon this Bench a man of stalwart independence, and of the purest character who, without a trace of intellectual arrogance, and always with respectful toleration for the views of colleagues who differed with him, fought stoutly for the constitutional guarantees of the liberty of the individual.[29]

[28] Oliver Wendell Holmes, *Collected Legal Papers*, New York, Harcourt Brace and Company, 1921, pp. 267-268.
[29] 323 U.S. xxi (1944).

APPENDIX A

Table of Cases in which Mr. Justice Sutherland Wrote an Opinion

A. A. Lewis & Co. v. *Commr.*, 301 U.S. 385
Adkins v. *Children's Hospital*, 261 U.S. 525
Aetna L. Ins. Co. v. *Dunken*, 266 U.S. 389
Alabama v. *U.S.*, 279 U.S. 229
Alabama Pow. Co. v. *Ickes*, 302 U.S. 464
Aluminum Castings Co. v. *Routzahn*, 282 U.S. 92 (concurring)
American Foundries v. *Robertson*, 269 U.S. 372
American Propeller Co. v. *U.S.*, 300 U.S. 475
American Ry. Exp. Co. v. *Lindenburg*, 260 U.S. 584
Anderson v. *Clune*, 269 U.S. 140
Anderson v. *Shipowners Assn.*, 272 U.S. 359
Arkansas Gas Co. v. *Railroad Comm.*, 261 U.S. 379
Arkansas Railroad Comm. v. *Arkansas Gas Co.*, 261 U.S. 379
Associated Press v. *Labor Board*, 301 U.S. 103 (dissent)
Atchison, T. & S. F. Ry. v. *Scarlett*, 300 U.S. 471
Atlantic Cleaners & Dyers v. *U.S.*, 286 U.S. 427
Atlantic C. L. R. Co. v. *Ford*, 287 U.S. 502
Atlantic Lumb. Co. v. *Commr.*, 298 U.S. 553
Atlantic & Pac. Tea Co. v. *Grosjean*, 301 U.S. 412 (dissent)
Austin Nichols & Co. v. *SS Isla de Panay*, 267 U.S. 260 (dissent)

Bainbridge v. *Merchants & Miners Trans. Co.*, 287 U.S. 278
Baltimore & O. R. Co. v. *U.S.*, 260 U.S. 565
Baltimore & O. R. Co. v. *U.S.*, 264 U.S. 258 (dissent)
Baltimore & O. S. W. R. v. *Burtch*, 263 U.S. 540
Baltimore & O. S. W. R. Co. v. *Carroll*, 280 U.S. 491
Baltimore S. S. Co. v. *Phillips*, 274 U.S. 316
Barry v. *U.S. ex rel. Cunningham*, 279 U.S. 597
Bayside Fish Flour Co. v. *Gentry*, 297 U.S. 422
Beaver Cement Co. v. *Calif. Ore. Pow. Co.*, 295 U.S. 142
Becker v. *St. Louis Un. Tr. Co.*, 296 U.S. 48
Bedford Co. v. *Stone Cutters Assn.*, 274 U.S. 37
Bengzon v. *Secty. of Justice*, 299 U.S. 410
Berger v. *U.S.*, 295 U.S. 78
Bergholm v. *Peoria L. Ins. Co.*, 284 U.S. 489
Binderup v. *Pathe Exchg.*, 263 U.S. 291
Bingaman v. *Golden Eagle Lines*, 297 U.S. 626

Connally v. *Gen. Const. Co.*, 269 U.S. 385
Continental Ill. Bank v. *C.R.I. & P. R. Co.*, 294 U.S. 648
Cook v. *U.S.*, 288 U.S. 102
Coombes v. *Getz*, 285 U.S. 434
Corona Co. v. *U.S.*, 263 U.S. 537
Cox v. *Hart*, 260 U.S. 427
Cramer v. *U.S.*, 261 U.S. 219
Crooks v. *Harrelson*, 282 U.S. 55
Cudahy Co. v. *Parramore*, 263 U.S. 418
Cunard S. S. Co. v. *Mellon*, 262 U.S. 100 (dissent)

Davis Co. v. *U.S.*, 273 U.S. 324
De Laval Co. v. *U.S.*, 284 U.S. 61
Denton v. *Yazoo & M.V.R. Co.*, 284 U.S. 305
Deutsche Bank v. *Humphrey*, 272 U.S. 517 (dissent)
Dimick v. *Schiedt*, 293 U.S. 474
District of Columbia v. *Colts*, 282 U.S. 63
Duffey v. *Central R.*, 268 U.S. 55
Duffey v. *Mutual Benefit Co.*, 272 U.S. 613
Duke v. *U.S.*, 301 U.S. 492
Duke Pow. Co. v. *Greenwood County*, 302 U.S. 485
Dupont de Nemours & Co. v. *Davis*, 264 U.S. 456

Early v. *Richardson*, 280 U.S. 496
Educational Films Corp. v. *Ward*, 282 U.S. 379 (dissent)
Erie R. Co. v. *Duplak*, 286 U.S. 440
Euclid v. *Ambler Co.*, 272 U.S. 365

Fairport, P. & E. R. Co. v. *Meredith*, 292 U.S. 589
Farmers Nat. Bank v. *Wilkinson*, 266 U.S. 503
Federal Res. Bank v. *Malloy*, 264 U.S. 160
Federal Trade Comm. v. *Raladam Co.*, 283 U.S. 643
Federal Trade Comm. v. *Royal Milling Co.*, 288 U.S. 212
Ferry v. *Ramsey*, 277 U.S. 88 (dissent)
Fetters v. *U.S.*, 283 U.S. 638
First Nat. Bank v. *Maine*, 284 U.S. 312
First Nat. Bank v. *Missouri*, 263 U.S. 540
First Nat. Bank v. *Weld County*, 264 U.S. 450
Fix v. *Philadelphia Barge Co.*, 290 U.S. 530
Florida v. *Mellon*, 273 U.S. 12
Fox Film Corp. v. *Muller*, 296 U.S. 207
Freshman v. *Atkins*, 269 U.S. 121

APPENDICES

APPENDICES

APPENDICES

APPENDIX B

Memorandum on *Gold Clause* Cases Prepared by Mr. Justice Sutherland

The various obligations involved, in varying terms, called for the payment of stipulated sums in gold coin of the United States of America of or equal to the then standard of weight and fineness. The provision was inserted not with the idea of requiring a literal payment in gold coin, but in gold coin or money the equivalent of gold dollars as they then existed. It seems clear that the contract cannot be satisfied by payment in legal-tender money of a less value, unless the act of Congress which undertakes to strike down the specific obligation and substitute another and lesser one is constitutional.

Congress has power to "coin money and regulate the value thereof and of foreign coin." It has power to make the money it authorizes legal tender for the payment and discharge of all obligations not payable in specified kinds of dollars. So much is decided by the *Legal Tender* cases.

But Congress cannot by law compel the acceptance of such money to discharge an obligation payable in specified kinds of dollars of greater value. Such is the effect of the *Bronson* v. *Rodes, Trebilcock,* and later cases. To do so would be not to regulate the value of money, but to regulate the value of the contract.

To prohibit by law the payment of *gold coin* may be justified upon the ground that that regulates money. But to prohibit the payment of the value of the gold coin in money, in respect of the use of which no limitation has been placed, cannot be justified, because that strikes down the obligation of the contract—a power which has not been vested in Congress by any provision of the Constitution and which is, moreover, forbidden by the due process of law clause. It seems to me that to uphold such a power would be equivalent to saying that Congress by law could compel the holder of a bond for $1000 to accept $800 in payment.

The argument that the gold clause constitutes an obstruction to the exercise of the power of Congress to fix the value of money seems to me utterly fallacious. Conceding the power of Congress to say that the weight of a gold dollar shall be reduced from 25 grains to 15 grains, it does not follow that the power of Congress is obstructed by the payment of enough of the 15-grain dollars to equal the stipulated amount of the 25-grain dollars. The result might be to greatly interfere with the business of the country. It might conceivably result in business chaos, of which the Attorney General spoke. That would not interfere in the slightest degree with the power of Congress to measure the value of the dollar by any quantity of gold it saw fit. The contemplation of such a result might induce Congress to a greater degree of care in exercising its power, but it does not interfere with the power itself.

The case against striking down the government obligation seems to me not to admit of any doubt. This court definitely held in the *Sinking Fund Cases*, 99 U.S. 700, 718, and more emphatically in Mr. Justice Strong's opinion, pp. 731-732, that when the government made a contract it took the status of an individual; that it had no more power to avoid its contracts or to curtail its obligations than an individual had; that it laid aside its sovereignty and stood on the same footing with private contracts. It follows, indubitably, that the government has no more power to vary the terms of its contract than a private individual has. That much, of course, is conceded by everybody. But it will be said that while all this is true, the government may escape under the claim that the private individual cannot receive gold because immediately it will become subject to seizure—that therefore, the damages must be measured by the dollars which alone are permitted to circulate. Such a view seems to me utterly dishonest. Can the government, which is forbidden to vary the terms of its contract, accomplish the same result by a legislative manipulation which prevents the terms being carried into effect? To state the proposition, as Chief Justice White would say, is to answer it. I think the best way to deal with it is to cite the history—to point out the fact that a bond issue was made by the present administration calling for gold-dollar payments a short time before the legislation under attack was passed; that, with callous indifference to its solemn engagement, it undertook to destroy its effect by the legislation last referred to; that it gathered the gold into its treasury, thereby impounding the very thing it had promised to pay; that it has cynically and in disregard of all moral principle boasted that the result of its gold manipulation has been to bring to it a profit of between two and three billions of dollars—a profit made possible, in part at least, by the dishonorable attempt to annul promises made to its own citizens who mistakenly trusted to its honor. An individual as a contractor has as much authority to avoid his obligations as the government. Suppose an individual, lacking the power to annul or lessen the amount of his monetary obligation, should attempt to secrete or manipulate his assets so as to put them beyond the reach of his creditors. The court would denounce that as a fraud, and sweep it aside as ineffective; and a boast on the part of a dishonest debtor that he had reaped a great profit by the fraud would not be received with a high degree of patience.

ADDENDUM:

The effect of the gold clause is to exact payment in an amount of legal tender depreciated money equivalent in value to the gold coin required by the bond. That contingency does not obstruct the exercise of the power of Congress under the money clause of the Constitution. Its effect is simply to admonish the law-making body to weigh the relative evils likely to result from passing or failing to pass any given act of legislation on the subject. It does not authorize that body to destroy contract rights which in every sense constitute property, which, in the opinion of Congress, if permitted to stand will tend to render the proposed legislation less effective or useful than would otherwise be the case.

In that connection, the words of Mr. Hamilton, quoted by Mr. Justice Strong in the *Sinking-Fund Cases*, 99 U.S. 731, cannot be too often repeated—

> When a government enters into a contract with an individual, it deposes, as to the matter of the contract, its constitutional authority, and exchanges the character of legislator for that of a moral agent, with the same rights and obligations as an individual. Its promises may be justly considered as excepted out of its power to legislate, unless in aid of them. It is in theory impossible to reconcile the idea of a promise which obliges, with a power to make a law which can vary the effect of it.

The soundness of this doctrine has never been doubted by this court; and in harmony with it, to quote the language of Mr. Justice Strong, at p. 732, "it is as much beyond the power of a legislature, under any pretense, to alter a contract into which the government has entered with a private individual, as it is for any other party to a contract to change its terms without the consent of the person contracting with him. As to its contract the government in all its departments has laid aside its sovereignty, and it stands on the same footing with private contractors."

Can the government, thus forbidden, as a private person is forbidden, to vary the terms of its contract, accomplish the same result by a legislative manipulation of money values so as to prevent the terms being carried into effect? Certainly, if an individual undertook to annul or lessen the amount of his monetary obligation by secreting or manipulating his assets so as to put them beyond the reach of his creditors, the court would denounce such an attempt as a fraud and sweep it aside as ineffective.

If it be conceded that the literal enforcement of the gold clause, by requiring payment in gold coin, would obstruct the exercise of the power of Congress under the money clause of the Constitution, it is clear that exaction of payment of the amount of the bond in legal tender money does not constitute an obstruction, since the right to exact such payment is recognized by the Congressional joint resolution itself. It seems equally clear that exaction of such payment in an amount of legal tender depreciated money which is equivalent in value to the gold coin required by the bond does not obstruct the exercise of the power. That contingency does no more than admonish the law-making body that it must consider the good and evil consequences destined to flow from the contemplated legislation. The fact that Congress is obliged to weigh the relative evils which would be likely to result from passing or failing to pass a given act of legislation does not confer upon that body the power to destroy property rights which, if permitted to stand, may in the opinion of Congress tend to render the operation of the act less effective or useful than would otherwise be the case.

It is no part of the constitutional power of Congress to strike down contractual obligations, valid when made, simply because the legislation which it contemplates, will impose hardship upon one of the contracting parties. That would be simply to relieve one of them at the expense of the other.

APPENDIX C

Memorandum of a Supreme Court Conference [1]

May 15, 1928

Memorandum for the Chief Justice.

Nos. 493, 532, 533. *Olmstead et. al.* v. *United States.* This is the wire tapping case in which there probably will be a vigorous dissent. In a general way my view is that the conversations which were heard as a result of the wire tapping did not relate to a past crime but were part of a crime then being committed. The question is whether there was an unlawful search and seizure; and plainly there was not. Neither papers nor information was surrendered under any form of compulsion. Consequently, the evidence was admissible however we may condemn the manner of obtaining it. I am inclined to think the opinion should squarely meet the proposition that there was probably a violation of the state law which we do not in any way attempt to excuse. That however is a matter for the state, and the federal courts cannot refuse to receive evidence plainly relevant and material because the state law may have been violated in obtaining it. The point made, that there was an unlawful search and seizure, being negatived, that is the end of the matter so far as we are concerned.

Nos. 7, 11, 12 Orig. *Wisconsin et al.* v. *Illinois et al.* This is also assigned to you. The vote was unanimous, and you may put me down for the opinion which you will write.

No. 551. *Boston Sand & Gravel Co.* v. *United States,* assigned to Holmes, J. Stone voted the other way, and Butler and I doubted. I shall not dissent, unless Butler does. I will drop him a note about the matter.

No. 139. *Quaker City Cab Co.* v. *Pennsylvania,* assigned to Van Devanter, J. This is an old case which we reversed a year ago. I hope it will be disposed of. Stone, Brandeis, and Holmes dissented but if Van Devanter writes the opinion I shall unhesitatingly agree to it. If written by anybody else, I will agree to what you and he accept.

No. 43. *New York ex rel.* v. *Zimmerman*; No. 64, *Kinney Coastal Oil Co.* v. *Kieffer,* and No. 131, *Mellon* v. *Goodyear.* My

---

[1] This memorandum was found in the papers of Mr. Justice Sutherland. It is reproduced here because of the glimpse it affords of the Court at work.

record shows Nos. 43 and 64 were assigned to Van Devanter, and probably No. 131 as well. In any event, I was absent and have nothing to say.

No. 168. *Nobles of Mystic Shrine* v. *Michaux*, assigned to Van Devanter. Holmes alone dissented. The comments as to No. 139 apply.

No. 205. *National Leather Co.* v. *Massachusetts*, assigned to Van Devanter. McReynolds and I voted to reverse; Butler voted to affirm with a question. I thought that the statute was an attempt to tax property outside the state. I am not very tenacious about it, and will go along with Butler.

No. 209. *Highland* v. *Russel Car & Snow Plow Co.*, assigned to Van Devanter. Comments respecting No. 139 apply here.

No. 554, 571. *Taft* v. *Bowers*. You sat out of this case. It was affirmed by a vote of five, McReynolds passing. Butler and I voted to reverse. I will drop Butler a note about it.

No. 343. *Hemphill* v. *Orloff*, assigned to McReynolds, J. The vote was unanimous, with Stone doubting. An opinion satisfactory to you will be satisfactory to me.

No. 228. *National Life Insurance Co.* v. *United States*, assigned to McReynolds. Stone, Brandeis and Holmes dissented, Holmes with a question. Comment in last case applies.

No. 16 Orig. *Ex parte: In re Williams*, assigned to Brandeis, J. My record shows a unanimous vote to discharge rule, except Stone doubting. Comment in No. 343 applies.

No. 425. *Midland National Bank* v. *Dakota Life Co.* The vote was unanimous, McReynolds passing. Comment in No. 343 applies.

No. 561. *Willing* v. *Chicago Auditorium Association*. I have just received Brandeis' opinion and will dispose of it before I go.

No. 337. *Williamsport Wire Rope Co.* v. *United States*, assigned to Brandeis. The vote was unanimous. Comment in No. 343 applies.

No. 404. *Baltimore & Ohio* v. *United States et al.*, assigned to Butler, J. Comment in No. 343 applies. The vote was to reverse, except McReynolds.

Nos. 768, 769. *Foster-Fountain Packing Co.* v. *Haydel*, assigned to Butler, J. Comment in No. 343 applies. The vote was to reverse, except McReynolds.

No. 744. *Reed* v. *Commissioners*, assigned to Butler, J. This is the well known case where the Senate thinks it may pass laws allowing its members to sue without the concurrence of the House and the President. Comment in No. 343 applies.

No. 403. *McCoy* v. *Shaw*, assigned to Sanford, J. The vote was to reverse, Brandeis passing. Sanford already has an opinion prepared which I have examined and agreed to.

No. 472, 733. *Southern Pacific Co.* v. *Haglund*, assigned to Sanford, J. The vote was to affirm, Brandeis passing. This was the "thoroughfare" collision case. Comment in No. 343 applies.

No. 496. *Sisseton & Wahpeton Bands* v. *United States*. I voted reluctantly with the others to affirm. Comment in No. 343 applies.

INDEX

INDEX

Criminal Code, 53-54
Critchlow, E. B., 49

Danbury Hatter's Case, 85
Davidson v. New Orleans, 118n
Day, William R., 115n
Debs, In Re, 33-34
Delano, Frederic A., 70
Depew, Chauncey M., 105n
Dickinson, John, 192
Dillon, John Forrest, 9, 28
Dimick v. Schiedt, 210-211
District of Columbia v. Colts, 209
Dolliver, Jonathan P., 25
Douglas, William O., 137
Dred Scott Case, 238

Educational Films Corp. v. Ward, 158
Edwards v. Kearzey, 173-174
Eight-hour Day, 63, 96
Elmore, A. R., 105n
Elmore, George Sutherland, 234
Employer's Liability Act, 56
Euclid v. Ambler, 126-127, 166, 242-243
Ex Parte Milligan, 171n

Farmers Loan & Trust Co. v. Minn., 159n
Federal Reserve Act, 83n, 97
Federal Trade Commission Act, 84, 97, 102
Ferrey v. Ramsey, 133
Field, Stephen J., 32-35, 153
First National Bank v. Maine, 159-160
Fish, Hamilton, 199
Fitch, Tom, 38-39
Fletcher, James, Jr., 105n
Fletcher v. Peck, 118n
Fla. v. Mellon, 139
Foster v. Ill., 215
Frankfurter, Felix, 3n, 122
Frazier-Lemke Act, 183
Frost v. Commission, 132
Frost Trucking Co. v. Commission, 134-135, 164-165
Fulcher, W. E., 105n
Fuller, Melville H., 111, 153

Fuller, T. Staples, 105n
Funk v. United States, 211n, 235-236
Furuseth, Andrew, 71-72, 97, 125

Garretson, A. B., 70
Garrison, L. H., 105n
Georgia Railroad & Power Co. v. Decatur, 125
Gibbons v. Ogden, 136n, 193
Gilmour, W. P., 105n
Gitlow v. New York, 216n, 219, 236
Glavis, L. R., 61
Gold Clause Cases, 179-182
Gompers, Samuel, 72, 97, 125
Green, William, 187
Grosjean v. American Press Co., 216-217
Guffey Coal Act, 188, 192-198
Guthrie, William D., 105n

Hamilton v. St. Louis County Court, 18
Hammer v. Dagenhart, 194
Hanna, Mark, 46n
Harding, Warren G., 105-108, 112
Hay-Pauncefote Treaty, 93
Heiner v. Donnan, 161-162
Hepburn Rate Bill, 56
Herbert v. La., 215
Herndon v. Ga., 212-213
Herndon v. Lowry, 213n
Hill, Samuel B., 188
Hilles, Charles D., 105n
Hobbes, Thomas, 101n
Holden v. Hardy, 36
Holmes, O. W., Jr., 68, 87, 104, 115-116, 122n, 124, 129, 130n, 131, 134, 152n, 156, 159, 194, 219, 236, 245
Home Building & Loan Ass'n v. Blaisdell, 167-174, 177, 179
Hoover, Herbert Clark, 156
Hughes, Charles Evans, 92, 105n, 159, 168-172, 175, 183, 204, 205, 220
Humphrey, William E., 183

Indian Motorcycle Co. v. United States, 142

{ 264 }

INDEX

{ 265 }